"Off the Straight Path"

Gender, Culture, and Politics in the Middle East
miriam cooke, Suad Joseph, and Simona Sharoni, *Series Editors*

"Off the
Straight
Path"

ILLICIT SEX, LAW,

AND COMMUNITY

IN OTTOMAN ALEPPO

Elyse Semerdjian

SYRACUSE UNIVERSITY PRESS

Copyright © 2008 by Syracuse University Press

Syracuse, New York 13244–5290

All Rights Reserved

First Paperback Edition 2016

16 17 18 19 20 21   6 5 4 3 2 1

∞ The paper used in this publication meets the minimum requirements
of the American National Standard for Information Sciences—Permanence
of Paper for Printed Library Materials, ANSI Z39.48–1992.

For a listing of books published and distributed by Syracuse University Press,
visit www.SyracuseUniversityPress.edu.

ISBN: 978-0-8156-3173-6 (cloth)

978-0-8156-3463-8 (paperback)

978-0-8156-5155-0 (e-book)

The Library of Congress has cataloged the cloth edition as follows:

Semerdjian, Elyse.

"Off the straight path" : illicit sex, law, and community in Ottoman Aleppo /
Elyse Semerdjian.

p. cm. —(Gender, culture, and politics in the Middle East)

Includes bibliographical references and index.

ISBN 978-0-8156-3173-6 (hardcover : alk. paper)

1. Adultery (Islamic law) 2. Fornication (Islamic law) 3. Rape (Islamic
law) 4. Domestic relations (Islamic law) 5. Customary law (Islamic
law)—Syria—Aleppo. 6. Punishment (Islamic law) I. Title.

KBP559.958.S46 2008

345.5691'0253—dc22

2008043095

Manufactured in the United States of America

To my parents, Nerses and Sandra Semerdjian

ELYSE SEMERDJIAN is an associate professor of Islamic and Middle Eastern history at Whitman College in Walla Walla, Washington. She has published articles on the subject of gender in Islamic law in *Beyond the Exotic: Women's Histories in Islamic Societies* (2005) and *Hawwa: Journal of Women of the Middle East and the Islamic World.*

Contents

Illustrations

MAPS

TABLES

Acknowledgments

I began this project in 1996 as a graduate student at Georgetown University, and it has taken more than a decade to complete. Along the way several individuals and institutions supported me and deserve recognition. Much of the material from the book was located in the Library of Congress, where I spent a great deal of time as a graduate student. I would like to thank the Middle East librarian in the law library, George Sfeir, who helped me and shared his own scholarly work. The library had a vast array of juridical materials (*fiqh,* fatwas, and commentaries) that I would like to encourage researchers to use more often than they do. The Middle East Reading Room of the Library of Congress was also extremely helpful during the course of this project.

As for my research in Syria, the majority of my time was spent in the Center for Historical Documents (Markaz al-Watha'iq al-Tarikhiyya). Both the late Dr. Da'd Hakim, former director of the center, and the current director, Dr. Ghassan Obeid, did much to facilitate this research. The center's staff has become my friends and family away from home. I would like to also thank the French Institute of Damascus (Institut Français d'Études Arabes de Damas–IFEAD/IFPO) which has been a source of great help for me. The staff, in particular Issam Chehadat and Ali al-Ali, was willing to help even when my book requests fell far into the recesses of the collection, including a far-away storage facility. Jen Johnson of Penrose Library at Whitman College is a miracle worker and has gone out of her way to find material for me to use in remote Walla Walla, Washington.

I also thank Fulbright, which provided me with a grant to conduct the core of this research in Syria from 1999 to 2001. The Ford Arab-American Chamber of Commerce provided me with a scholarship in 2002 that paid for my final semester of tuition at Georgetown University, for which I am eternally grateful.

I also thank the Syrian Studies Association for awarding me the Syrian Studies Association Best Dissertation Prize in 2003, for which I am truly humbled.

Several professors helped me along the way, and without their help and guidance I would have never completed the project. I would like to thank Müge Göçek for introducing me to the world of Ottoman studies and, in particular, the shari'a court records. Salim Khaldieh, instructor of Arabic at the University of Michigan in the early 1990s, was an amazing spirit who died much too young and is truly missed. I do not know how to thank Denise Spellberg for her mentoring that eventually led to me to Georgetown University. John Esposito, the director of the Center for Muslim-Christian Understanding, and the School of Foreign Service at Georgetown provided me with teaching assistantships that kept me out of Washington, D.C.'s soup kitchens. I would like to thank my adviser, John Voll, for his guidance throughout the years. Special thanks to Amira Sonbol, who became my mentor at Georgetown and saw me through to the end. Her Arabic Sources course was one of a kind and produced some of the early research in my dissertation. Course work offered by Judith Tucker, the late Hisham Sharabi, and Yvonne Seng provided further inspiration for some of the ideas contained within the book. I would like to thank my Ottoman language instructors: the late James Stewart Robinson of the University of Michigan and Yvonne Seng and Gábor Ágoston of Georgetown University. I add the disclaimer that any mistakes made in translation are my very own.

I would also like to thank friends who have been a sounding board for my ideas, read some chapters of this book, and been a source of moral support throughout the years: Theresa Alfaro-Velcamp, Faedah Totah, and Hibba Abugideri. The bond I share with these Arab women inspired me to finish this book and turn a new page in my career. A special thanks to my longtime friend Kathleen LaTosch, who edited an earlier version of this work. Abdul Karim Rafeq has lent crucial advice and expertise throughout the years for which I am grateful. Peter Sluglett read a few chapters and offered amazing comments that helped immensely. I would like to thank Charles Wilkins, my comrade in the archives, who held a common interest in Aleppo that developed into a friendship during some very cold days huddled around the *sobiya* in *bayt* Khalid al-'Azm.

I am most grateful to Mary Selden Evans for her early interest in my work, which has resulted in a working relationship with her and Syracuse University Press, and Annette Wenda, my copy editor, whose amazing pen caught many inconsistencies prior to publication. My colleagues in the History Department at Whitman College have read and commented on chapters during our "First Friday" research meetings. I am very thankful to Nina Lerman, David Schmitz, Lynn Sharp, Julie Charlip, Brian Dott, Kyra Nourse, Mike Bottoms, and Trey Proctor for the insights and comments about my project along the way. Damascene lawyer Thaier Mourad read and discussed documents with me, offering his perspective on the cases. The Dean of Faculty's office at Whitman College along with the History Department have always been generous in funding some of my trips back to Syria over the past few years that were crucial to accessing important sources in Damascus. I would like to thank Bryan Lubbers for listening to my ideas and lending his computer expertise that aided the construction of a database containing all of my court records. Cartographer Joseph Stoll of Syracuse University created beautiful maps for the book for which I am grateful.

I would like to thank my family and friends in 'Aziziya, Aleppo, including my aunt, *tantig* Elyse Semerdjian, and our close family friend and neighbor, former Aleppo municipality chief and head of the Ministry of Awqaf, Sulayman Nasr (Abu Imad), who passed away in 2006; Abu Imad personally escorted me to various government agencies in my pursuit of missing documents; he was an Aleppo icon and is missed by all.

Finally, my best thanks to Nerses and Sandra Semerdjian, my parents, who came to my rescue with a bag of groceries when I was down to my last pita in graduate school.

A Note on Transliteration

Transliterations are based on a modified version of the system used in the *International Journal of Middle East Studies.* All Ottoman Turkish terms are transliterated into their contemporary Turkish equivalents. To avoid confusion and to offer more uniformity in the text the Arabic term *fatwa* (Ottoman Turkish *fetva*) is used throughout. Ottoman transliteration is used in Ottoman texts. Names of plaintiffs and defendants are transliterated exactly as they appeared in the court record. For clarification, an example of a woman's name is Fatima bint Muhammad, which literally means "Fatima the daughter of Muhammad." Similarly, a man's name such as Taha ibn Husayn literally means "Taha the son of Husayn." The father's name is provided in the lineage, as last names were not widely used until the nineteenth century. Only prominent notable families such as the Amirzade and Kawakabi families had recognizable last names in earlier periods.

Introduction

On September 26, 1660, a woman named Zahra from the neighborhood of Jami' 'Ubays on Aleppo's southern wall was brought to court by her neighbors, including the local imam, Hajj Ahmad ibn Bashar. The residents of the quarter accused Zahra of being "mischievous," an "evildoer," a fallen woman who had veered "off the straight path" of Islam. "She brings strange men into her home," the residents informed the judge, using a common euphemism for prostitution frequently found in the Aleppo court records. The residents requested that Zahra be removed from their neighborhood, and the court granted their request.[1]

This case of illicit sexual intercourse is one of several that appeared before shari'a court judges in early modern Aleppo. The verdict against Zahra was consistent with that reached in other cases, namely, removal from the city quarter. However, many Islamists today would promote more severe punishments for illicit sexual intercourse, the crime of *zina* in Islamic law. Violent punishments for this crime, such as death by stoning, have been advocated by contemporary Islamic movements and incorporated into the legal codes of some Muslim countries as punishment for breaches of sexual morality in the name of a return to a more "authentic" Islamic law.[2] Of course, the basis for stoning is not completely unfounded; it is a tradition that can be found in the hadiths of the Prophet Muhammad and the caliph 'Umar ibn al-Khattab (634–44) who apparently encouraged the practice after the Prophet's death. Later juridical writings gave the practice more support, but the sentences handed down by the courts in the Ottoman period tell another story. In Ottoman Aleppo, the shari'a court regularly recorded nonviolent, noncorporal punishments in cases like Zahra's. Not a single documented case of stoning was found in more than three hundred years of shari'a court records studied.[3] So, how is it possible that the punishments handed down by the shari'a courts in Aleppo are so radically different both from the precedents established in the early Islamic period and from the punishments prescribed by later Islamic legal theorists? How did jurists reconcile the contradictions between the theoretical, doctrinal law that they were trained in as students and the law they practiced in the shari'a courts?

According to the shari'a, Zahra's crime was *zina,* which Joseph Schacht has defined as "fornication" or "any sexual intercourse between persons who are not in a state of legal matrimony or concubinage."[4] Many discussions of Islamic law seek a normative definition for crimes in an attempt to create parallels with legal concepts that Western readers would find familiar. However, in the end they fail to flesh out all the dimensions of crimes that have been discussed and debated in a vibrant Islamic juridical discourse over many centuries. *Zina,* as defined through the volumes of juridical writings produced by Muslim scholars, encompasses a wide range of sexual violations: it is an umbrella category for several offenses found in modern Western codes of law, including adultery, prostitution, procurement, abduction, incest, bestiality, sodomy, and rape. To redefine our concept of the crime demands an examination of some of these complex juridical conversations; hence, I have conducted an archaeology of *zina* crime beginning with its earliest references in the Qur'an. Later, criminal cases of *zina* will be tested in one locality, Aleppo, Syria, in order to better understand, as much as can be done given the limitations of the sources, the way in which *zina*-related cases were treated in the court of law.[5] Furthermore, *zina* is discussed within the larger context of public morality in a specific geographical setting, in order to understand the way that a local court and its surrounding community defined the boundaries between permissible and forbidden behaviors.

Several studies of law and society have been produced in recent years, but Aleppo has not been part of that conversation. Historians have been engaged in various kinds of study with court records, using them to reconstruct the social and political history of Aleppo, such as the works of Abraham Marcus and Margaret Meriwether. Aleppo's economic history and its non-Muslim communities have been discussed in two carefully crafted monographs by Bruce Masters, but for Syria as a whole, no one has contributed as much as Abdul Karim Rafeq, who has used court records from four major cities in the Syrian archives, including Aleppo, and has written on numerous political, economic, and social issues.[6] One study in particular focuses on public morality in eighteenth-century Damascus and raises important questions of gender and morality. Rafeq argues that the century marked an increase in various forms of moral breaches, including prostitution, suicide, and troublemaking. Importantly, for this study, he argued that "quarter solidarity" provided the vehicle for adjudication of crimes against the moral order. Many of the arguments advanced in this important article are tested in this study.[7]

All the cases used in this study were found in the shariʿa court records (sijillat al-mahakam sharʿiyya) of Aleppo, an invaluable source for our understanding of the practice of Islamic law. Aleppo's court records illustrate the workings of the Ottoman administration in the period under study. Almost all the records are in Arabic, although a few are in Ottoman Turkish. I have also consulted collections of Ottoman kanunnames and Ottoman fatwas, which present the perspective of imperial law, in an attempt to give a holistic approach and to cover some historical and legal material pertaining to the practice of the central Ottoman state. A combination of materials, including selections from the vast amount of fiqh documents available in Arabic, particularly those from the Hanafi school of law, have been used in an attempt to compare legal theory with court practice. The virtual absence of secondary studies dealing with zina and Islamic law has led me to rely predominately on primary sources from Syria, namely, the records in the Syrian National Archives (Markaz al-Wathaʾiq al-Tarikhiyya) and juridical literature (fiqh and fatwas). As a result, the scope of the Islamic legal literature was quite large, so I selected volumes that would have influenced a Hanafi jurist in the period under study.

The methodology I have chosen has been influenced by several fields; comparative studies in Islamic law and society have been particularly influential.[8] Several studies in the past decade have chosen to compare the shariʿa court records to juridical writings found in fiqh and fatwas in order to compare doctrine with the actual practice of the court. This has been the methodology of Amira Sonbol, who has cross-referenced Egyptian court cases with juridical texts. Judith Tucker has compared fatwa literature with court records in her study of gender discourses in Ottoman Syria and Palestine. Leslie Peirce's microhistory of Ottoman ʿAintab also compares and contrasts the body of juridical literature with an examination of practice as shown in the court records.[9] I have chosen to borrow this comparative model of analysis in my examination of Aleppo court records, with two exceptions.

First, after examining the state of the archives in Damascus, including the manuscripts now housed in the Asad Library, I discovered that there were only a few fragments of fatwa collections from Aleppo; however, none of the ones with a discussion of *zina* were from Aleppine jurists, which made it impossible to compare Aleppine fatwas with the local court records in a systematic way. That being said, a few fatwas are used from those collections and other fatwas that were cited within the court records themselves, composed by the hand of the court scribe. Hence, I have used the imperial fatwas of Ebu's Su'ud Efendi, supreme religious leader (*sheikhul-islam* of the Ottoman Empire from 1545 to 1574) during the reign of Süleyman I in order to understand better the imperial discourse on gender and sexual criminality. These fatwas are examined in chapter 2 in conjunction with the imperial law codes, the *kanunnames*.

The second way that I depart from some of the models I have chosen is that I do not engage in a microhistory of Aleppo based on the court records. Microhistory has been popular in the field in recent years, but there are a number of reasons for my not having chosen that approach.[10] To begin with, the court records found in Aleppo, as will be demonstrated, are quite formulaic and rarely provide the lengthy narratives and richness of detail of, for example, the Inquisition cases that have formed the microhistories of other parts of the world.[11] Furthermore, the nature of the sources and the way in which the material is recorded make it difficult to understand the underlying motivations of the individual participants. Any attempt to understand those motivations is quite speculative.[12] Therefore, I have chosen to analyze only the bits of data I found useful from the *sijills*—names of defendants and plaintiffs, neighborhoods, social titles, narrative choices—and use this information to understand the adjudication process.

My method of digging through the layers of *zina* discourse in order to understand the history of this crime and the way it was treated in court is intended as an attack on the pervasive discourse of Muslim sexuality that has real effects on the way shari'a is interpreted today. By systematically documenting a legal discourse on illicit sexuality, I seek to fill in a crucial gap in both academic and lay understanding of the shari'a and to continue a conversation initiated by Fatima Mernissi in the late 1980s, when she broke down a centuries-old barrier to female interpretation of Muslim traditions.[13] Her original critique published twenty years ago is just as important today as it was then.

Current Islamist discourse often looks to the doctrinal prescriptions of the law and takes them at face value, ignoring the ways that Islam allowed for flexibility of interpretation. In many ways, the Islamist understanding of Islamic law is similar to that of the Orientalist tradition: timeless, stagnant, and rigid in its interpretation of law.[14] Even historical precedents are often taken out of context in order to suit political agendas. Feminists like Mernissi, who discusses this preoccupation with the past and the way that it has been used to advance the patriarchal interests of contemporary politicians, call it the "misuse of memory."[15] This problem is by no means exclusive to the postcolonial Muslim world; rather, it is a cross-cultural phenomenon. The "misuse of memory" can be seen in various aspects of twentieth-century Islamic revivalism, in which crimes against the moral order, specifically *zina*, have often been punished with the death penalty, ignoring the larger legal process established by jurists as well as the way in which such cases have been treated historically. Hence, the process of resuscitating draconian punishments found in Islamic doctrine but not in judicial practice has been in many ways ahistorical, an example of the all too familiar process of the invention of tradition to shore up a supposedly failing moral order. Advocates have selected some passages of hadith to support the implementation of stoning, since it is suspiciously absent from the Qur'an, yet have simultaneously disregarded hadiths that provide strict criteria for conviction. This revivalism has also been encouraged through the republication of several classic treatises on the law that advocate corporal punishment for *zina*. Browsing through bookstores in the Arab world reveals a flood of newly (re)published works on women and morality in Islam, most of which, it should be emphasized, were originally written during the first five Muslim centuries. These publications, coupled with a dynamic contemporary Islamic discourse on morality and gender, have resulted in a particular convergence of the past and the present—the use of history to justify an authoritarian political agenda concerning women and morality. Therefore, exploring the "actual" historical position of women, gender, and morality becomes even more pressing as it stakes out the ground upon which the battle over morality in Islamic law will be fought.

This project is also part of an ongoing conversation about the theories and practice of Islamic law. Much of our understanding of Islamic law has been shaped by Western theories, such as those of Max Weber, who embraced the Oriental despotism model originally formulated by Marx and Engels (and elaborated further by Karl Wittfogel in the 1950s) to describe the political development of Asia.[16] In this theory, the court of law is a microcosm of the despotic state, in which the judge *(qadi)* sits as the patriarch of his courthouse. Weber, and others, on the basis of no particular body of evidence, argued that the judge arbitrarily meted out punishments as he saw fit, without rhyme or reason. The system, called *kadijustiz,* has been described as one in which "judges never refer to a settled group of norms or rules but are simply licensed to decide each case according to what they see as its individual merits."[17] Weber argued that the reason *kadijustiz* was prominent in Islamic society was owing to the legal structure in which outside forces wielded little influence on the decisions of the judge, a position that parallels the stance of the sultan vis-à-vis the state. The judge administered justice alone, his decision was final, there was no appeal system, and justice was swift and immediate. Hence, there were no lawyers to influence judicial decisions, nor did the Islamic world have a commercial class that could influence legislation and check the powers of the polity. For Weber, this situation marked a departure from the Western legal system, making Islamic law exceptional.[18] Orientalists long held that Islamic law was practiced arbitrarily and its legal tradition was stagnant, although such fundamentally inaccurate notions have been challenged by recent scholarship.[19] A revisionist approach to Islamic law and society has developed over the past two decades in the work of Brinkley Messick, David Powers, Muhammad Khaled Masud, Judith Tucker, Wael Hallaq, and others, who have demonstrated convincingly that Islamic law developed as positive law, based on historical precedent and as part of a rational body of legal thought.[20]

A major part of the debate has been centered on the history of Islamic law and its development throughout the centuries. Scholars have claimed that (Sunni) Islamic law was stagnant because of a process called "the closing of the gates of *ijtihad* (legal reasoning)" in the ninth century. It was in that century that after two centuries of debate jurists began to view the corpus of work developed as exhaustive and complete. It was indeed a real debate, discussed by both foreigners and Arabs, including the travel narrative of Mouradgea D'Ohsson and the writings of Syrian jurist Husayn al-Jisr, respectively.[21] Whereas Orientalist scholars argued that the gate was closed, new scholarship has argued to the contrary. This revisionist school in the field of Islamic law and society developed after 1984, when an important article by Wael Hallaq entitled "Was the Gate of *Ijtihad* Closed?" was published. Hallaq demonstrated that although Orientalist scholars argued that *ijtihad* had been stifled, jurists continued to refer to the process in their writings. Soon after Hallaq opened the debate, several books were published that focused on the consistent use of *ijtihad* in the formulation of fatwas. Authors such as Messick, Powers, and Tucker have worked extensively with fatwa literature that existed after the alleged disappearance of *ijtihad* to in fact show that it was a vibrant, ongoing tradition in Islamic law.[22] Later, Hallaq published an article that connected the process of issuing fatwas *(ifta')* to legal manuals to demonstrate the connection between doctrinal law found in juridical writings and fatwas, both of which use legal reasoning but also have a basis in the living law in Muslim communities.[23]

One of the overarching goals of this study is to determine the way Islamic law was practiced in the courts of early modern Aleppo. The examination of multiple sources reveals a discrepancy between the theoretical prescriptions of the law found in legal manuals, that is, what could be called *doctrine,* and the practice of law in the courts.[24] Doctrine produces what could be called a "symbolic construction" of gender relations that can be found in the writings of Muslim jurists versus the sometimes complicated "social relationship of gender" that is, to quote Judith Tucker, "the product of the historical development of human experience, a relationship that changes, evolves, and adapts in rhythm with a changing society."[25] Does this adaptation mean that law was practiced arbitrarily as *kadijustiz?* The answer to that question is an unequivocal no. Despite the disparity between the theory and the practice of law in Aleppo, there is a consistency in the verdicts that judges issued in matters of public morality and the crime of *zina.* In fact, it is quite difficult to find much change in the way these crimes were punished throughout the 359 years of court cases used in this study.[26] I argue that this lack of change in punishment is a result of the consistent application of the local interpretations of law by the numerous judges who entered the court. It was customary for judges to take traditions of law into consideration so long as it did not overtly contradict the shari'a. This consistency should not be mistaken for stagnation or lack of development. The cases themselves vary in frequency and type within various periods, marking social and political changes in Aleppine society. Through these changes, societal norms for treating deviancy, rather than regulations laid down by the state, were consistently upheld by the courts.

This study of moral deviancy is useful for challenging the dominant paradigms found in Orientalist scholarship about law and society for several reasons.

First, the study of morality and deviancy forces us to throw out Orientalist misconceptions about sexuality and law in the Islamic world. The fact that an active, illegal flesh trade existed in Aleppo demonstrates that an underground economy functioned there, as in many other places, and opens the door to possible comparative histories of gender and morality in the future. Second, it forces us to look at the way in which law functioned in society, rather than isolated solely as a text. Textual analysis alone simply does not get at the agency of local actors shaping the practice of law in their own communities. This book will demonstrate that communities defined deviant behavior outside the Islamic juridical framework, yet the courts adapted to those definitions. This process of negotiation between the community and the court emphasizes the effects that communities had on their own legal culture. So we are dealing with not only divine law as found in the shari'a, and Ottoman imperial law, but also the way in which law operated on its most local level, in Aleppo's neighborhoods. Michel Foucault has argued that nineteenth-century European notions of the normal and the abnormal "actually originated in social practices of control and supervision [surveillance]."[27] Therefore, to write a history on the subject of deviancy, one must take into account the various social practices that enforce these definitions, as well as the discourse that develops on an official level, particularly through the law because of its special influence in shaping views toward sexuality by delineating the boundary between licit and illicit sexuality. Law is a reflection of power that is diffuse in society on the local level and in its legal discourses on illicit sexuality. The way that the community used the court in Aleppo illuminates the reciprocal relationship between the court and society. The court itself, in order to be deemed legitimate, needed public approval, which can be seen in the accommodations to local conceptions of morality illuminated by instances of community policing and en masse testimony illustrated in this volume. This notion stands in stark contrast to scholarship that has presented the courts as neutral. As demonstrated in this study, the court accommodates the interests of the community in several ways, sometimes even allowing the community to use hearsay and circumstantial evidence in *zina*-related crimes, that overrun the rules of evidence outlined in the shari'a.

Therefore, following this methodological example, the process of historicizing and contextualizing the legal discourse on *zina* is documented in two parts: *zina* discourses and law in practice. The first two chapters of the book deal with legal theory found in early Islamic juridical writings and in Ottoman law. Chapter 1, "*Zina* in Islamic Legal Discourse," outlines the way in which Islamic law viewed the crime of *zina,* using some of the Hanafi juridical literature available on the subject. This chapter situates Islamic law within the context of prescriptive literature that contains variations in interpretation presented by different jurists, focusing on writings of the Hanafi school, the dominant legal school in the Ottoman Empire. Chapter 2, "*Zina* in Ottoman Law," looks at the way in which the crime was dealt with by Ottoman jurists. The Ottomans converted the draconian punishments found in the shari'a into a set code of imperial laws, the *kanunnames,* which prescribed a system of fines and lashing instead of the death penalty in most cases. Use of Ottoman fatwas in this chapter also demonstrates a continued interpretative tradition of the shari'a and the ongoing development of a legal discourse during a period that some have argued marked a closure of legal interpretation.

The second part of the book looks at the practice of law in Aleppo. Chapter 3, "People and Court: Policing Public Morality in the Streets of Aleppo," is an introduction to the city of Aleppo and its historical background from the sixteenth to the nineteenth centuries, exploring the city's structure and its connections to the rest of the world. This chapter introduces the shari'a court record as a source for social history. Class composition and the role that class and communities played in policing crime in the city are also detailed. Local neighborhood representatives policed their own neighborhoods, apprehending those residents who violated the moral code and bringing them to justice. The fact that neighborhoods initiated these cases reflects the civic function of the court as a mediator in public affairs. By focusing on the local interpretation of law and local initiatives of neighborhoods in the court, the importance of the people in shaping and implementing the law is revealed. Chapter 4, "Prostitutes, Soldiers, and the People: Monitoring Morality Through Customary Law," discusses the way in which prostitution was policed and punished in Aleppo. It compares data found in Aleppo with studies of other parts of the Ottoman Empire and argues that a consistent pattern of banishment for prostitution existed in the empire as a whole, despite shari'a prescriptions to the contrary.

Chapter 5, titled "In Harm's Way: Domestic Violence and Rape in the Shari'a Courts of Aleppo," investigates cases of violence against women in the court. It seeks to dispel the Orientalist notion that the crime of rape did not exist in Islamic law, pointing out that language has been a major cause of this misconception; therefore, an analysis of terminology is included to illuminate the presence of rape as a legal category in Islamic rulings. This discussion will also highlight cases of rape and domestic violence that appeared in court. Together, these chapters attempt to challenge some pervasive assumptions about the nature of law and Ottoman rule that continue to persist in the field of Middle East studies. The study of law and vice in Aleppo will, I hope, generate future discussion about the nature of law and society in other parts of the Ottoman Empire.

ALEPPO AND ITS HISTORY

"The Aleppine is a gentleman, the Damascene is a pessimist, the Jerusalemite is a helper and the Egyptian is a thief."[28] This saying conveys the popular attitudes and stereotypes toward the residents of some of the Ottoman Empire's major metropoles. The fact that the Aleppine was considered a gentleman *(Halabi chalabi)* tells us something about the way the northern province of what is today Syria was perceived in the early modern period. It is a city with a vast history that can be traced as far back as the second millennium B.C.[29] The local name for the city, Halab, is derived from the Arabic verb meaning "to milk," relating to the popular belief among Aleppo's residents that the Prophet Abraham once stopped in Aleppo to milk his flocks there.[30] The city has been the site of several invasions throughout history, from the Hittites, Aramaeans, Assyrians, Persians, Greeks, Romans, Arabs, Crusaders, and Turks. Because of its many cultural influences throughout the centuries, Aleppo has a distinct local identity (ill. I.1).

Despite its importance in regional trade and strategic location at the crossroads between Anatolia and the Arab world, Aleppo was never used as a capital center, except for a brief period under the rule of the Hamdanid Sayf al-Dawla (r. 944–67). Although it lacked the political title of capital, it was long considered the economic capital of the region, attracting a diverse set of immigrants from all over the Middle East, including vibrant Christian and Jewish communities that date back to pre-Islamic Byzantine rule. Khalid ibn Walid's conquest of the city in 636 brought it under Muslim rule. It is at this time that the first mosque was built in the city, situated along a colonnaded street constructed during the Roman period.[31] Well after the Muslim conquest, Umayyad Aleppo still had a

I.1. Sketch of Aleppo in the eighteenth century, from A. Drummond's *Travels Through Different Cities . . . and Several Parts of Asia* (London, 1754). Courtesy of the Harry Ransom Humanities Research Center, University of Texas at Austin.

large population of Christians. It took more than a century for the authorities to build a Great Mosque on the site of the Roman-era market to serve the small but growing Muslim population.

Aleppo had a tumultuous history after the massive influx of Turkish nomads into the region who set up a series of independent and often mutually hostile Seljuk emirates (1058–1194). The general instability of the region was evident during the Crusades (1096–1291) in which the city-states of Tripoli, Aleppo, and Damascus were some of the first to be captured, largely because these Seljuk states were bitter rivals, which put the Crusaders at a military advantage. Nur al-Din Zangi (r. 1154–74) would eventually put an end to these rivalries by taking over the region and creating a united front against the Crusaders. Salah al-Din (r. 1169–93), in many ways Nur al-Din's "successor," took advantage of that unification and eventually conquered Jerusalem in 1187 (maps I.1 and I.2).

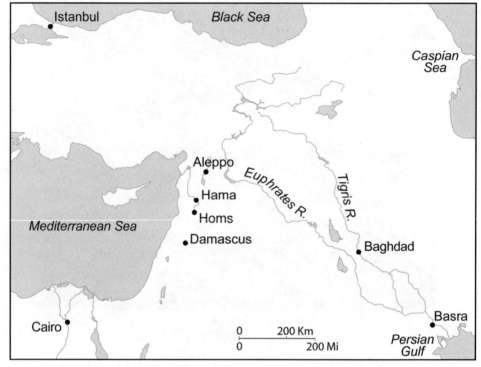

Map I.1. Regional map of the East Mediterranean. Produced by Joseph Stoll.

After the Crusades subsided, new power struggles took place in the region, particularly between the ailing Byzantine Empire and other waves of invading Turkish nomads who would later unite under the leadership of Osman (d. 1324), after whom the Ottoman Empire would be named. In 1453, the Byzantines were dealt a crushing blow when their capital, Constantinople, was conquered by Mehmet II (1444–46 and 1451–81). This defeat was only the first of several steps toward the consolidation of Ottoman rule throughout the region over the next century, culminating in the capture of Syria by Sultan Selim I (r. 1512–20), followed by the conquest of Palestine, Egypt, and the holy cities of Mecca and Medina in the Arabian Peninsula. The conquest of Mamluk Syria (1250–1517) took place as a result of the Battle of Marj Dabiq on August 23, 1516, when the Mamluk leader Sultan Qansuh al-Ghawri was defeated by the Ottoman army. Although Aleppo welcomed its new Ottoman ruler, Ottoman authority was not left unchallenged. By the time Süleyman I (r. 1520–66) took

Map I.2. Aleppo and its environs. Produced by Joseph Stoll.

the throne, the governor of Aleppo, Janbirdi al-Ghazali, had inspired a revolt against the empire. Al-Ghazali did not have the support of the local population, who resisted him until the Ottomans returned with reinforcements, retaking the city in 1520 (ill. I.2).

With the further expansion of the Ottomans into Iraq (Baghdad was captured in 1534 and Mosul in 1549), the trade routes from East Asia were secured and Aleppo continued to prosper.[32] As had been true of many of their predecessors, the Ottoman rulers generally absorbed the cultures of areas they conquered, which left local custom and tradition relatively undisturbed. As the Ottomans conquered Arab lands, they formed links with local elites and employed them

I.2. The citadel of Aleppo from its main entrance. Library of Congress, Prints and Photographs Division, G. Eric and Edith Matson Photograph Collection, LC-DIG-matpc-07217.

in state service as members of the *'ulama,* neighborhood representatives, heads of guilds, and representatives of the urban noble class *(a'yan).* These Ottoman employees served as the eyes and ears of the sultan in the provinces and facilitated the absorption and management of the Arab lands. The Ottomans chose to continue some local traditions, such as the use of neighborhood representatives as mediators between the state and the local population, as will be demonstrated later. Furthermore, in the area of law, the Ottomans continued the tradition of using Arabic as the primary language of the courts in these newly conquered lands. The fact that the Ottomans, in the Arab lands as earlier in the Balkans, administered the provinces without imposing Ottoman Turkish on the population kept local identity intact. In Aleppo, locals would eventually acquire some Turkish expressions because of the city's proximity to Anatolia, the effects of acculturation, and because of the opportunities for advancement that knowledge of the language presented, but they were under no pressure from the imperial authorities to do so. Instead, local identities were based on language and custom, and sometimes on ethnicity or region.[33]

Aleppo in the Ottoman period consisted of what is now the city center overshadowed by a massive citadel, surrounded by walls and nine gates, encompassing about one and a half square miles. Such walls served a protective role for the residents; within the walls were clusters of narrow alleys and closed culs-de-sac that constituted up to 50 percent of the total streets in the city.[34] Many alleys were gated at night in order to protect residents. The nine gates of the old city also had doors that were closed and locked to protect the city from both domestic crime and foreign invasion. Homes were packed closely together; the close proximity of houses increased the amount of surveillance in neighborhoods, but made privacy a difficult commodity to come by. Therefore, although limited privacy could be viewed as a drawback, it offered residents a level of security as a benefit (ill. I.3).

The city, located at a cultural, geographical, and economic crossroads in the region, contained a diversity of ethnic and religious groups within its borders. Ethnic Arab, Kurdish, Turkish, Armenian, Albanian, Bulgarian, Romanian, Serbian, Jewish, Assyrian, Greek, Maronite, and Gypsy populations lived within the city. The urban geography of Aleppo is a reflection of the mosaic of cultures that have inhabited the city throughout its history. For example, neighborhood names reflect the historic Kurdish and Persian residents who dwelled within them. Quarters such as Banqusa, Karliq, Tatarlar, and Maydanjik in the eastern suburbs of the city were full of tribal migrants such as Turkmen, Kurds, and Bedouin. Inhabitants of these same neighborhoods often appear in the court records "as perpetrators of theft and murder."[35]

Aleppo's economic success increased with an influx of Venetian and other Italian traders who sought goods such as silks, carpets, glass, steel, and spices.[36] The trade routes shifted after the fall of the Armenian Kingdom of Cilicia in 1375, and by the fifteenth century Aleppo had become the principal center for the commerce between Iran and Europe, and increasing demand for Iranian silk would keep the economy of the city alive.

Aleppo had advantages over Damascus in that it was easily accessible to European traders, lay relatively close to the port of Alexandretta, and possessed goods in its market that Europeans sought to buy and export to their homelands. Damascus, on the other hand, was closer to the Lebanese ports, but the Lebanon and Anti-Lebanon mountains lay between it and the Mediterranean, making

I.3. A scene from a residential neighborhood in Aleppo. Library of Congress, Prints and Photographs Division, G. Eric and Edith Matson Photograph Collection, LC-DIG-matpc-02164.

travel hazardous.[37] As the major economic hub of the region, Aleppo had a reputation as a sophisticated cosmopolitan center, which is reflected in popular sayings such as "The people of Aleppo have taste and manners."[38]

By the seventeenth and eighteenth centuries, Aleppo was one of the largest and most prosperous cities in the Ottoman Empire, ranking third after Istanbul and Cairo. Its location between Europe and East Asia made it a crossroads of trade. The city was full of foreign merchants within its caravansaries, conducting business by day and lodging on the upper levels of the structures by night. Merchants from Asia and Europe were engaged in the lucrative silk trade, and many Europeans lived as expatriates in Aleppo; members of these expatriate communities often appeared in the courts of Aleppo in both commercial contracts and criminal cases. As a result, the city had a diverse population of Italian, French, and British traders. Bruce Masters notes that by 1750, Aleppo was fully integrated into the world economy dominated by Europe and capitalism, but he is careful to note that this position was mostly the result of specific Ottoman economic policies that granted more and more leniency to foreign traders. These traders were given commercial privileges through the Capitulations *(imtiyazat)* that "granted an extraterritoriality to the European merchant trading communities, in effect making them mini-nations in the Ottomans' midst."[39] Aleppo's strategic location next to Anatolia gave it special proximity to the Ottoman capital and other Turkish cities that lay to the north, an advantage for local and foreign merchants alike.

The Ottomans offered opportunities to these foreign traders in hopes of strengthening the domestic economy, but for various reasons it did not happen. What followed was a reversal of the sixteenth-century Muslim domination of the world economy, particularly the East Asian spice trade, and the seventeenth century eventually saw the emergence of English and Dutch commercial supremacy.[40] Their prominence was especially notable in the spice trade, where English naval power succeeded in increasing its economic hegemony in the eastern Mediterranean and the Indian Ocean after the defeat of the Ottomans at the Battle of Lepanto in 1571.

As European traders flooded the global market, they were quick to make alliances with local minorities involved in commerce.[41] In Aleppo, these minorities consisted principally of Armenians, Maronites, Chaldeans, Jews, Catholics, Assyrians, and Greek Orthodox Christians. According to Masters, the Christian population in the seventeenth century constituted 20 percent of the city's population. The close relationship between non-Muslims and foreign merchants in the city cannot be underestimated. Non-Muslim merchants were quick to form alliances with their European counterparts. At times, non-Muslim merchants were given citizenship by European countries that afforded them privileges usually offered to foreign merchants. This entitlement included capitulatory benefits such as protection, tax exemptions, and immunities *(berat)* that were offered to some Christians and Jews who were protégés of the various foreign consulates in Aleppo.

The northwest quadrant of the city was an important zone for several reasons. It hosted most of the non-Muslim neighborhoods such as Bab al-Nasr and Kharij (Outside) Bab al-Nasr, al-Bandara, and Bab al-Janayn (see map I.3). The southwest part of the city, on the other hand, was predominately Muslim.[42] It is important to note that no neighborhood was exclusively Christian or Jewish, and neighborhoods were not segregated according to religion or even social class.[43] The area outside of Bab al-Nasr, particularly the quarter of Saliba al-Judayda, was a predominately Christian neighborhood, and the quarters of al-Bandara, al-Masabin, and Bahsita were heavily populated by Jewish residents. The area of Bab al-Nasr happened to be the industrial zone of the city, with the highest concentration of workshops and artisans.[44] This section of the city contained blacksmiths' shops, wood merchants, and copper and brass foundries. The majority of the artisans were Christian, but there were some Muslim workers as well.[45] The Bab al-Nasr region attracted the attention of foreign traders who did business and sometimes chose to live there. Traders who chose not to live there could be found in the caravansaries just south of Bab al-Nasr, close to the Central Market that extended between Antakya Gate and the citadel.

As much as these neighborhoods buzzed with daily business dealings, complaints of criminal activity were heard in the shariʿa courts. As demonstrated in court cases highlighted throughout later chapters, the court was accessed by Muslims and non-Muslims alike. In fact, cases involving only Christians and Jews were also brought to the shariʿa court for trial despite the fact that these communities had their own courts.[46] The use of the shariʿa court by non-Muslims has been the topic of several histories in recent years.[47] However, not unexpectedly, since the Muslims formed the overwhelming majority of the population, the majority of cases brought before the court involved Muslims alone.

The diverse range of participants in the courts has made the records an invaluable source for unearthing some of the history from below. The source can tell a scholar much about the elite Muslim families and wealthy non-Muslim merchants of the city. But the records also tell us something about the lives of Aleppo's marginal poor, religious minorities, and women. Some schools of history, such as the French Annales school, have been able to create statistical studies from the records. I have used some of the data collected in this way, but I have done so with considerable caution. Since the collection of Aleppo court records is incomplete, it is not possible to determine exact quantities of any given group that appeared in court.

Throughout its history, Aleppo was periodically shaken by political and social power struggles. In the early seventeenth century there were several rebellions called the Jelali (meaning "rebel" or "outlaw") Revolts that posed a serious threat to the empire. Although many of these revolts were based in Anatolia, Aleppo was also the scene of much fighting. One rebel leader, 'Ali Canpulatoğlu, was a Kurd from a clan based in the small towns of Kilis and 'Azaz, near Aleppo. The Canpulatoğlu were recognized as political bosses in the region by the Ottomans who attempted to integrate these local tribesmen within the empire in hopes of pacifying them. The result was a clash between the Kurdish clan and the Janissaries of Damascus who appeared "in 1603, as in 1599 and 1601 . . . pillaging and looting, while the Ottoman governor looked on from the security of the city's citadel unable to restore order." The Canpulatoğlu clan subdued the Janissaries and protected the city, and in return for this service the Ottomans granted Husayn, chief of the clan, the governorship of Aleppo. Soon afterward, in 1605, the Ottomans were at war with Iran and demanded Husayn's assistance, but their army suffered a defeat before Husayn and his troops arrived. When Husayn heard the news of this defeat, his troops turned back and camped in Van. In return for his failure to defend the state when in need, the Ottoman general Çağalzade Sinan Paşa executed him.[48] Husayn's nephew 'Ali then initiated another rebellion in revenge, and the Ottomans immediately granted him the position of governor in 1606 yet, at the same time, secretly prepared an army to attack him. The Ottoman army attacked him the following year, and 'Ali's forces were defeated. He was given a pardon and granted a position in Romania, but in 1610 he was found guilty of treason and executed. After this period of rebellion, the Ottoman authorities did not appoint locals to the governorship, with one exception, Ibrahim Agha Qattar Aghasi, who was appointed governor in 1799 and held the office for five years.[49] He was an illiterate and relatively unknown member of the local notables (a'yan) who had been a tax farmer in Aleppo. It was common for governors throughout the empire to buy their position from the Ottomans, which intensified the strong links of patronage to Istanbul.

Most often, the Ottomans rotated their officials in order to discourage the continuous contact necessary to build a power base, but it did not exclude other social groups from ascending to power, most notably the Janissaries. Local military commanders had been fighting each other since the late sixteenth century. The Janissaries had dominated the city and were eventually expelled in 1604, only to rebuild their power base in later years. The power of the Janissaries was also increasingly checked by a new rising force in the city, the dominance of the *ashraf*, nobility who traced their blood lineage to the Prophet Muhammad.

These power struggles took place in the context of a weakening economy. In 1619, the Ottoman economy was seriously affected by the Safavids' attempt to create a monopoly on the silk trade by sending exports by sea instead of by land. It would have severely hurt the Ottoman economy, which partly depended on the revenues generated from transit taxes on the caravan trade.[50] In fact, the Safavid monopoly was short-lived, and foreign traders resumed business in the Levant by 1629. Over the next century, foreign traders created closer links with the local economy of Aleppo, but eventually the decline in the demand for Middle Eastern silk, as a result of the opening up of new sources of supply, caused the merchants to look elsewhere. Other economic factors included cheaper textile production in France, which undermined the traditional trade relations between European merchants and Levantine textile manufacturers. Eventually, only raw materials were sought from Aleppo, and the caravan trade had greatly declined by 1750, which effectively cut out the middleman role of Aleppo's merchants.[51]

The late eighteenth century was a period of increased political instability as several groups struggled for political ascendancy and challenged Ottoman authority. Three groups, the Janissaries, the *ashraf* (descendants of the Prophet Muhammad), and the Ottoman government, all competed for power in Aleppo.[52] Ottoman attempts to install their own appointees as governors of the city were met with stiff resistance from both the Janissary garrison and the *ashraf*; allied against the Ottoman authorities, the two groups often rivaled each other. The eighteenth century also saw popular riots in a protest led by the *ashraf* against high bread prices and taxes in 1770. Soon after, in 1775, another riot, this time led by the Janissaries, was directed against the appointment of 'Ali Pasha as governor, whose bad reputation had become known to the residents prior to his arrival. Ultimately, 'Ali Pasha left Aleppo in humiliation. This banishment was not an unusual occurrence, as it happened again in 1787 with Governor 'Uthman Pasha and in 1791 with Governor Kusa Mustafa Pasha, who were removed in popular protests orchestrated by the local *ashraf* and Janissaries. "Such resounding success of the two dominant groups of Aleppo no doubt explains why the Imperial Government several times attempted to crush their power."[53] Increased localism is demonstrated in the resulting short-lived dominance of the Janissaries between 1808 and 1812. During this period of Janissary rule, soldiers controlled quarters of the city, the guilds, and the city's food supply. The Janissaries also robbed homes, extorted money, and broke into small businesses throughout the city.[54] Another revolt in 1819 was not easily suppressed by the Ottomans. The Ottomans attempted to reassert direct control over Aleppo, but were also distracted by external events, particularly wars.

As much as the eighteenth century was dominated by internal tensions within the empire, it marked an intense period of warfare in which the Ottoman Empire struggled to defend its borders from rival powers. The Ottomans went to war with Iran in 1723 and again in 1746, and wars with the Russians and the Austrians (1768–74 and 1787–92) soon followed. This series of wars undermined the strength of the Janissaries and made way for a stronger *ashraf* in Aleppo. Wars continued to affect Ottoman borders as the empire lost control over Egypt after Napoleon's invasion in 1798. The French controlled Egypt for only three years, but when they left the power vacuum was filled by the ambitious governor Muhammad 'Ali, who had imperial ambitions of his own. He built an army and sent his son Ibrahim to invade the Ottoman lands to the east, conquering Palestine and Syria in 1831. Some of the policies initiated by the Egyptians included conscription and direct taxation. Egyptian rule over the Levant was characterized by the increased participation of non-Muslims in government, particularly in the administrative bodies *(majlis)* that the Egyptians set up in every town. They recruited members from among both Muslims and non-Muslims to be representatives within the *majlis*.[55] The system was eventually dismantled after the British put an end to Muhammad 'Ali's threat to the Ottoman Empire in 1839, although the return to Ottoman rule after the Egyptian occupation proved particularly disruptive.

The Ottomans continued the system of conscription and taxation that the Egyptians had instituted. Furthermore, they attempted to ease the growing tensions between the Muslim and non-Muslim populations by initiating a period of reform. It was intended not only to reformulate the conception of the empire and of citizenship and nationality within it but also to centralize the empire— something that had fallen by the wayside since 1760.[56] The first initiative, the 1839 *Hatt-i Sharif* of Gülhane, or the Imperial Rescript of the Rose Chamber, contained several areas of legal reform, one of which included Muslim and non-Muslim equality under the law.[57] It marked a sharp departure from the previous *millet* (or *zimmi*) that characterized Muslim empires in the past. It was at this point that the Ottomans viewed their non-Muslim subjects as equal under the law, and subject, for example, to military service as their Muslim counterparts but also given rights to political participation in provincial councils.[58] The edict was meant to appeal to Europe, but it was not fully accepted by the Ottoman public. It does mark a period of reform in the Ottoman Empire known as the Tanzimat (Reorganization) that would last until 1876. Events in Aleppo demonstrate the effects of these reforms. In 1850, just a decade after the proclamation of the *Hatt-i Sharif*, tensions between the Muslim and non-Muslim community in Aleppo resulted in riots, the culmination of increasing resentment toward Ottoman centralization and the legal reforms as well as economic hardship. The 1850 attacks were focused on both non-Muslims and Ottoman authorities.[59]

Such difficulties resulted in yet another edict, the *Hatt-i Hümayun* of 1856, reiterating the principles of the 1839 *Hatt-i Sharif*. Some of the reasons for the reissuing of the edict were diplomatic. The Ottomans had fought another war in the Crimean with the Russians (1853–56) and sought European favor through increased reforms, improving the quality of life for Christians within its realm. This period forever affected the relations between Muslims and non-Muslims. Non-Muslims were now legally equals, subjected to military service, and no longer required to pay the *jizya* (a poll tax paid by Christian and Jewish adult men to the Ottoman state). However, this period also had drastic effects on the legal system that had been in place for centuries. My study ends before the initiation of these changes in the court system, a topic discussed by other scholars.[60] The reforms would result in a split in legal jurisdictions and the creation of several courts, including a *nizami* court for criminal matters in 1871. These records would have proved ideal for my study: alas, the records of the Aleppo *nizami* court have not so far been located.[61]

PART ONE
Zina Discourses

1

Zina in Islamic Legal Discourse

A long tradition of legal debate among Muslim jurists dating back to the seventh century produced thousands of legal treatises that are a testament to this lively discourse. Khaled Abou el Fadl, a contemporary Muslim scholar based at the University of California at Los Angeles, has lamented the loss of this lively, pluralistic tradition of the past that has been replaced by the current authoritarian trend that seeks to codify the law into uniformity. This trend can be traced back to the Tanzimat (1839–71) reform era of the nineteenth-century Ottoman Empire whereby centuries of legal opinions were distilled into one all-encompassing legal code. The purpose of this codification of the shari'a was to centralize the Ottoman Empire using a Western modernization model, as well as Western legal codes, as a guideline.[1] The results of this reform have been widely criticized by historians, particularly gender historians who have found that the appropriation of Western codes of law, in some cases, had negative effects for women.[2] In the modern Middle East, trends toward codification have become increasingly authoritarian. Today, government agencies, such as the Saudi Permanent Council, legislate the shari'a, issuing opinions in Saudi Arabia that often become law even as they often lack sound juridical underpinnings.[3] Classical Islamic law, in Abou el Fadl's opinion, has always resisted codification and encouraged interpretation through *ijtihad*. In fact, he argues that such uniformity through codification contradicts the very nature of Islamic law.[4]

The current authoritarian trend in Islamic thought attempts to halt discussion and juridical progress and is reminiscent of the calls for the "closing of the gates of *ijtihad*" by ninth-century Muslim clerics. This attempt to halt Islamic discourse was based on the belief that all legal matters had been settled in the formative period; it sought to silence debate and codify Islamic law. However, Muslim scholars continued to elaborate on the law and invoke *ijtihad* despite this

3

ninth-century discussion, and we have volumes of legal documents produced in those "dark ages" of the closing.[5] Much of the juridical literature *(fiqh)* in this chapter was composed long after the so-called closing of the gates of *ijtihad,* a point that lends further evidence to revisionist arguments that *ijtihad* continued beyond the ninth century.[6]

This chapter investigates some of the layers of Islamic juridical thought on the topic of *zina* in order to demonstrate its origins and development from the early Islamic period onward. An analysis of these writings underscores the liveliness of juridical debates on sexual indiscretion wherein jurists consistently advocated corporeal punishment for *zina,* namely, lashing for unmarried offenders and stoning for married offenders. Jurists advocated these punishments in accordance with legal precedents established in hadith literature upon which they relied. Working with a few brief references to stoning, jurists elaborated on the law using the techniques in legal reasoning in which they were trained. The result was a diversity of opinions in terms of procedure and criteria for punishment—a conclusion that reveals the way readings of the text produced some varied interpretations but also views the precedents that occurred under the Prophet Muhammad as setting clear guidelines through the Prophet's example *(sunna)* upon which law would be based. This emphasis on precedent conforms to the criteria of substantive law; however, jurists also engaged in debates and disagreements in the literature, demonstrating an open discourse among scholars.

ZINA IN THE QUR'AN AND HADITH

In terms of historical practice of stoning among Muslims, the hadith, or the preserved practices of the Prophet Muhammad, are the best source for historians of law. The hadiths claim that the Prophet did not always practice stoning for cases of *zina.* He often advocated one hundred lashes for *zina* and one year's banishment from the community. This punishment is related in a hadith in which the Prophet is reported as saying, "Take it from me! Take it from me! God has now appointed a process for females; the unmarried with the unmarried, one hundred lashes and twelve months' banishment; the married with the married, one hundred lashes and death by stoning."[7] Contradictory reports indicate that the Prophet was disinclined to combine the punishment of flogging and stoning, which explains why later jurists would prohibit dual punishment.

Stoning was of great concern to the second caliph, 'Umar, who insisted that it was a part of the Qur'an but had been excluded in the process of transmission. This claim, as controversial as it may seem in that it implies imperfection in the version of the Qur'an compiled by the third caliph, 'Uthman (644 56), is related in the writings of Ibn Ishaq (704–68). To some Muslims, the claim of a missing "Verse of *rajam* [stoning]" adds veracity to the opinion that stoning is a practice that is mandated, or should have been, in the Qur'an. However, for most Muslims, the hadith sets a historical and legal precedent, laid down by the Prophet, for the tradition of stoning.

So in order to uncover those early precedents, we will look at the Qur'an and hadith, as they form the pillars upon which jurists formulated Islamic law. The first source constitutes the slow accumulation of Qur'anic revelations in the Muslim holy text, and the second, the documented actions of the Prophet and his successors in the hadith, forms the legal precedents used to justify the punishment. Muslim jurists used these sources to develop the corpus of Islamic law. This scholarly discourse resulted in a great body of juridical literature that attempts to cover every aspect of the crime of *zina* in order to provide guidance to the community of believers.

As we begin an archaeology of the legal discourse on *zina*, it is important to discuss the way in which jurists obtained their evidence. There are four main sources of Islamic law. The first source is the Qur'an. The second is the practices of the Prophet Muhammad, collectively called the *sunna,* which is expressed through the hadith. A third source of law is analogy *(qiyas),* by which jurists can develop new rulings for a given situation based on analogous situations found in the Qur'an and the *sunna.* The fourth source is evidence that a consensus *(ijma')* of scholars from the formative period has been found. In addition to these four main sources, other sources are available to the jurist, such as the ability to apply human reason *('aql, ra'y)* in order to solve a legal puzzle, even though much debate surrounds the practice of *ijtihad,* discussed in the introduction. Aside from the shari'a, jurists always took local customary law *('urf)* into consideration, recognizing it as a legitimate source of law so long as it did not contradict the Qur'an and the *sunna.* "The theory of the sacred law did not fail to influence practice and custom considerably, albeit in varying degrees at different places and times, but it never succeeded in imposing itself on them completely."[8] The customary *'urf* laws of a region were in constant tension with and sometimes contradicted the shariʿa, as we will see with the case of *zina* in Aleppo. As *ʿurf* was considered by jurists when making legal rulings, it offered a flexibility that resulted in a diversity of legal interpretations in Islamic law.[9] In fact, entire genres were constructed around the possibility of diverging opinions *(ikhtilaf)* in the law. Other sources sometimes available included consideration of the common good through *istihsan* and *istislah* and the laws promulgated by the state *(siyasa).*[10]

Islamic law divides sex acts into legal and illegal sexual intercourse. Legal intercourse occurs between a married man and woman, but also encompasses a number of permissible sex acts such as masturbation, sex with female concubines, and the practice of birth control.[11] Illegal sex acts include any heterosexual intercourse between free Muslims who are not married to each other. Each offender is given his or her own distinct punishment regardless of gender and marital status. In a hypothetical scenario where a married woman committed *zina* with an unmarried man, each would be given the punishment prescribed according to their status. Jurists would also include sex between a Muslim woman and a non-Muslim man as a punishable transgression.[12]

Jurists debated other forms of *zina,* which included same-sex intercourse; however, jurists were more interested in prohibiting same sex intercourse among men rather than women. Other forbidden practices include anal intercourse, which is forbidden even to married couples, and constitutes a *zina* crime in the Hanbali and Shiite tradition.[13]

To find the original references to *zina* in the shariʿa, one must consult the primary sources—the Qurʾan and the hadith.[14] The Qurʾan cautions against *zina* in three instances. The first verse in *Surat al-Israʾ,* or *Surat Bani Israʾil* 17:32, states that *zina* "is a shameful [deed] and an evil, opening the road [to other evils]." Further elaboration on the issue of *zina* is found in *Surat al-Nur* 24:2–5. It is the only passage that advocates punishment for *zina* in the Qurʾan; more specifically, it promotes the punishment of flogging for the crime. "The woman [zaniah] and man [zani] guilty of adultery or fornication, flog [ajildu] each of them with a hundred stripes." In this passage, the Qurʾan does not make a distinction between married or unmarried adulterers, which becomes an important detail in later discussions of *zina.* The fact that this brief reference will become a foundation for future law demonstrates the complexities of legal reasoning used by jurists in later years.

The third reference to *zina* is found in *Surat al-Nur* where Muslim believers are instructed not to marry an adulterer. It continues to warn that if an accusation of adultery is made, it must be supported by four witnesses. "And those who launch a charge against chaste women, and produce not four witnesses [to support their allegations], flog them with eighty stripes" (17:32). First, the verse *(aya)* establishes the rule for four witnesses, discussed at greater length below. Second, the passage sets into practice a law known as *qadhf,* or false accusation of *zina,* which is an important preventative clause against slanderous accusations and an attempt to dissuade false testimony. The verses intended to warn those Muslims who may attempt to abuse the law and to protect those individuals who may be wrongly accused of the crime by severely punishing wrongful accusations. The historical context for these verses is the accusation of adultery made against the Prophet's favorite wife, 'A'isha bint Abi Bakr, in 627.

The incident that has been called "the account of the lie" *(hadith al-ifk)* has been well documented by both Muslim accounts and modern gender histories of the early Islamic period.[15] The accusation finds its basis in an incident in which 'A'isha accompanied the Prophet Muhammad on a journey but was mistakenly left behind when she dismounted her litter to search for a necklace that had been inadvertently dropped. The caravan, assuming she was still seated in her litter, left without her. She was rescued and reunited with the caravan that she was traveling with the following morning, led by a young man named Safwan ibn Mu'attal al-Sulami.[16] Soon after, rumors of impropriety circulated in the Muslim community. After a period of silence, the Prophet came forth with several verses, including the ones found in the *Surat al-Nur* discussing *zina* and, most important, the wrongful accusation of *zina (qadhf).*

These revelations set forth the criteria of evidence for *zina* outlined above but, importantly, punish anyone who wrongfully accuses without four witnesses. In the case of 'A'isha's accusation of adultery, three individuals were punished with eighty lashes: Hamna bint Jahsh, who was the sister of the Prophet's wife Zaynab, Mistah ibn Uthatha, and Hasan ibn Thabit, a poet.[17] Most notable is the fact that verses of the Qur'an were revealed to support a wife of the Prophet in this unique case. *Surat al-Nur* 11:20 is intended to serve as a warning to anyone who indulges in shameless gossip and slander.

The Qur'an also admonishes same sex intercourse among men in verse 7:81 when it states: "For ye practice your lusts on men in preference to women: ye are indeed a people transgressing beyond bounds." Yet the Qur'an does not pronounce judgment on men who engage in such acts. Even Lot's words to the people of Sodom and Gomorrah in the Qur'an do not threaten punishment. In 26:165–73, Lot says, "and leave those whom God has created for you to be your mates? Nay, ye are a people transgressing (all limits)! They said; 'If thou desist not, O Lut [Lot]! Thou will assuredly be cast out!' He said: 'I do detest your doings.'" The verse conveys disapproval but no legal recourse for acts of sodomy.

The lack of legal recourse for sodomy in the Qur'an left room for debate among jurists. At the popular level, verses relating to the ever after in Muslim heaven were sometimes read with a homoerotic lens by future poets. The Qur'an describes heaven where men will have endless access to overflowing cups of an unnamed nonintoxicating drink and sexual gratification in the presence of both male cupbearers *(saqi)* and heavenly, big-eyed virgins *(houri)*. "Round about them will (serve) youths of perpetual (freshness), with goblets, (shining) beakers, and cups (filled) out of clear-flowing fountains" (56:16). The same chapter describes the companions with big lustrous eyes "like unto pearls" awarded to men in heaven. This image of Muslim heaven was articulated in even more detail in the homoerotic poetry of Abu Nuwas (756–810) and others who played on the image of the young boys "doing nothing but making love and pleasure," as one poem relates.[18] Such popular images of heaven contradicted Qur'anic injunctions against homosexuality, demonstrating that the subject was open to debate.

The second source of Islamic law is the hadiths, which are the traditions and sayings of the Prophet Muhammad, the early caliphs, and the companions of the Prophet. Compiling the hadith was a long historical process in which oral histories were transmitted from one professional memorizer to another and eventually written down. They are the subject of much debate, as some historians view the hadith as the earliest form of Arab history writing.[19] It must be kept in mind that not all hadiths are accepted as authentic by hadith scholars. Checking the authenticity of hadiths is an Islamic science in which the chain of transmission *(isnad)* is subjected to rigorous testing. The viability of transmission is checked through the veracity of its *isnad.* The *isnad* represents those persons who orally memorized the hadith from generation to generation until they were finally compiled into volumes. By checking the *isnad,* many hadiths have been dismissed by scholars who "have advocated its partial or complete abandonment as a pillar of *shari'a.*"[20] There are several hadiths that contradict each other and are still considered authentic. One example of contradictory hadiths is the Prophet Muhammad's wife 'A'isha bint Abi Bakr, whose hadiths often contradict those of other companions of the Prophet.[21] Nonetheless, hadiths are continually invoked by jurists to support their juridical opinions; they are also used in everyday conversation to promote particular social and political conventions as well as patriarchal attitudes.[22]

With respect to *zina*, the hadiths are generally consistent with the prescriptions from the Qur'an that advocate flogging; however, some hadiths add another punishment which is *rajam* (stoning) for a free, married *(muhsan)* man or woman *(muhsana)* who commits *zina*.[23] A hadith in *Sahih al-Bukhari,* one of the most respected collections of Sunni hadiths compiled by Abu 'Abdallah Muhammad ibn Isma'il al-Bukhari (d. 869), affirms the practice of stoning when it states, "The stone is for the adulterer *(lil-'ahir al-hajar)*."[24]

Despite this frequently cited injunction, there is great discrepancy between the Qur'an and the hadiths on the issue of stoning. This incongruity stems from a major problem in the sources, namely, stoning was never advocated as punishment for *zina* in the Qur'an. The inconsistency was noted in a hadith of Caliph 'Umar, who attempted to reenforce the punishment of stoning, despite its lack of textual references. A hadith states:

> 'Umar said, "I am afraid that after a long time has passed, people may say, 'We do not find the Verses of Rajam (stoning to death) in the Holy Book,' and consequently they may go astray by leaving an obligation that Allah has revealed. Lo! I confirm that the penalty of Rajam be inflicted on him who commits illegal sexual intercourse if he is already married and the crime is proved by witnesses or pregnancy or confession. . . . " 'Umar added, "Surely Allah's apostle (peace be upon him) carried out the penalty of Rajam, and so did we after him."[25]

These hadith sources convey an urgency to emphasize the legal precedence of stoning despite its absence in the Qur'an. 'Umar clearly demonstrated in this hadith that local customary practice of law should be carried out, even where the Qur'an is silent presenting, in the view of Muslim jurists, a clear point of abrogation *(naskh)* of the Qur'an in favor of the hadith.[26]

The hadiths claim that stoning was practiced under the Prophet Muhammad and under the rule of the second and fourth caliphs, 'Umar and 'Ali, respectively. These stonings were recounted in several hadiths and formed the foundation for its practice in *zina* cases. However, some hadiths rightly place the foundations of stoning in earlier Jewish traditions. Some popular legends among Muslims have traced the practice of lapidation (casting stones in order to drive away evil) to the early prophet Abraham.[27] The Qur'an does not mention stoning as punishment for *zina,* yet the hadith and even more so Islamic jurisprudence *(fiqh)* create an entire juridical discourse on the topic. There are several references to stoning in the hadith; one particular account stands out from the rest and connects the Islamic practice to the Judeo-Christian tradition. The hadith relates the story of a Jewish man and woman who were caught in the act of adultery:

> Jew and Jewess were brought to Allah's Apostle [*rasul*] on a charge of committing illegal sexual intercourse. The Prophet asked them, "What is the legal punishment [for this sin] in your Book [the Torah]?" They replied, "Our priests have innovated the punishment of blackening the faces with charcoal and *Tajbiya.*"[28] 'Abdullah ibn Salam said, "O Allah's Apostle, tell them to bring the Torah." The Torah was brought, and then one of the Jews put his hand over the Divine Verse of the Rajam [stoning to death] and started reading what preceded and what followed it. On that, Ibn Salam said to the Jew, "Lift up your hand." Behold! The Divine Verse of the Rajam was under his hand. So Allah's Apostle ordered that the two [sinners] be stoned to death, and so they were stoned. Ibn 'Umar added: "So both of them were stoned at the Balat and I saw the Jew sheltering the Jewess."[29]

This hadith offers a dramatic portrayal of the male adulterer attempting to protect the adulteress as they are stoned together. Importantly, it points to the shared Judeo-Christian tradition of stoning as punishment for adultery or sexual indiscretion.

Possibly one of the most memorable scenes of stoning is related in John 8:7 with the image of Jesus protecting the unnamed prostitute about to be stoned. He challenges the Pharisees who condemn her by saying, "Let anyone among you who is without sin be the first to throw a stone at her." This verse attempts to overhaul a practice prevalent in earlier Jewish traditions. The Torah contains several instances of stoning that contain similar patriarchal notions of proprietorship over female sexuality. One case involves a girl who marries, but then afterward her husband states that she was not a virgin at the time of her marriage. "Then the girl shall be brought out to the entrance of her father's house, and the men of her town shall stone her to death; for she did a shameful thing in Israel, committing fornication while under her father's authority. Thus you will sweep away evil from your midst" (Deut. 23:21). This passage points to the community's duty to stone an adulteress in order to purify its town from any form of chaos. It also attaches a woman's sexual propriety to her family since the stoning is to take place on her father's property.

Another case of stoning in the Torah involves a betrothed virgin who has sexual intercourse with a man who is not her fiancé. "In the case of a virgin who is engaged to a man, if a man comes upon her, you shall take the two of them out to the gate of that town and stone them to death: the girl because she did not cry for help in the town, and the man because he violated another man's wife" (Deut. 23:21). This case shows that both the male and the female fornicator were to be punished, just as in Islamic law. What is unique about this case is that if the very same case were to occur in the open country, the girl would not be stoned, only the man. It is assumed that if she were in the open and forced to have intercourse, no one would have heard her screams for help.

These earlier examples are telling of dominant patriarchal attitudes toward women's sexuality that are informative as we begin to study early Islamic traditions on *zina* and stoning. It is in the broader context of the Abrahamic tradition that the hadith describe stoning as it was gradually incorporated into the practices of the early Islamic community; several hadiths report that the Prophet Muhammad and subsequent caliphs may have stoned *zina* convicts. One of the most frequently cited hadith regarding stoning ordered by the Prophet Muhammad was that of Ma'iz. In this hadith, the Prophet tried to dissuade Ma'iz from his confession of *zina,* but ultimately accepted his single confession instead of insisting on four separate witnesses, as the shari'a prescribes. The hadith is as follows: "Narrated Ibn 'Abbas: When Ma'iz ibn Malik came to the Prophet (peace be upon him) [in order to confess], the Prophet (peace be upon him) said to him, 'Probably you have only kissed [the lady], or winked, or looked at her?' He said, 'No, O Allah's Apostle!' The Prophet (peace be upon him) said, using no euphemism, 'Did you have sexual intercourse with her?' The narrator added: At that, the Prophet (peace be upon him) ordered that he be stoned [to death]" (8:534).

Bukhari's rendition of this hadith is not complete. In fact, without a longer version of the hadith we would not know that the Prophet reportedly interrogated Ma'iz to the point of four confessions before stoning him. In the longer version of this hadith Ma'iz is questioned by the Prophet Muhammad, who seeks more precise details of the sex act, inquiring:

> "Did you fuck her [*a-niktaha*]?" He said, "yes." Then he asked, "Did that thing of yours enter that thing of hers?" He answered, "Yes." He asked, "Like the kohl stick disappears into the kohl container and the bucket into the well?" He answered, "Yes." Then he asked, "Do you know what *zina* means?" He said, "Yes, I did with her unlawfully what a man does with his wife lawfully." Then the Prophet said, "What do you intend with these words?" He answered "That you purify me." Then he ordered him to be stoned.[30]

Therefore, this hadith demonstrates that it was only after this series of questioning in which Ma'iz testified against himself four times that the Prophet finally ordered him to be stoned.

Even as earlier punishments found in the Qur'an prescribed one hundred lashings, and one year of banishment as punishment in a hadith tradition, the Prophet prescribed only stoning in the case of Ma'iz.[31] The hadith of Ma'iz has been an important hadith owing to its complexity. This fact is demonstrated in Shafi'i law since it supports a single confession for a *zina* conviction and punishment. "According to Shafei [*sic*], a single confession, in a case of whoredom, is sufficient, because he considers the law to be the same here as in all other cases, the confession or acknowledgement of any circumstance being the means of disclosing or discovering that which is so confessed or acknowledged."[32] On the other hand, in Hanafi jurisprudence, four confessions must be given in order to prove a case of *zina*. These confessions, as stated in the Qur'an, must occur on four separate occasions and in front of a judge. The judge must refuse to accept the confession on three separate occasions, but ultimately accept the fourth confession.[33] Other criteria include that the confession must come from a person of a mature age and of sound mind. It is for this reason that several hadiths concern inquiries about the sanity of anyone who confesses to *zina*.[34] Sanity is a required criteria for punishment in these cases; if one is insane, the case is dismissed. The Hanafis later expanded the clauses for dismissing punishment to include underage offenders. Punishment was generally discouraged in hadith sources; for instance, the Prophet said, "Seek a pretext to prevent punishment according to your ability."[35] Attempts to avert punishment can be seen in examples in which the Prophet tried to discourage confession. One hadith reads:

> Narrated Jabir (peace be upon him): A man from the tribe of Aslam came to the Prophet (peace be upon him) and confessed that he had committed illegal sexual intercourse. The Prophet (peace be upon him) turned his face away from him four times; still the man bore witness against himself four times. The Prophet said to him, "Are you mad?" He said, "No." He said, "Are you married?" He said, "Yes." Then the Prophet (peace be upon him) ordered that he be stoned to death at the Musalla. When the stones troubled him, he fled, but he was caught and was stoned till he died. The Prophet (peace be upon him) spoke well of him and offered his funeral prayer.[36]

This hadith highlights a number of legal issues related to *zina*. First, it clearly establishes the status of the offender as married, warranting the death penalty for the *zina* offense. Second, the hadith notes that the confessions occurred four times, which was equivalent to four witness accounts. Last, the scene emphasizes the important prerequisite of sanity for *zina* conviction. Islamic law, as other codes of law, holds that an offender needs to have the intellectual capacity to understand the unlawfulness of the act he has committed, what is called in legal theory "mens rea," literally "guilty mind."[37]

Aside from adultery cases, hadith sources, more than the Qur'an, illuminate the Prophet's stance on punishment for sodomy. Although the Qur'an makes only brief references to homosexuality, hadiths provide more details on the Prophet's point of view regarding the practice. The Prophet Muhammad stated in one hadith, "Whenever a male mounts another male the throne of God trembles; the angels look on in loathing and say, Lord, why do you not command the earth to punish them and the heavens to rain stones upon them?"[38] Another account states, "The Prophet, peace be upon him, cursed the effeminate men and women who act like men, and said expel them from your homes."[39] Later, a conservative twelfth-century Hanbali jurist, Ibn Jawzi, recalled a hadith of the Prophet, stating, "The thing I fear most for my community is the act of the people of Lot." The Prophet also warned the Muslim community about what would happen if they allowed same-sex relationships in their midst: "Indeed, my community will suffer punishment if men go with men and women with women."[40] Despite these repeated warnings, one hadith acknowledged the temptation to indulge in sex with young men: "Do not gaze at the beardless youths, for verily they have eyes more tempting than the *houris* [big-eyed maidens]."[41] These beardless boys are also described in hadith sources as wearing sumptuous robes and having perfumed hair. One can note differences between the hadith and the Qur'an as the hadith increasingly condemn the practice of sodomy.

The prescriptive literature also reflects an increased interest in punishing anyone who engaged in sodomy. For instance, Malik ibn Anas, the founder of the Maliki school of Islamic law dominant in North Africa, advocated stoning for sodomy. He also argued that both active and passive sodomites will be among the first to burn in the fires of hell, along with men who drink wine, men who masturbate (where he held a dissenting view from other jurists, such as Ibn Hanbal), men who beat their parents, men who offend their neighbors until they are compelled to curse him, and men who have intercourse with their neighbors' wives.[42]

Despite Maliki injunctions, other schools including the Hanafi had mixed rulings on the issue of same sex intercourse. Abu Hanifa placed sex acts with men or boys *(wati'a)* outside the boundaries of *zina,* yet other jurists such as 'Ala' al-Din al-Kasani (d. 1191) argued that sodomy was not *zina,* and therefore it should be punished differently from other *zina* crimes.[43] Another Hanafi jurist, Ibn Nujaym, argued that sodomy constituted *zina* crime. Damascene jurist 'Abd al-Ghani al-Nabulusi (1640–1731), who himself was accused of sexual relations with men and boys, an accusation challenged by Barbara von Schlegell, had a very strong stance against sodomy, arguing that it constituted *kufr* (unbelief) and should be punished with stoning.[44] Such disagreements were clearly possible (even within the same school of legal thought) in Islamic legal discourse. Shafi'i and Hanbali jurists disagreed with some of the more lax rulings of the Hanafis, even prescribing death by the sword for the offense.[45]

As for another category of *zina,* prostitution, there are some early traditions on the subject. The Prophet intervened in a dispute between two concubines (that is, female slaves) and 'Abdallah ibn Ubayy. The women complained that their master was procuring his six female slaves in order to earn money. Upon hearing the case, the Prophet Muhammad received a revelation that swiftly prohibited the practice. In *Surat al-Nur* the Qur'an states, "But force not your maids to prostitution when they desire chastity, in order that ye may make a gain in the goods of this life. But if anyone compels them, yet after such compulsion, is God Oft-Forgiving most Merciful [to them]" (24:33).[46] Prophetic traditions found in the corpus of hadiths describe another man who approached the Prophet Muhammad with a slave girl and asked if it was permissible for the slave to prostitute herself in order to earn money for orphans. The Prophet rejected the request, prompting another revelation on the subject.[47]

Prostitution was addressed yet again in 627 by the Prophet during the Battle of the Trench. The Prophet received complaints that the men of Medina were making sexual advances *(ta'arrad)* toward Muslim women in the community. It was at this moment that the verse on veiling was revealed. In fact, prostitution may have been one of the major underlying factors that encouraged the adoption of the veil that intended to distinguish morally upright Muslim women from prostitutes and slaves in the streets of Medina.[48] The compulsion to differentiate rather than punish prostitutes emphasizes that early Islamic society did not attempt to punish prostitutes so much as place Muslim women in a position of reverence.

THE HANAFI SCHOOL

A vast body of writing developed from the systematic study of the Qur'an and hadith resulted in two genres of Islamic writing, *fiqh* (Islamic juridical writings) and *tafsir* (interpretation of the Qur'an). In the early Islamic period, juridical movements were abundant, resulting in hundreds of schools of legal thought, later narrowed down to four major schools *(madhahab)* in the Sunni tradition: the Hanafi, Shafi'i, Maliki, and Hanbali. These schools are by no means uniform, as there are differences in opinions within legal schools, as exemplified in the debate concerning sodomy above.

The origins of Islamic schools of law stem from Iraq under the Umayyad Dynasty (661–749) in the early second century of Islam. The Iraqi school later influenced the development of other schools in the Hijaz.[49] One of the major schools of thought was founded by Abu Hanifa al-Nu'man ibn Thabit (d. A.H. 150/A.D. 767), who was known for his adherence to the traditions established by the Prophet Muhammad in the *sunna*. The Hanafi school grew out of the great Kufa school and eventually absorbed the Basra school.[50] Muslim jurists expanded the shari'a, elaborating in more detail the Muslim obligations and areas of law that were only briefly mentioned in the Qur'an. By employing reason and logic, jurists developed a science by which law was interpreted and composed into volumes of *fiqh.*

Several legal schools existed along with the Hanafi school, all having a discursive relationship among each other. Legal manuals *(furu')* consistently address the differences between these schools and address the debates among the schools on key issues. The legal schools included the Maliki tradition, founded by Malik ibn Anas (d. A.H. 179/A.D. 795) that was based on the Medinan school, yet was considered underdeveloped when compared to the Iraqi tradition of law. The Maliki school is marked by its "material considerations" that influenced its doctrines.[51] That is, the Malikis not only looked to the traditions of the early Islamic community to base its laws but also valued *'amal,* or tradition, in making its judgments on legal matters. The Maliki school was dominant in several North African communities.

A second school was founded by Imam Shafi'i (d. A.H. 204/A.D. 820), who placed himself within the Iraqi school like the Hanafis. Imam Shafi'i is noted for his successful separation of legal elements from moral elements in his judgments. In this respect, he differed from traditionalists *(ahl al-hadith),* such as the Hanbalis, who disagreed with the use of subjective reasoning *(ra'y)* in Islamic law. "In theory, Shafi'i distinguished sharply between the argument taken from traditions and the result of systematic thought," which, Joseph Schacht argues, created a new system of thought.[52] This legal philosophy later became a discipline of its own when Imam Shafi'i created the *usul al-fiqh,* a discipline that studies the legal theory underlying Islamic shari'a. With these characteristics in mind, the various Islamic schools demonstrate a wide range of opinions on given issues; these differences are often pointed out in the legal texts themselves.

A number of legal commentaries produced by jurists of the Hanafi *madhhab* outline the doctrine embraced by its school of thought. The *fiqh* writings used in this study are works commonly cited by Ottoman and Syrian jurists. The Ottomans chose the Hanafi *madhhab* as the basis for imperial law. Authors have suspected that the Hanafi school was chosen because it was well established in Anatolia from the time it was brought there by the Seljuq Turks.[53] Others have argued that the Hanafi school was chosen over others because it was seen as more favorable to commerce because of its emphasis on binding contracts.[54] Colin Imber argues that the Hanafi school offered more latitude to

Muslim rulers to enforce their own laws (Arabic: *siyasa;* Ottoman Turkish: *siya-set*), which may have been another motivation for its selection.[55] What we know for sure is that the major Ottoman courts were Hanafi, and even though other schools of law existed alongside the Hanafis, in the Ottoman period jurists who administered Hanafi justice found themselves more easily promoted to Ottoman administrative positions. The influence of the school extended to other parts of the Islamic world, such as the region that encompasses today's Afghanistan and Pakistan.

There are several volumes of juridical writings in the Hanafi school that were widely read by jurists in the period under study, many of which were written after the so-called closing of the gates of *ijtihad*. One such source is the *Mabsut* of Muhammad ibn Ahmad al-Sarakhsi (d. A.H. 490/A.D. 1090), one of the earliest books to outline Hanafi law. The *Hedaya* (Guide) of Abi Bakr al-Farghani al-Marginani (d. A.H. 953/A.D. 1196) is another popular Hanafi legal manual in the Ottoman period that was referenced by jurists. Yet a third *fiqh* commentary is Zayn al-Din ibn Nujaym's (d. 1563) *Al-Bahr al-Ra'iq Sharh Kanz al-Duqa'iq* (Commentary on the Treasury of Subtleties). And, finally, Ibrahim al-Halabi's (d. 1549) *Multaqa al-Abhur* (The Confluence of Seas) was highly influential in sixteenth-century Ottoman juridical thought. The work was commissioned by Selim I, was completed in 1517, and soon replaced other juridical texts as the authoritative text in the empire.[56] These volumes form a core of Hanafi juridical thought in the period under study, but should be understood primarily as the doctrine and ideals of the authors who composed these texts. One author has written, "It is possible perhaps to characterize the *shari'a* as an ideal law, in part practical, but whose fulfillment in total remains a pious aspiration rather than an achievable goal." These laws are not a uniform legal code of justice. "Normative legal discourses were designed not to be rigidly applied but rather to be used as legal guidelines whose interpretation depended on local particulars."[57]

Aspects of Hanafi law were later incorporated into the early Ottoman legal codes, called the *kanunnames*. These laws are discussed in detail in the next chapter. The Ottoman legal system became, in effect, ossified in 1877 when the Ottoman Empire codified the Hanafi laws into the *Mecelle,* a secular code that synthesized both the Swiss code and Hanafi law, thereby attempting to emulate Western-style models of law. This legal reform greatly impacted the practice of law in the region, as the population had considerably less access to outside interpretations as in the previous four-school model whereby those individuals who used the court could use not only the Hanafi judge but also deputies *(na'ib)* representing the other three schools of law, who were present to offer their interpretations of law. Postreform, only a singular interpretation could be accessed, the reformed code.

What is the definition of *zina* in the Islamic juridical writings? According to al-Marginani, *zina* is defined as "the carnal conjunction of a man with a woman who is not his *property* either by right of marriage or of bondage."[58] Ownership of a slave woman gives a man the right to sexual access to her according to the law. For a free woman, it is necessary for the union to be legal, which can only be through marriage. The interesting choice of the term *property* to describe legal unions conveys the idea that a woman's sexuality can be owned through the marriage contract, whereby her sexuality belongs to her husband. It is unfortunate that this idea of women as property evokes stereotypical images of the Muslim world when in fact it is found in the earliest laws of the Mediterranean. In several legal cultures women were viewed only as a means of procreation, a body from which children could be reproduced. Within some of the earliest civilizations, such as the Phoenicians, Assyrians, and Babylonians, women were completely subservient to male authority, and married women were owned exclusively by their husbands. For that reason, when a woman was involved in a case of adultery or sexual indiscretion, the matter was comparable to an issue of stolen or usurped property.[59] Other ancient Mesopotamian legal practices in the pre-Islamic period included the proprietorship of the patriarch over his family. For example, Hammurabi Code relegated wives and children as property to the extent that they could be forced into servitude for debts unpaid by the patriarch. This practice also extended to the degree that a man could hand over his child or wife to be punished for crimes that he committed.

It is in this wider context that the notion of woman as property needs to be understood. Muslim jurists described various damages that included damaged property and even abduction under the category of usurpation *(ghasb).* Today, the word for rape in modern Arabic is *ightisab,* which is derived from the verb meaning "to usurp" or "to take illegal possession" of something. Joseph Schacht argues that among tribesmen in the pre-Islamic period, *zina* was not so much a sin as it was "an injury to the rights of property of a fellow tribesman."[60] There is a noticeable continuity with the pre-Islamic past in which the crime of rape, as well as sexual impropriety, held the same status as theft of property. Some of the patriarchal residue of these earlier practices has even been imprinted on the language used to describe such crimes.

Marriage relations also demonstrate a continuation of the notion of proprietorship. For example, the Hanafi school emphasizes the binding nature of contracts, be they business or personal. This stress is particularly noticeable in marriage contracts, since it is difficult for a woman to obtain a divorce in Hanafi courts of law. A woman could obtain a divorce, with her husband's consent, by giving up her final dowry *(mu'akhkhar)* in a *khul'* (a mutual repudiation resulting in the dissolution of a marriage). Outside of that measure she could not obtain a divorce except in cases of the husband's proven death or impotency. The Hanafi school stressed the ownership *(mulk)* of the wife's sexuality on the part of the husband; this ownership makes the sexual intercourse between man and wife legal. The legal contract is sealed by the husband's gift to the wife in the form of *mahr* (dowry or bridal gift), which awards him this ownership. In a much referenced volume of Hanafi *fiqh,* the *Mabsut,* it states explicitly, "The dowry [*mahr*] is an exchange for the vulva [*al-mahr 'iwad 'an al-budh'*]."[61] In turn, if a couple is married and does not consummate the marriage, Abu Hanifa states in a fatwa that "the whole of the dower [*mahr*] is due because the husband did not make use of his possession."[62] In such a case, the husband would be forced to return the dowry to his wife, reinforcing the Hanafi connection between the *mahr* and access to a woman's sexuality. However, this connection also underscores another important concept in Islamic law, namely, *diya* (blood money).

The Prophet declared that "there is no dower less than ten *darahim.*" Although each woman has the right to determine her own dowry, ten *darahim* is declared a minimum because it marks the "lowest amount of a theft including the punishment of amputation of a limb."[63] The correlation between the payment of *diya* for the crime of theft and a woman's dowry is worth discussing. They are connected through the way in which Islamic law treats issues of bodily harm *(arsh).* In the case of murder, whether intentional or unintentional, one pays a *diya.* If one has been harmed, the perpetrator will pay for bodily harm in proportion with a body part lost, that is, an arm, leg, or eye.[64] Muslim jurists assigned value to various body parts, as they were viewed as property *(amwal)* of the individual, and if they were in some way injured, the offender "must suffer a loss of precisely equivalent value."[65] This restitution includes sexual offenses; for example, this type of compensation was paid to rape victims in the Ottoman period as will be discussed in chapter 5. On the other hand, in the case of murder, *diya* can also take the form of monetary punishment and instead of the death penalty.

As licit sexual relations hinge on the marital contract between a man and his wife sealed in the *mahr* exchange, the criminal definition of *zina* becomes more complex. In most legal manuals *zina* is either given its own heading or listed as a *hadd* (plural, *hudud*) crime. In the context of Islamic law, *hadd* designates crimes that have fixed punishments in the shari'a. Ibrahim al-Halabi calls this category of crime "the claims of God [*haq Allah*]," which describes the offense as one against religion.[66] What this classification means in theory is that the judge cannot use his own discretion when administering punishment but instead must administer the fixed punishment established by the shari'a. *Hadd* crimes are the most severe violations of moral and religious code. These crimes include *zina,* false accusation of *zina (qadhf),* theft, apostasy, highway robbery or banditry, and drinking alcohol.[67] The punishments for these crimes are prescribed in juridical writings; they are severe and can range from amputation to flogging and death, depending on the crime and circumstance. The reason for the severity of punishment relates to the way in which the law divides the world of punishment. Some crimes, such as the ones in the *hadd* category, have "the potential for social chaos," and therefore needed to be checked. The punishments for those crimes need to be established by God, since "these offenses are regarded as acts that violate the bounds, rights and claims of God [and therefore] it is not up to human beings to interpose their own judgment as to appropriate remedies."[68] A second form of punishment found in juridical writings is *ta'zir,* which in the context of Islamic legal theory refers to the discretionary punishment of the judge.[69] From the perspective of Islamic law, these crimes are punishable at the discretion of the judge because they do not threaten social order or the authority of God. In theory, the punishments for *hadd* crimes are not at the discretion of the judge; however, it has been argued that judges used their discretion, rather than the prescribed punishments, when they were unable to apply the appropriate punishments when evidentiary requirements were unfulfilled, when judicial doubt was present *(shubha),* or when the offender was pardoned by the victim's family.[70]

Under the shari'a's clearly defined criminal categories, *zina* fits squarely within the bounds of a *hadd* crime. Because punishment for *zina* could produce lethal results, jurists drafted procedures by which conviction was acceptable.

Hanafi jurists agreed that confession was to take place on four separate occasions in the presence of a *qadi*. However, the law also became more complicated concerning the admission of one party and the denial of another. If a man confesses to adultery with a given woman and she denies it, he is subject to punishment alone, according to Hanafi code. The man in question would not be punished for *zina*, but for *qadhf* (false accusation of *zina*), and his punishment would be eighty lashes.[71]

Along with *qadhf*, jurists often discussed a third concept, the *li'an* divorce. This divorce allows one to leave the marriage without enduring any punishment for committing *zina*. In this case, the husband is not responsible for any children born after the marriage is dissolved. In order to enact this divorce, the wife must make a financial sacrifice in the form of her final dowry *(mu'akhkhar)*.[72]

In the Hanafi school, the *qadi*'s duty was to do everything in his power to prevent punishment from taking place, in the tradition of the Prophet Muhammad found in the hadith of Ma'iz, noted above. Furthermore, jurists established rigid conditions upon which a person can be convicted of *zina* in order to prevent punishment in most cases.

There were some precedents for milder punishments in *zina* cases (or *zina* as rape in this particular example). A hadith from the reign of Caliph 'Umar states "And Safiya bint 'Ubayd said: A state-owned slave had sexual intercourse with a girl from among the *khumus* [a fifth of a share of war booty]. He had coerced her until he [ultimately] raped her. Therefore, 'Umar flogged him according to the *hadd* and banished him, but he did not flog the girl because she was forced."[73] This hadith from *Sahih al-Bukhari* is the earliest report of rape in these sources. Its importance lies in its vivid description of the way Islamic law differentiates between consensual and nonconsensual sexual intercourse and shows a distinction between a general type of sexual crime *(zina)* and the crime of rape. The hadith explicitly describes the rape victim as forced into the act and, as a consequence, not subject to punishment. Even as he called for stoning on several occasions, in another incident Caliph 'Umar allowed punishment for rape to take the form of incarceration or flogging, unless a confession took place four times.[74]

Later-sixteenth-century jurist Ibrahim al-Halabi, whose work *Multaqa al-Abhur* was influential among the Ottomans, questioned whether rape should be included as a *zina* offense. It shared both characteristics of crimes of injury and

crimes that violated religion *(hudud)*. This ambiguity over whether rape constituted *zina* was mostly owing to the absence of consent on the part of the victim,
which caused jurists to set it apart from other offenses.[75]

As for confession, the Hanafis held that a confession of innocence after one
of guilt could release the person from the charge. The Shafi'is and the Hanbalis
disagreed with the Hanafi school on this issue; some jurists within those schools
argued that punishment must be instituted, despite the denial.[76] Islamic doctrine
does not offer a reduction in penalty for any confessions to the crime. Crime
accumulates debt, a debt that must be paid either in this life or in the next. This
debt can be either physical punishment or monetary compensation. For instance,
in the case of murder, the victim's family can decide whether to accept physical
punishment or payment of blood money. In Islamic law, if the perpetrator has
not been caught, the victim's family is still entitled to compensation that will
be paid to them through the civil treasury *(bayt al-mal)*. This example reaffirms
the importance of criminal debt being paid to society and victims through punishment. The same holds true for *zina,* whereby jurists deliberated on the form
punishments would take.

PUNISHMENT, GENDER, AND THE BODY

The punishment of stoning until dead *(rajam)* is not found in the Qur'an. *Rajam,*
as used in the Qur'an, does not advocate stoning; instead, the word conveys the
concept of "murder," "the devil," and "the accursed."[77] In terms of its other meaning as "lapidation," its origins lie in the Muslim pilgrimage ritual at Mina, where
pilgrims throw stones, symbolizing the casting off of evil. It is in this sense that
jurists use the term to describe the punishment of stoning until dead. Hanafi
and Hanbali jurists required that both parties to the act of *zina* have the status
of *muhsan* in order for stoning to be applicable.[78] The term *muhsan* has many
meanings, describing the person as free, adult, of sound mind, married, having
had sexual relations in marriage in the past, and Muslim (except in the Shafi'i
tradition). It has an alternate meaning in some juridical discussions that describe
someone who has not been convicted of any crime, including *zina.*[79]

Juridical writings describe, in explicit detail, the instructions for the treatment of the body while it endures the sentence of stoning. There are two aspects
of the body that are revealed in Hanafi legal thought: the actual positioning of

the body during stoning for men and for women and the treatment of the body after death.

Islamic law describes two types of stoning cases. The first is for someone punished based on their confession *(iqrar)*. In these cases, it is not mandatory to stone them, and if the person flees from the site while being stoned, they are free to leave.[80] The second type of case is mandatory punishment based on concrete evidence *(bayyina)* in the form of four male eyewitnesses. This situation is problematic, as the four-male-witness requirement greatly restricts the witnessing power of women, whose testimony is, according to the law, worth only half that of a man. There are to be four witnesses in order to support a *zina* conviction, though some jurists have disagreed on this point, including Hanbali jurists Ibn Taymiyya, Ibn al-Qayyim al-Jawziyya, and al-Tabari.[81] In the case of *zina* proven through evidence rather than personal confession, the offender must be bound and is not free to leave. Juridical writings specify that stoning should take place far away from mosques, holy places, or any other places of worship.[82] Furthermore, Islamic law has varying opinions about who should execute the punishment of stoning. Abu Hanifa and later Hanafi jurist Ibrahim al-Halabi argued that witnesses used in the conviction should be the first to cast stones at the convict, since it presents a good opportunity for any weary witnesses to recant their statements and stop the process before it is too late.[83] The imam, or religious leader, and the wider community were to join in the process and throw stones at the offender. If the conviction was based not on the testimony of witnesses but instead on personal confession, the head of state or a judge *(qadi)* should cast the first stone.[84] The Shafi'i school of law disagreed with the Hanafi ruling, arguing that it was not the duty of the witnesses to begin the process; rather, the imam or his deputy should initiate the punishment. Ibrahim al-Halabi writes that after the witnesses and the imam cast their stones, the community can join them. However, both schools agree that the behavior of witnesses should be observed throughout the process in case there is any doubt about their testimony. Furthermore, the juridical writings even discuss the size of the stones that should be used during the stoning. Stones should not be too large, causing death too quickly, nor should they be too small, causing unnecessary suffering. For that reason, the Hanafis ruled that stones should be the size of one's hand.[85]

Juridical writings discuss in detail the way in which the body should be positioned during stoning. Immediately apparent is the difference in posture during stoning based on the gender of the accused. These positions were established in hadith, such as the precedent set in the stoning of Maʿiz, who was left unbound during punishment. The hadith related earlier about the man from the tribe of Aslam describes him as unbound during the stoning and actually fleeing the scene; he was eventually caught and killed. Men are not to be bound except in cases where the offender is exceptionally strong.[86] The stoning of women differs greatly because it is based on two precedents: the stoning of Ghamidiyya during the life of the Prophet and the stoning of Shoraha under Caliph ʿAli.[87] Both of these women were stoned while part of their body was buried in the ground.

The hadith of al-Ghamidiyya (meaning woman from Ghamid, a tribe and district in western Arabia) relates the story of an unnamed pregnant woman who confessed to *zina* before the Prophet Muhammad. Although al-ʿAsqalani documents four versions of this hadith, all of them fail to describe the marital status of the woman.[88] Still, the stories all document the same interaction, whereby al-Ghamidiyya says, "Oh Prophet of God, I have sinned, purify me." Some of the hadiths add that the woman repeated her confession on more than one occasion. The hadith describes that the Prophet was impressed by her honesty. He reportedly said, "I urge you to ask for God's forgiveness and repent." And she said, "I see that you wish to dissuade me as you dissuaded Maʿiz ibn Malik," indicating her familiarity with the earlier instance of stoning related above. The Prophet said to her, "What is that?" apparently referring to her abdomen. She said, "I am pregnant from *zina*." He said, "You?" and she answered, "Yes." This conversation resulted in two more confessions of *zina*.

The Prophet then said, "Wait until you give birth to that which is in your stomach." In the meantime, a man from among the Ansar (Medinans) provided her with financial support until she gave birth. He later notified the Prophet Muhammad when she had given birth but noted, "If we stone her we will drive away her small son and he will not be able to suckle." So they waited until her son was weaned and began to eat food on his own. It was then that they executed her by burying her up to her chest and stoning her to death, which the hadith describes in graphic detail. During the stoning, Khalid ibn al-Walid "aimed a stone right at her head and blood spurted on his face and he cursed her, and the Prophet Muhammad (peace be upon him) heard his curse at her, and said, 'Oh Khalid, that soul has repented and turned to God in repentance.'" Khalid begged for forgiveness, and the Prophet also forgave him. After they stoned her they prayed and buried her.

A number of important legal precedents are established in this hadith. First, the hadith deals with the treatment of pregnant offenders. Both Hanafi and Shafi'i schools contain variations in punishment in the case of pregnancy. Stoning cannot be postponed because of illness but can be postponed if the recipient is pregnant, "for if she were to be stoned whilst pregnant, the child would be destroyed in her womb, and its blood is not to be taken; and if her punishment be scourging, the execution must be deferred until she shall have recovered from her labour."[89]

Second, the hadith provides a detailed account of the treatment of the female body during stoning. Some jurists would establish it as the norm as the Hanafi text, the *Hedaya,* states that "where a woman is to be stoned, a hole or excavation should be dug to receive her, as deep as her waist."[90] In contrast, the hadith of the Jew and Jewess describes neither party as bound during the stoning. Although the hadith specifically references Jewish law, and Muslim empires often allowed religious communities to adjudicate their own cases, debates ensued over jurisdiction. The Hanafis hold non-Muslims punishable in accordance with Islamic law, unlike the Shafi'i school, which places the responsibility on each non-Muslim *(dhimmi)* community to administer its own punishments.[91] As for the variation in practice, the Prophet may have been applying Jewish law, as evidenced by the explicit reference to the Torah, which may explain why the couple was punished unbound.

A third precedent established in the hadith of Ghamidiyya is the treatment of the body of the executed after punishment. In modern versions of stoning, women have not been given a proper burial after stoning; instead, as in one stoning case in modern Iran, the body was left outside the city to be eaten by wild dogs—a punishment reminiscent of the biblical execution of Jezebel.[92] Yet traditions for a proper Islamic burial were clearly established with the stoning of Ghamidiyya. Furthermore, the Prophet demanded an Islamic burial after the stoning of Ma'iz: "Do by the body as ye do those of other believers." Islamic jurisprudence incorporates these earlier traditions when it states that "the offender thus put to death is slain in vindication of the laws of God, wherefore ablution is not refused, as in the case of one put to death by a sentence of retaliation. Moreover, the Prophet allowed the prayers for the death of Ghamdia [Ghamidiyya], after lapidation."[93] In other words, committing the crime does not render the offender a nonbeliever or undeserving of a respectable interment. Once payment is made for the crime, in this case stoning, the offender is to be treated as any other believer and given a proper burial.

In stoning cases, the Hanafi school argues that the woman need not fully recover from labor before punishment, since the child is to be taken from her upon its birth. In Hanafi code, there is but one exemption: if the mother is the only possible guardian of the child. In that instance, her punishment will be delayed until the child is old enough to be independent of its mother, namely, when it has finished nursing. This tradition is based on a hadith of the Prophet in which he said to Ghamidiyya after her bearing a child, "Go and remain until such a time as your child is independent of you."[94] Such imprisonment is not unusual, as one tradition notes that the Prophet once prescribed imprisonment for the crime of *zina*.[95] By advocating imprisonment, the Prophet also created a legal precedent by which corporal punishment could be overruled in favor of imprisonment.

The Hanafi literature addresses flogging, applicable in cases where the status of the *zina* offender is unmarried. There are distinctions made based on free or slave status; if the offender is a slave, he will receive fifty lashes, whereas free men and women receive one hundred lashes.[96] Furthermore, the body is treated differently according to gender, as the flogging differs for male and female offenders.[97] The shari'a urges moderation; punishments like stoning and banishment cannot be combined with lashing (or any kind of *ta'zir*).[98] The Shafi'i code differs on this point, saying the two should be united, because the Prophet once prescribed one hundred lashes and one year of banishment for an unmarried person guilty of *zina* and one hundred lashes and stoning for a married offender.[99]

Flogging, as with stoning, differs according to gender. Caliph 'Ali gave a directive on punishment for unmarried men and women guilty of *zina*, stating, "When punishment is to be inflicted on any person, it is necessary that he be stripped naked; that is to say, that all clothes be taken off except the girdle."[100] However, a woman's body is problematic in the juridical literature. The legal sources prescribe lashing of the skin, something that contradicts the standards of modest dress for women. Because an important aspect of flogging is the necessity for it to be a public event, a spectacle, in order to deter future offenses, the Hanafi code explicitly states that lashes are to be given to women as they sit as opposed to men while they stand.[101]

The reason for such variations in posture could again be attributed to the fear of nakedness, as in the burying of a woman during stoning. The impact of the stones could cause her dress to tear, and her nakedness could evoke lust among the executioners, causing yet another form of *zina*. Another possible reason for burying women during stoning could be that the gendered worldview of the jurist held that men, as the "stronger sex," could endure more punishment than women. The buried position of women would focus blows to the skull until death and possibly result in a more speedy execution. Hanafi shari'a is just as specific in its formulations regarding flogging. It is not to be given lengthwise, because doing so would damage the body more than necessary. The attention given to inflicting no more than the minimum amount of punishment necessary is indicative of the concerted effort of jurists to institute moderation among executioners of punishment. Lashings are to take place on the back so as to cause the least amount of damage to the offender's body.[102] Furthermore, individual limbs are not to be flogged. "None of the stripes must be inflicted on the face, the head, or the privities, because the Prophet once said to an executioner, 'In inflicting the punishment, take care not to strike the face, head, to the privities (al-Halabi notes the vulva [*farj*] in particular is not to be targeted).'"[103]

These areas are to be left undamaged during the flogging for several reasons, which al-Marginani lists. One reason is that lashing one's head could cause damage to the brain and could destroy one's mental capacity. Punishment should not permanently damage the mental faculties of the criminal and is therefore forbidden. The literature also adds that it is forbidden to target genitalia during punishment. The *Hedaya* says the privates are to be avoided because they are "a part which cannot be wounded without danger to life."[104] Lashings are supposed to be moderate and not cause any permanent scarring. Furthermore, the punishment is not to take place if the weather is too hot or too cold or if the offender is ill.[105] The *hadd* punishments for theft, drinking, and *zina* committed by an unmarried Muslim will be delayed if the party is ill. In these circumstances, the offender will be imprisoned until healthy enough to endure the punishment.

The sources overwhelmingly point toward physical punishment. The body becomes the space upon which the shari'a draws the connection between the crime committed and the punishment prescribed. The care given to the treatment of the body in juridical writings emphasizes only that the procedures were meant to ritualize punishment so that it could be displayed to a viewing public.

Khaled Fahmy discusses the ritual of public punishment with reference to the Ottoman criminal code, discussed in the next chapter: "The intention of all these punishments that exhibited itself so spectacularly on the body of the culprit was, in one sense, to make the body of the culprit a book to be read, as it were, by the illiterate spectators, urging them to draw connections, however vague, between the crime committed and what was believed to be its appropriate punishment."[106] The vivid details offered by Muslim jurists on the subject of stoning and flogging emphasize that urge to make punishment a spectacle.

At the same time, moderation is urged through the example of the Prophet, which is reiterated by jurists. In these instances, the punished are not to be permanently maimed or even killed during flogging, and innocents, like unborn fetuses, are not to bear the burden of their mothers' sins. It is in this discussion that one notes the care that jurists gave to the matter of directing punishment only where it was due and under the strictest criteria of evidence in order to ensure that only the guilty were punished.

Furthermore, through the constant discussion of *zina* in the legal literature, the punishment guidelines based on the Qur'an and earlier codes became more sophisticated and complex. The detail by which Muslim jurists described the punishment of stoning leaves one to question how these guidelines were interpreted in later centuries. The best illustration is to look at the Ottoman Empire, where Islamic law underwent a major transformation and was codified into Ottoman criminal law. The next chapter will look at the Ottoman *kanunnames* and fatwas and the way in which the shari'a continued to develop into an imperial code of law under the Ottomans.

2

Zina in Ottoman Law

As a major city in the Ottoman Empire, Aleppo was subject to the laws of its rulers. The Ottomans viewed themselves as the protectors of Muslim tradition, which included upholding the shari'a. Yet the shari'a was not always practical for handling the day-to-day issues that arose in the empire. Therefore, by necessity, the Ottomans established their own imperial laws called *kanunnames* that covered a wide range of areas, including taxation policies, the responsibilities of Ottoman officials, land regulations, and criminal codes. The usefulness of *kanunnames* can best be understood when they are studied in combination with other sources of law. The *kanunnames* not only show the imperial position on gender relations and concerns for maintaining civil order but also document the historical development of Islamic law in the Ottoman period, namely, the distilling of the shari'a into a set code of imperial law. The result of this process was sharp differences in interpretation of the shari'a, especially in penal law.[1]

Ottoman fatwas (juridical opinions) were yet another source of law in the Ottoman Empire.[2] Fatwas were issued in several cities throughout the Ottoman Empire; many of them, particularly the fatwas from the Arabic-speaking lands, have been explored by historians in recent decades.[3] Ottoman imperial fatwas were issued by the chief mufti of the empire *(shaykhul-islam)*, who was, in effect, the spiritual leader of the sultan and the official Muslim leader of the empire. The chief mufti's fatwas often reflected a more imperial point of view than the ones issued by provincial muftis in other parts of the empire, which have been examined by other scholars.[4] Both imperial fatwas and *kanunnames* contained detailed discussions of *zina* that will be explored in this chapter.

This discussion of Ottoman sources will include the *kanunnames* of Selim I (r. 1512–20) and Süleyman the Lawgiver (r. 1520–66) along with the fatwas of Ebu's Su'ud Efendi, who served as his *shaykhul-islam* (1545–74). The documents used in this chapter date back to the sixteenth century and reveal some of the earliest insights into the perception of both gender and public morality at that time. These laws set the stage for the study of law in Ottoman Aleppo that will be undertaken in the next chapter. How did the Ottomans treat *zina* in their criminal codes as compared to the Muslim jurists discussed in the previous chapter? What kinds of gender issues was the empire preoccupied with and why?

A noticeable departure from our previous discussion is that Ottoman law transformed the physical punishments found in the shari'a into a fine-based punishment system. Ottoman law, embodied in the *kanunnames,* differed in the way that it defined *zina* and how punishment was to be administered. Ultimately, the differences between shari'a and *kanunname* with respect to *zina* lie in variations in punishment, whereby the mandated prescriptions for *hadd* in the form of physical punishment were omitted from the *kanunnames.*

HADD IN OTTOMAN LAW: A STRATEGY TO ESCAPE THE STONE

> Ward off the fixed punishments from the Muslims on the strength of *shubha* as much as you can.
> —The Prophet Muhammad

Ottoman legal sources present a very different picture of punishment than the Islamic juridical writings discussed in the previous chapter. There are a number of reasons for this variation, an important cultural consideration being the vast boundaries of the empire extending through Mesopotamia, across North Africa, and as far north as the Balkans during its height in the sixteenth century. Ottoman law differs so drastically from the shari'a on the subject of punishment that one may speculate it was an attempt to reconcile the law with the needs of the empire's diverse population. It is worth considering the context of legal pluralism during this investigation of Ottoman law. The Ottomans had a tradition of accommodation of local legal traditions among tribesmen and villagers. Christians and Jews were able to practice their own traditions within their communities under the jurisdiction of their churches and synagogues. Shari'a courts in many ways belonged to the Muslim community but were open to anyone who sought to use them. It is this view of the court as more than a Muslim court, but rather a civil court, that is its best description.[5] Ottoman law lay under the supreme jurisdiction of the sultan. As earthly ruler, the sultan sought an accommodation between God's law and his own. "Jurists gave wide discretion to the Sultan outside the realm of *fiqh* to preserve order, protect the interests of the community *(maslaha)* and make examples out of those who defied his authority." Streamlining these two divergent legal traditions was a challenge. The Ottomans may have chosen the Hanafi *madhhab* as their major school of choice because its interpretation of law accommodated the autonomy of the ruler, giving him more room to administer his own laws (Arabic: *siyasa;* Ottoman: *siyaset*) outside of the shari'a. Leslie Peirce defines this area of law "as the right to inflict severe corporal or capital punishment—almost always violence to the body, sometimes execution—if the public interest or the integrity of the state or its religion demanded it."[6] It is in this way that the Ottoman sultan, according to Hanafi legal theory, could promulgate codes that differed from the shari'a and still maintain his authority as a Muslim head of state.

When it came to the crime of *zina,* the Ottomans embraced two legal principles that offered strategies for preventing the implementation of *hadd* punishments such as stoning. First, it created a system of fines in which compensation was paid for physical damages. Second, it relied on the notion of *shubha* (judicial doubt), which provided a legal loophole for escaping punishment altogether. With regards to the first principle, the system of fines used in the Ottoman laws is fully documented in the Ottoman *kanunnames.* This system marks a major departure from the shari'a, as "the *shari'a* treats *zina* as a criminal offence for which conviction in court incurs fixed *(hadd)* penalties. The *kanunname* does the same, but commutes the fixed penalties of the *shari'a* for a fixed scale of fines." Why the Ottomans modified some of the most severe punishments in Islamic law is debatable, but there are legal precedents for commuting prescribed *hadd* punishments to lighter penalties. For example, "the Prophet once ordered a person charged with whoredom to be imprisoned." Uriel Heyd has argued that the shift from physical punishment to fine-based punishment was a result of the legal teachings of Hanafi jurist Abu Yusuf, who argued that rulers could "inflict discretionary punishment by taking money," or *ta'zir b'il-mal.* Overall, *hadd* crimes found in *fiqh* (which includes fatwas) called for stoning but were commuted to lighter punishments of flogging and fines in the *kanunnames.* This shift has been attributed to "the increasing rigidity of the *shari'a* itself [that] prevented it from keeping pace with actual practice."[7] Even as fines were applied, they did not increase with time but remained fixed, despite inflation. Thus, the fines would have been nominal after the first few *kanunnames* that set the rates at sixteenth-century standards.[8]

There were several legal strategies available to the Ottomans that allowed them to discard violent corporal punishment in cases of sexual indiscretion. There were the precedents of Caliph 'Umar, discussed in the previous chapter, that allowed for alternative punishments, like flogging, instead of stoning. The Ottomans also took full advantage of an important feature of the shari'a, the notion of *shubha,* meaning "resemblance" or "judicial doubt."

The epigraph at the beginning of this section is a hadith of the Prophet Muhammad, calling for believers to avoid implementing *hadd* punishments where judicial doubt or resemblance *(shubha)* is present. *Shubha* can be used to create a legal loophole for avoiding punishment for *zina* in cases in which the accused claims that he perceived the act as lawful.[9] This loophole works primarily in cases where a man and a woman believe they are legally married, lacking the intent to commit *zina.* The foundations for this principle are found in the *Hedaya,* which states, "The person who has carnal conjunction does not incur punishment, provided he declares—'I conceived that this woman was lawful to me';—but if he should acknowledge his consciousness that the woman was unlawful to him, he incurs punishments." Perceived "ownership" can be used to discourage punishment in cases of prostitution as well. This passage indicates that in Ottoman law a perpetrator needs to have intent, or knowledge that he is in fact committing a crime, for it to be an offense. Colin Imber writes, "The offender(s) must plead ignorance of the act's legality in order to avoid punishment." Again, this plea is made through judicial doubt. In this case, the offender perceived that the act was legal *(shubhat al-milk;* literally, "resemblance of ownership").[10]

Later jurists continued to endorse *shubha* as a way to avoid the *hadd* punishments outlined in the shari'a. The sixteenth-century legal treatise *Multaqa al-Abhur* of Ibrahim al-Halabi notes, "'There is no *hadd* punishment due for intercourse . . . with a strange woman [*mahrama*] whom a man has hired in order to fornicate with her. . . .' Ibn Nujaym, following Abu Hanifa, explains the ruling by assimilating prostitution to quasi-ownership, the prostitute's fee representing the dowry."[11]

Seventeenth-century Ottoman jurist Sadiq ibn Muhammad al-Saqazi (d. 1688) agreed with al-Halabi, that sex for hire did not warrant the *hadd* punishment required for *zina*. Later chapters of this book will show that in the Ottoman period, physical punishment was rarely administered in cases where prostitution was proven. The notion of *shubha* is essential to understanding how prostitution as well as other sexual offenses were not punished with the prescribed whip and stone. Judith Tucker, discussing seventeenth- and eighteenth-century fatwas of Ottoman Syria and Palestine, writes that the "concept of *shubha* allowed the muftis to convert the usually draconian punishment for rape into the relatively mild requirement of an indemnity." This manipulation of the law may have been necessary in order to align the practice of law with social realities on the ground and could explain why sixteenth-century Ottoman legal codes did not subject prostitutes to corporal punishment.[12]

The Hanafi school held firmly to a tradition of the Prophet Muhammad that urged believers to avert *hadd* punishments through judicial doubt. In order to deter convictions of *zina*, Hanafi law makes it virtually impossible to witness it. "The witnesses must explicitly state: 'We saw him having intercourse with her using the description posed by the Prophet Muhammad to Maʿiz "like the kohl stick disappears into the kohl container and the bucket into the well."'"[13] The *qadi*, once again following the tradition of Prophet Muhammad, was supposed to discourage confession to the crime of *zina* altogether.

The specificity of the *fiqh* leads one to ask why such detail would be given to these matters if it were not practiced after all. Was it just a scholarly exercise? The reluctance to practice these punishments may in part be owing to the diversity of the Ottoman Empire. The empire ruled over a heterogeneous group of people and faiths, and incorporated the customs and traditions of many earlier empires into its fold. All the while, it negotiated these traditions with the legal principles found in the shariʿa.[14] But it is also important to note that the very mechanisms utilized by the Ottoman laws to divert corporal punishment have their foundations in principles of Islamic jurisprudence.

OTTOMAN *KANUNNAMES*

Officially, the Ottomans viewed the law through the doctrine of the Circle of Justice that defined power relations throughout the empire.[15] Justice was the maintenance of harmony, whereas the notion of injustice was defined as the abuse of power by those individuals who governed in the sultan's name. The Circle of

Justice was the ideal; it was paternalistic and utopian. Any kind of infraction, whether by the masses *(ra'aya)* or administrators of the empire, would find its way back to the sultan, where justice would be served. The sultan invoked this symbolism as much as possible, even making it a habit to adjudicate cases personally in his court, located in the Topkapi Palace, so as to reassure the masses that justice was at the forefront of his mission as ruler. The preamble of many *kanunnames* explicitly declares its goal as the "prevention of oppression [*zulm*]."[16] Similarly, official documents such as the *adaletnames* (rescripts of justice) made similar proclamations, claiming to protect the subjects of the empire in the name of the sultan.[17] A recent trend in scholarship has critiqued this idyllic vision of Ottoman justice perpetuated by the imperial tone of the documents the empire produced and the scholars of Ottoman history who have accepted these Ottoman sources at face value.[18] However, in this rendering, I am looking only at the way the Ottomans understood themselves through this philosophy of justice, as it forms the subtext of the legal sources used in this chapter.

The Circle of Justice worked to legitimate the rule of the Ottoman sultan as upholding justice, and Islamic justice in particular. However, this philosophy of rule had a direct relationship with dynastic preservation. The sultan had absolute power where justice was concerned and ruled in the name of the shari'a. In order to efficiently maintain justice, the empire separated its juridical apparatus from the general administration of the empire. Thus, *sipahis* (cavalrymen) were responsible for collecting revenues from the subjects who lived on the land but, ideally, would be held accountable for any abuses by the juridical branch of government embodied in the *qadi*.[19] The sultan viewed his subjects as a constant source of revenue, a precious resource that could be extracted by the ruling class. "The administration of justice implied that the population had to be protected against the excessive demands of the local administrators and military."[20] So, through all these elements we can see that the circle is the balance of these competing forces: the drive for revenue, with the demands of Ottoman officials, and the sultan's need to maintain order and justice to legitimate his rule.

The sultan issued his own edicts to maintain this balance of power among various constituencies. The shari'a, in whose name he ruled, was insufficient in regulating the complex everyday transactions in this heavily bureaucratic empire. The sultan needed to carefully balance the secular aspects of his empire with the religious symbols that were necessary to keep him in the people's good graces.

Therefore, when Ottoman law is examined, it is evident that there are two kinds of law, shari'a and *kanun*. Shari'a is religious law found in the Islamic juristic tradition. However, it has been argued that "the jurists never intended large areas of the *shari'a* to function as a practical system of law. In part, of course, it did provide the basis of a working system of law and religious ritual, although custom and expedience often modified the exact prescriptions of the jurists." For practical matters, such as conducting the affairs of the state, *kanun,* or secular law, was necessary. Such laws were promulgated by the sultan in times of need in the form of edicts. Hanafi political theory in this respect exercised some influence on the Ottoman theory of rule. The sultan was placed in a mediatory position between the shari'a and the *kanun*. The *kanun* represented his own edicts, his own authority that he could impress upon areas of land tenure, taxation, and criminal matters. The shari'a was something outside of his power to regulate, thereby limiting his authority in some areas.[21]

One may ask how these two aspects of the law were reconciled. It was certainly possible through the adoption of the Hanafi interpretation of the shari'a, owing to its deference to Muslim rulers. Muslim juridical writings recognized the authority of rulers as the leaders of prayer, the leviers of taxes, the benefactors of the spoils of war, and the executors of fixed penalties. It is in this sense that the final authority over legal matters requiring fixed penalties, crimes that would include *zina*, were left up to the ruler to execute. Imber presents an intriguing argument on the subject. He argues that Hanafi jurists found that the ruler's authority applied only in theory in prosecuting crimes in the category of fixed penalties, as it was virtually impossible to prosecute them because the criteria for evidence presented procedural deterrents. Crimes that are religious violations, like *zina*, apostasy, and drinking, are, therefore, left to divine retribution. Only highway robbery, in Imber's opinion, constituted an actual crime that could be prosecuted by the state.[22]

The sultan's authority is best demonstrated through the imperial laws of the empire. The first *kanunname* was issued under Mehmet II, "the Conqueror" (r. 1444–46 and 1451–81) and was a tradition continued by subsequent sultans, all of whom elaborated on the original.[23] The *kanunnames* are composed in the imperial language, Ottoman Turkish, a language that combines vocabulary and syntax from three languages: Turkish, Persian, and Arabic. The *kanunnames* sometimes had subtle variations from one sultan to the next, as they were based on sultanic edicts *(firman),* but overall contained a variety of laws dealing with several areas of crime (theft, murder, and illicit sexual intercourse) as well as details of land and taxation. *Kanunnames* were issued for each *sancak* (administrative subdivision of a province) of the Ottoman Empire. "The *defter* [register] containing the *sancak kanun-name* was written in only two copies per *sancak*: one for the *defterhane,* a department attached to the central government in Istanbul, the other for the use of the *belerbegi* [*sic*] in the *sancak*."[24] The *kanunname* was usually copied into the judge's *(qadi)* books. In this context, the *kanunnames* are a part of the body of law accessed by *qadis,* although legal manuals of shari'a and *'urf* were also used in court cases. In fact, the *kanunnames* were not meant to be a formal law book to be followed by *qadis,* but were a set of imperial guidelines.

The *kanunnames* were an attempt to organize the shari'a into a code that was needed to unify a diverse population. In fact, the Ottomans went so far as to write different *kanunnames* for each province of the empire. For example, Aleppo had its own *kanunname,* but it was not copied into the court notebooks, as some scholars have argued.[25] Notably, the *kanunname* for the province of Aleppo does not contain references to criminal matters; instead, it focuses on matters of land tenure, taxation, and applicable fines, and for that reason this study will focus on the Anatolian *kanunnames,* as they discuss criminal matters in more detail. In one category, the *kanunname* of the province of Aleppo discusses communal responsibility that city quarters bear for crimes that occur within them.[26] The fact that criminal matters were not addressed in the *kanunname* of Aleppo may be a further indication that matters of crime were to be handled at the judge's discretion and help to explain the profound variations in the law found at the local level, as discussed in chapter 4 of this book.

Two criminal codes are examined in this chapter, the *kanunname* of Selim I, which has yet to be translated into English) and the *kanunname* of his son and successor, Süleyman I, translated by Uriel Heyd.[27] Both *kanunnames* contain numerous entries concerning theft, homicide, taxation, and categories of fines. They also include a discussion of *zina* crime, different forms of gender violence, and public morality more generally. Halil Inalcik, who consequently challenges the epithet *kanuni*, or lawgiver, bestowed on Süleyman, argues that these laws were originally composed during the reign of Bayezid II, around or before 1501.[28] The *kanunname* of Süleyman is considered the most developed of the *kanunnames* owing to his reorganization of the codes, yet its similarity to the *kanunname* of

Selim I demonstrates that the *kanunnames* were in the process of development long before the organization of Süleyman. The *kanunnames* were often an amalgamation of earlier *kanunnames* and laws, and it has also been argued that the imperial codes sometimes reflected folk understanding of the shari'a.[29]

Zina crime is discussed in the first chapter of both *kanunnames*, emphasizing its importance in terms of imperial concerns. In reading this chapter it is important to note the division of punishments according to social classes. The codes outline in detail the fines and punishments allotted to those men and women guilty of *zina* and make a sharp distinction in the penalties paid by persons of rich, average, and poor incomes. One example of this class-sensitive system is the following edict concerning fornication: "If the fornicator is unmarried and is rich, his property amounting to one thousand akçe or more, a fine of 100 akçe shall be collected; if he is in average circumstances, a fine of 50 akçe; and if he is poor, [a fine of] 30 akçes collected."[30] With this payment scale based on income, the Ottoman code created a reasonable system of fines based on one's ability to pay. This Ottoman innovation stands in contrast to the shari'a, which does not differentiate punishments according to class or income level.

The Ottoman criminal codes punish *zina* crime with fines, not stoning or lashing, as found in the juridical writings of *fiqh*. Moreover, the payment of fines for *zina* in the Ottoman code was directed at both sexes. The following clause, for instance, stipulates fines to be paid by a woman found guilty of *zina:* "If a married Muslim woman commits fornication, she shall, if she is rich, pay the fine [imposed on a rich man after her offense] has been proved; if she is in average circumstances, she shall pay the fine [imposed] on a man in those circumstances." This case may suppose that the woman's husband has left her after the accusation of *zina* and that she is forced to pay the fine herself. Yet another law states, "If it is a married woman who commits fornication, her husband shall pay the fine. If he [nevertheless] accepts [her] and he is rich, he shall pay 100 akçe by way of a fine [imposed] on a [consenting] cuckold." In this case, the wife is still with her legal husband, and he must pay the fine for her. Interestingly, despite the wife's crime, her property (money) is still protected, whereas the husband pays the fine for her.[31]

As previously discussed in chapter 1, *zina,* as it constitutes the crime of prostitution, is presented as an issue of temporary or quasi ownership *(shubhat milk)* in Hanafi *fiqh*. In the early *kanunnames*, prostitution does not appear as a distinct crime. In the juridical writings of al-Marginani, he writes in his section on banishment that for banished adulteresses, "cutting off their means of subsistence" might lead them to prostitution, which he considers to be "the ugliest form of *zina*." Other sources are silent about the position of prostitution in the early period. Imber offers an explanation, arguing that "procuring" and "pimping" were the central issues of law in the sixteenth century, more than prostitution itself. The focus on procuring is evident in Selim I's *kanunname* that contains an entry concerning the punishment for the crime of *püzavinklik,* or "pimping," as a *zina* crime. The original text reads: "If a person is procuring, the judge will make discretionary punishment and will parade him or her publicly, and a fine of one akçe for every two strokes should be taken."[32] The *kanunname* of Süleyman has several laws regarding procuring prostitution that call for the chastisement of guilty parties. These laws explicitly implicate both women and men as procurers.[33] The *kanunnames* discuss prostitution most often in the form of forcing or coercing one to commit *zina*.[34] Coercing someone to commit *zina* was considered a more severe crime by the Ottomans than prostitution, because the prostitute was viewed as having committed the act against her will. In turn, the *kanunname* of Süleyman calls for severe punishment for procuring prostitution, including the branding of a procurer's forehead. Some *siyasetnames,* yet another legal manual that contains prescriptions for corporal punishments, prescribe that female procurers have their noses cut off.[35]

Along with procurement, another subcategory of *zina* in the *kanunnames* is abduction. During the sixteenth and seventeenth centuries, the Ottoman Porte was preoccupied with the suppression of rebels against the state, called Jelalis. These rebels, made up of tribal peoples of Anatolia, raided and pillaged throughout the countryside. The spoils of these raids were captured peoples who made valuable slaves. Eventually, the state stationed Janissaries in provincial towns to protect the residents and eventually suppress the rebellions.[36] The Ottoman criminal codes contain references to the abductions, as political instability made them more likely. In fact, the *kanunname* of Selim I specifically discusses the case of "a girl or woman [who] is abducted with force."[37] For such an abduction, the most severe punishment is given, namely, castration (*siyaset için sikra kısla,* which literally means "his manhood should be cut").[38] The *kanunname* of Süleyman includes penalties for women who willingly participate in the abduction: "If the woman or girl is willing and runs away from her house, her vulva shall be branded [*onların farcalarını dağlılar*]."[39] This punishment is meant to be quite literal, as Süleyman's codes include similar branding and maiming. However, there is no evidence of its ever being practiced as a punishment in existing studies.

It has been argued that in Ottoman Syria and Palestine, cases of abduction (and rape, for that matter) were not brought to court—a problem more often found in the village than the urban center.[40] Other historians have argued more broadly that many cases, criminal or otherwise, never made it to court because often they were negotiated through an indigenous tradition of mediation *(sulh)*.[41] Local neighborhood or village leadership often resolved disputes privately through mediation; therefore, several cases remained undocumented in a courtroom. In this case, the *kanunnames* are addressing the empire's desire to discourage abduction in an attempt to maintain civil order by prescribing severe punishments for any who perpetrate the crime.

It is possible that the tumultuous context of sixteenth-century Ottoman expansion coupled with the suppression of local rebellions played into a preoccupation with civil order. Ottoman laws deal with a number of issues related to maintaining civil order, as well as sexual propriety. Many of these scenarios painted in the imperial codes point toward gender violence more frequently than the earlier Hanafi codes, suggesting concern over such matters on the imperial level. The codes describe several levels of infractions: "If a person enters a woman's house or approaches her on her way and cuts off her hair or takes away her garment or kerchief, [thus] offering [her] a gross indignity, the *cadi* shall, after [the offense] has been proved, chastise [him]; he shall have [him] imprisoned."[42] The statute remarks that the case is to be proven before punishment, unlike the earlier cases that were based on intent to commit the crime. This, in turn, leaves the victim of the attack to defend her case in court, and in some cases there may be no witnesses. Furthermore, from this passage it is apparent that the documents are still in search of a language for rape. Both sets of *kanunnames* deal with the issue of rape euphemistically, referring to someone who "crosses the path" of a woman and "cuts her hair" or "takes away her garment or kerchief."[43] These phrases convey the nature of the attack by mentioning hair, a symbol of female beauty, and a woman's modesty as covered by her garment, all of which emphasize the sexual nature of the violation.[44]

Other forms of violence against women, such as spousal abuse, are addressed in the *kanunnames*. One law reads: "And if a person beats a woman who is a stranger [*ecnebiye*] to him, [the *qadi*] shall chastise [him] severely and a fine of one akçe shall be collected for each stroke."[45] In this case the perpetrator pays a fine for attacking a woman stranger. The fact that the passage identifies the woman as a stranger suggests that a woman known to the offender may be treated otherwise. The *kanunnames* are vague on this point, unlike the fatwas, which are forthright in granting the woman/victim the right to self-defense. This difference between the *kanunnames* and fatwas demonstrates the variations even within the Ottoman legal tradition. That two forms of imperial law can diverge on a single issue exemplifies the diversity of interpretation that can be found within Ottoman law.

So-called honor crimes, otherwise known as "crimes of passion," are dealt with in the *kanunname* of Süleyman. The *kanunnames* are consistent with the fatwas issued by Ebu's Su'ud in the same period. The code reads: "If a person finds his wife somewhere committing fornication with [another] person [and] kills both of them together—provided he immediately calls people into his house and takes them to witness, the claims of the heirs of those killed shall not be heard [in court]."[46] A man who finds his wife with another man, in flagrante delicto, has the right to kill them both, without suffering punishment or being required to pay *diya* to the surviving heirs. A man also has the right to murder his daughter if he finds her in the same circumstance. This right includes cases where a stranger is found in the house; in such cases, the male proprietor will not suffer recourse if he strikes and wounds the man.

Another category of *zina* crime discussed in the *kanunname* is sodomy. Abu Hanifa argued that sodomy is not *zina* because it is not a mutual sex act. Furthermore, he argued that there is no punishment since no progeny is produced. In this respect Hanafi law makes a distinction between mutual and nonmutual sex acts and in many cases does not call for either of the parties to be punished if there is mutual consent. This lack of punishment is mostly owing to disagreement on the part of the early traditions, "for some of them have said that offenders of this kind should be burnt, some that they should be buried alive, others that they should be cast headlong from some high place, such as the top of a house, and then be stoned to death."[47] Alternatively, Imam Shafi'i argues that both parties are to be punished for an act of sodomy. According to his ruling, the punishment of stoning should be meted to both the "passive" and the "active" agent in sodomy. Juridical writings are explicit and use the term *forced* to convey nonconsensual sex acts, like forced sex (rape) and forced sodomy, that are punishable by law. In turn, sodomy is included in the list of fornication crimes in the Ottoman code. The statutes place a 300 *akçe* fine on sodomy involving a rich person, and for one of average income, 200 akçe. Furthermore, the Ottoman code states that "if little boys from among the townspeople or peasants [*türk*] perform sexual acts with one another, [the *qadi*] shall punish [them and] a fine of 30 akçe shall be collected from each one."[48] The boys in question are "dancing boys," and are subject to the smallest fines for sodomy in the code. "Dancing boys" was the epithet given to young boys used as entertainers and sometimes male prostitutes in coffeehouses and taverns.[49]

The crime of sodomy arises again in the *kanunnames* in the context of rape committed against young boys. In the *kanunname* of Selim I, punishment for sodomy *(kenizlik)* performed on a young boy is listed among other *zina* offenses. The code states that the father is to be punished for not protecting his minor son *(balağ oğlu)*. Thus, the father, according to the *kanunname*, will receive *ta'zir* punishment, though there is no mention of punishment for the abductor.[50] The same law is found in a later *kanunname* of Süleyman, but with an even more severe punishment. One code reads: "And if a boy is abducted, [the abductors] shall be castrated or else be fined 24 gold pieces. And if [the abducted person] is a catamite *(muhannes)*, the legal punishment *(hadd)* for fornication shall be inflicted on both parties; if it is not inflicted, each of them shall pay a fine like that for fornication."[51] Punishment for the abduction of a boy is the same as the *kanunname* of Selim I. Yet the *kanunname* of Süleyman presents a variation on the law; it calls for punishment of both the victim and the culprit if the victim is an effeminate male *(muhannes)* in his majority.

There are important aspects of Ottoman law to bear in mind while reading the *kanunnames*. The Ottoman codes often describe cases in which people are subject to punishment on the basis of the intent *(qasd)* to commit the crime, regardless of whether any illegal act was committed. For example, the *kanunname* of Selim I states, "If a person enters someone else's house with the intention to commit *zina*, if this person (the attacker) happens to be married, let the married fine be given. If he is unmarried, he should be given the boy's fine."[52]

What did intent mean in sixteenth-century Ottoman criminal codes? Intent is a concept in several modern legal codes that describes a premeditated crime. In the Ottoman texts, the word *qasd* is used for certain crimes, which translates as "purposing to do," or as "intending or endeavoring to kill or injure a person."[53] The word conveys the meaning of a direct and deliberate act made on the part of the perpetrator. In modern law, intent implies that a criminal must know that he or she is committing a crime in order for it to constitute a crime. An illustrative definition of intent is found in Egyptian criminal law: "The intentional character of the act may be analysed into foreknowledge of the act, coupled with desire for its accomplishment. . . . Thus it is true to say that all volitional acts are intentional, and no person can exercise his will to act unless he has foreseen the act and directs himself towards its accomplishment."[54] From this example one can see that the notion of intent, as found in modern law, is in some ways similar to what is found in Ottoman law. Intent used in Ottoman cases of rape means to enter a house for the purpose of raping, as opposed to entering the house to steal or commit another crime that would entitle a different punishment. Haim Gerber illustrates intent in Ottoman law with the case of a man who approached a woman with the intent of killing her; however, before attacking her, he screamed at her, inadvertently scaring her so severely that she died. He writes, "Although this man had a well known intention to kill, what he actually did was not considered murder."[55] In this case, the verdict with regard to intent is not all that different from the modern interpretation of intent. With respect to cases of illicit sexual relations, however, the *kanun* and shari'a contain clauses that treat intent or even the opportunity to commit *zina* as a crime, regardless of the stipulations of four male witnesses to prove *zina* cases found in the shari'a.

The notion of intent as a necessary component of guilt is found more often in the *kanunnames* than in other sources of Islamic law and is used more often as evidence toward indictment. In other words, the *kanunname* holds persons responsible for *zina* based on an opportunity to commit the crime or circumstantial evidence. In this passage of the *kanunname* of Süleyman, even speculation of misconduct has repercussions: "If a woman is spoken ill of (as having secret and illicit relations) with a certain man and her husband divorces her, that ill-reputed woman shall not be married to that man. If the marriage has (nevertheless) been contracted (between them), [the *qadi*] shall immediately separate (them) by force and compulsion and shall severely and heavily punish the *danishmend* [one who is learned in law] who married (them)."[56] This law specifically bars the marriage of a woman to a man she was suspected of having an affair with during her previous marriage. Note that this prohibition is based on suspicion rather than conviction of wrongdoing, which further illustrates the impact one's reputation can have in legal matters. The law goes even further and punishes any judge who marries the two after the affair. Both *kanunnames* studied also advocate punishing the *qadi* who marries a woman to the man who abducted her; in this case, the *qadi* would be publicly scorned, in this case his beard cut off.[57]

The case of the aforementioned adulterous wife describes her as being "spoken ill of" but does not discuss eyewitnesses to the illicit acts that she is accused of committing. Here it is evident that the *kanunnames* sometimes treat speculation of criminal activity as the crime itself. A woman suspected of committing adultery suffers punishment in kind. The intention to commit crimes or, in some cases, simply being placed in proximity to a person of the opposite sex can facilitate a conviction of *zina*. Moreover, if a woman was accused of committing *zina* with a man and is later divorced, she could not marry the man she was alleged to have committed the act with.[58] In another law, if a woman is seen with a man she is rumored to have committed *zina* with, "[and people] see the two at a secluded spot and testify [to that effect]," they will be subject to fines. These laws are a far cry from the strict criteria for *zina* conviction found in shari'a doctrine outlined in the previous chapter. Suspicion alone can be used for *zina* conviction, which in turn empowers communities in the policing process since they are often the source of such charges, a subject pursued in later chapters.

The *kanunnames* describe several crimes that involve sexual solicitations, including breaking and entering and the invasion of female privacy. It is in these cases that the Ottoman definition of *zina* becomes broader, as sexual innuendo and moral impropriety are included, both outside of the more physical offenses of *zina* found in the shari'a. For example, in the *kanunname* of Süleyman, there is a 20 *akçe* fine for Peeping Toms, which include those individuals who are "peeping through a hole [into another man's harem], or coming into someone's house . . . or kissing [another man's] wife or daughter, or approaching them on the way, or telling [them], 'I love [you].'"[59]

Likewise, the *kanunname* of Selim I also warns if a person "kisses someone's wife or daughter, or crosses their path and if he speaks to them, the judge will make strong punishment." Furthermore, the same laws add, "if he insinuates [flirtation] or kisses a person's slave the judge will give *ta'zir*," or discretionary punishment.[60] In these two instances, kissing *(öpsa)*, approaching or "crossing their path" *(yolına varup)*, and innuendo through speaking *(söylese)* are all considered acts of *zina* and punishable breaches of the moral code.

These laws demonstrate that in Ottoman imperial law, several forms of flirting are included in the definition of *zina* crime and include approaching, accosting, kissing, and speaking to women. Exemplified in these cases is the legal concept of intent, often perceived to be a primary difference between the *kanun* and the shari'a, as Imber writes: "The principles on which the *kanun* differs from the *shari'a* appear to be in treating amorous association as *zina;* in treating intent to commit *zina* as equivalent, in certain cases to the offence itself." However, the precedent for intention to commit *zina* may lie in the foundations of Hanafi interpretation of Islamic law. In Ottoman law the "intent" to commit the crime of *zina,* rather than an actual criminal act, may in fact prove guilt. In this case, an unmarried and unrelated man and woman alone in a house may provide enough evidence for a *zina* conviction. The *Hedaya* states that "zinna [*sic*] may mean something not directly amounting to carnal conjunction (such as *seeing* and *touching*)." Accepting these broader activities as intent to commit *zina* is found in earlier sources, such as the hadith where the Prophet Muhammad is reported as saying that "the adultery of the legs is walking [toward an unlawful woman with bad intention] and the adultery of the hands is touching and patting [an unlawful woman] and the adultery of the eyes is casting passionate glances [at a woman]."[61] In other words, both the hadith and the *Hedaya* have pointed toward sexual innuendo, rather than the definition of copulation found in the shari'a, as *zina* crimes. Therefore, the Ottoman *kanun* are not alone in defining *zina* crime broadly, as the shari'a sometimes includes the notion of adulterous intent in its definition.

That being said, not all Hanafi jurists were eager to point out that the amorous intention had to be present in order to make an association with *zina.* Late-seventeenth- and early-eighteenth-century jurist 'Abd al-Ghani al-Nabulusi was angered by "one of those morons who claim to be members of the *ulema* [*sic*] who say 'looking at the face of anyone with no beard is *haram* (illicit).'" He wrote more extensively on the subject, describing the way that such an injunction would hinder all sorts of social interaction among men young and old. Al-Nabulusi wrote to the man who made the statement:

"So, this must include your sons and brothers? Oh, you say you mean beardless boys who don't belong to one's family? Then what about your servants, or boys in the bathhouse? The rulers and *qadis* who have youths in their homes? Are they all *zindiqs* [heretics]? What of the teachers at the Umayyad mosque who sit with their students? Or men with their apprentices?" I wash my hands of this matter since these cows cannot fathom my reasoning. He says gazing [*nazar*] always involves desire. Does he not see that he can occasionally look at even his wife or slave-girl without lust? And, besides, how can he read other men's hidden thoughts?[62]

From this passage it is evident that debates existed concerning defining the boundaries of adulterous intent to the point that some questioned even looking at young men.

Intent becomes especially important when the *kanunnames* condone so-called honor crimes, whereby a husband can kill his wife and the man with whom she is committing *zina,* without fear of retaliation. There is no female equivalent in this category of *diya* or retaliation-free murder of her husband; it is exclusively the right of her husband and male relatives.

The explicit guidelines for *zina* in the shari'a that demand the direct witnessing of the act of physical penetration give way to the notion of intention in the *kanunname.* The intent to commit the crime is punished, albeit with lighter fines than the actual crime. Surprisingly, there is no evidence of other speculative indictments for crimes of murder and theft where physical evidence and witnesses are necessary for conviction. The evidentiary requirement in the *kanunname* of Selim I is otherwise very rigid; it is most evident in its treatment of murder cases, where evidence must be gathered in order to facilitate an indictment; a dead body alone is not enough.[63]

Although the notion of intent was meant to distinguish premeditated from accidental murder cases, it is a contentious point in modern law because the intent of the victims in rape cases is often questioned in courtrooms. This legal strategy of questioning the intent of the victim has hindered the ability of lawyers to prosecute rape cases effectively, namely, the defense questions whether the victim enticed her attacker through her actions or provocative dress. The controversial rape case that took place in a crowded Cairo public subway station in 1992 raised a question in the media: was the rape victim "asking for it" by going out alone?[64] Questioning the intent of the rape victim has also become a way of questioning the "virtue" of these women and implies that a woman of low morals deserves to be raped. These issues, especially in Muslim countries today, are central to problems in adjudicating rape cases. Yet, historically, Islamic law, as found in Arab and Ottoman traditions, does not question whether rape is first and foremost non-consensual by its very definition. The intent of the rape victim is not questioned in premodern Islamic law, either. Rather, on a deeper cultural level, two consenting adults, alone together in a room without supervision, are treated as though they had the intent to commit a crime. This standard is based on a hadith of the Prophet Muhammad: "A man is not alone with a woman but that the devil makes a third."[65] This suspicion has been used as justification for many forms of violence against women suspected of sexual impropriety, focusing more on the intent to commit *zina* than the actual act that was once a focal point of jurists. Several modern cases of "intent" to commit *zina* have resulted in stoning, imprisonment, and outright murder in what have been called "honor crimes."[66]

Furthermore, such cultural assumptions of women's sexual lasciviousness have their basis in popular literature. These patriarchal notions have been well documented in Arab-Islamic cultural production, where literary studies have noted a recurring theme of women's sexual desire and social conflict. These themes can be found in the earliest traditions of the Qur'an, in the story of Zulaykha and Joseph, wherein Potipher's wife attempts to seduce the handsome prophet.[67] Interesting in the case of both Surat Yusuf in the Qur'an and the *1001 Nights* is their popularity with the public; the attempted seduction by the cunning Zulaykha is a favorite for recitation, and the *1001 Nights* was common literature recited for the masses.[68] The stories of Shahrazade often contain tales of seduction and betrayal, as in the frame story of the *1001 Nights* in which Shahrayar's wife holds an orgy in the courtyard while he is believed to be traveling with his brother.[69] The two brothers later encounter the Ifrit's wife, who forces them to sleep with her while her monstrous husband sleeps nearby. The combination of these tales impairs King Shahrayar to the point that he undertakes what Fedwa Malti-Douglas has called a "gynocide" against women, marrying a young bride and murdering her by dawn, to ensure that he will not suffer such a betrayal at the hands of a woman again. It is in this context that Shahrazade steps up to rescue womankind from the hands of the psychologically damaged king.[70]

What can these examples of literature tell us about popular attitudes about women? A recurring theme is the notion of women's sexuality as a force that can cause "chaos" (*fitna*) if left unsupervised by patriarchal authority. It is not a mistake that the word *fitna* itself can also mean "civil war" in Arabic. 'A'isha's entry into the Battle of Camel (A.D. 656), and resulting defeat, has been used as an example of the kind of chaos that can occur when women are unchecked by male authority. Shahrayar's betrayal is yet another literary example of the chaos caused by his wife's unchecked sexuality. The notion of *fitna* is also used in conjunction with the belief that women are cunning *(kayd)* by nature. Women can sometimes deceive, as the Ifrit's woman did, in order to cuckold her husband. A fifteenth-century text by Ibn al-Batanuni catalogs women's cunning and trickery from both sacred histories and Arabic literature in the *Kitab al-'Unwan fi Maka'id al-Niswan*. In her analysis of the text, Malti-Douglas comments that "story follows story as Adam leads a parade of prophets, rulers, and various other dignitaries of Islamic sacred and secular history who have all been somehow or other the subject of woman's trickery and guile. . . . Ibn al-Batanuni has a knack for construing events in such a way that the female turns into the source of all evil."[71] The compiler, she adds, also includes various incantations that can be recited to protect men from women's trickery.

These well-documented examples in Arab-Islamic literature are laden with patriarchal assumptions about female sexuality that cannot be dismissed when considering the larger cultural context of Islamic and Ottoman law. Jurists were a part of the communities that they lived in, and products of both their legal training and the cultural influences of their time. It, therefore, aids in our understanding of the onus placed on women's sexual propriety to take into account patriarchal cultural assumptions in Arabic literature and sacred Islamic texts. It becomes particularly evident in some of the fatwas produced by Ottoman *shaykhul-islam* Ebu's Su'ud that contain within them patriarchal notions of honor, which more often than not refer to the honor of men that is at stake when women deviate from morality.[72] However, the cultural assumptions above help us understand why it is female morality, more than male, that is likely to falter.

THE OTTOMAN FATWA

An examination of Ottoman law would not be complete without a discussion of the fatwa. A fatwa is a juridical opinion that can be issued by any *mujtahid,* one who is qualified to interpret the law using legal reasoning. Usually muftis, the highest-ranking Muslim jurists in the Ottoman Empire, issued fatwas. The fatwa is meant to present an informed juridical opinion on a subject for personal use, or possibly use in court, but it is not a legally binding document. To be enacted into law, a fatwa must be adopted by either a judge in the shari'a court as a basis for a ruling or, in the case of the Ottoman state, adopted as imperial law by the sultan.[73] The most frequently cited Ottoman fatwas are those of Ebu's Su'ud Efendi, the sixteenth-century *shaykhul-islam* under Sultan Süleyman I. His fatwas are most valuable for gender historians because they deal with issues such as marriage, divorce, and spousal support *(nafaqa)*. Ebu's Su'ud's most revealing fatwas are the ones dealing with issues of gender violence, in particular rape, "honor crime," sodomy, and spousal abuse. His fatwas were far-reaching and were often cited in the Aleppo court records to support local cases. For historians interested in the sixteenth-century official position on these issues, consulting Ebu's Su'ud's fatwas provides unique insight, especially when combined with another source like the *kanunnames*.[74]

Ottoman fatwas have been used by scholars in classic studies to show their relationship to imperial power, the methodology employed by the mufti, and the way in which fatwas were issued. According to Uriel Heyd, prior to the accession of Sultan Süleyman, the question posed in the fatwa would originate from the mufti himself. However, "[by] the first quarter of the sixteenth century, [the mufti] had a small basket hung from his window in which everyone could place his question. On his moving a string, it is said, the mufti pulled up the basket, wrote his reply on the same paper and sent it down [sic] the basket."[75]

Imperial muftis actually wrote several hundred fatwas per day. According to several Ottoman historians who were contemporaries of Ebu's Su'ud, he once claimed he had written 1,412 fatwas between morning and afternoon prayers, and 1,413 fatwas the day after. Because of the huge quantity of fatwas written by Ebu's Su'ud, it is common to find his answers brief as compared to the fatwas issued by provincial muftis.[76]

Why did Ebu's Su'ud issue so many fatwas, and what was their social significance? Understanding the impact of fatwas has been the goal of many historians who aim to employ them as a source of social history. One must note the outstanding number of fatwas issued by Ebu's Su'ud during the heyday of Ottoman power. Moreover, the frankness and specificity of issues dealt with in the fatwas suggest urgency for social control in areas of violent crime. As fatwas were issued in different localities, with varying contexts and verdicts, they are a rich source for anyone interested in social history and legal interpretation.

Several authors have pondered the use of fatwas and their importance to social historians. Brinkley Messick did much to draw attention to fatwas in his work on Yemen and argued that the mufti is an essential link between the legal administrative chain and the living community.[77] The mufti, Messick argues, is a *mujtahid* who is obliged to engage in legal interpretation *(ijtihad)* and elaborate on law through fatwas. Furthermore, fatwas are linked to the community of believers, since in many cases the questions originate from the public, however anonymously. Whereas some questions are fictitious scenarios, possibly legal puzzles that faced the jurist, others are based on real events. This fact is proven through court records in which defendants and plaintiffs appeared in court with fatwas that they had requested from the local mufti. Such consultation was usually done before litigation, and the court usually backed the fatwas, but not always.[78]

A counterexample is found in a February 1719 case from one of Aleppo's shari'a courts in which a fatwa was brought to court by the Armenians who lived in the neighborhoods outside Bab al-Nasr in Aleppo.[79] The case concerned a church in which men and women were using the same entrance alongside a major street. Muslim neighbors complained about the mixing of the sexes in the doorway and brought the case to court, insisting that the second church doorway be used by women only. The Armenian community produced a fatwa arguing that it was permissible to use the door. This case is unusual because many fatwas brought success to the plaintiffs and defendants who used them in court. It may be that the aforementioned Armenian fatwa was overruled by the greater interest of the Muslim community, namely, to limit the amount of harmful mixing of the sexes, even in predominately Christian neighborhoods. Residents of the empire had access to *mujtahids* from different schools with varying opinions on the law whereby a particular mufti could be sought if his opinion would have supported a more favorable outcome.

Judith Tucker has used fatwas as a lens to examine gender relations in seventeenth- and eighteenth-century Ottoman Syria and Palestine.[80] Her study reinforces Messick's conclusions and affirms the role of the mufti as providing a link between the beliefs of the community and the shari'a. More important, Tucker compares her findings with court records and notes the similarity of the cases that appeared before the mufti and the *qadi*—a similarity that strengthens the historical relevance of the cases being dealt with by the mufti. Indeed, the difficulty of using fatwas as a source has been in determining whether the mufti is dealing with a real case or engaging in an intellectual exercise. Although on occasion fatwas and court records contain similar cases, not all fatwas are based on real cases. This point leads one to question the very nature of the fatwa and its relationship to lived reality. Simply put, a fatwa is a legal opinion and is located within the category of *fiqh,* which is technically an area of doctrinal law, not reflecting the legal practice of the courts. However, more often than not, it does have the potential to be used in the courts to tilt the judge's verdict one way or the other.

Other studies, such as Wael Hallaq's, investigated the connections between fatwas and their influence on substantive law *(furu').* Hallaq writes, "Fatwas that contained *ijtihad* were, as a rule, included in the manuals of substantive law *(furu')* as well as in commentaries and super-commentaries on such manuals."[81] Therefore, there is a triadic relationship among the living community, the fatwa, and juridical writings on the law *(fiqh* and *furu').* Altogether these studies have convincingly shown the importance of fatwas for social historians who are only beginning to use them to construct social history and gender studies of the Ottoman Empire.[82]

As in the earlier Ottoman *kanunname,* the legal opinions of the empire's *shaykhul-islam* reflected a similar preoccupation with gender relations and sex crime. Ebu's Su'ud's rulings on social issues such as prostitution situate it as a *zina* crime, to be punished accordingly:

> Question: If a group makes it a custom to go from village to village, causing their wives, daughters and female slaves to commit fornication, what is their sentence according to the shari'a?
>
> Answer: They should all, without exception, suffer an extremely severe chastisement and not be released from prison until their reform becomes evident. Those women whose fornication is proven should all be stoned.[83]

Ebu's Su'ud's ruling in this fatwa is consistent with the shari'a as it confirms the punishment of stoning for married *zina* offenders. The *shaykhul-islam* prescribed similar punishment in a fatwa concerning rape:

> Question: If Zeyd without being married to Hind takes her by force, what should happen to Zeyd?
>
> Answer: If he is a *muhsan* [a married Muslim], he will be killed.[84]

Ebu's Su'ud clearly places rape under the category of *zina* in this case, as he calls for the death penalty in accordance with the shari'a formulations. Yet the form of execution remains unspecified. The *Kitab al-Mabsut,* as well as other works of Hanafi law, states that *zina* by a *muhsan* is punishable by stoning to death *(rajam).*[85] However, contemporary scholarship has documented that other punishments for *zina* crimes sometimes took the form of banishment, flogging, and fines.[86] Unique to this fatwa is its description of Zeyd as unmarried to Hind. It implies that if they were indeed married, there would be either a different punishment or none at all. There is little literature concerning marital rape in Islamic law, because it is a modern and Western legal concept. In fact, modern laws are still struggling with how to deal with such cases, as according to Muslim family law the husband is entitled to sexual access to his wife in his marriage contract.[87] However, we can induce from the fatwa above that the jurist recognized only those rape cases in which the couple was not married to each other.

Many of Ebu's Su'ud's fatwas dealt with aspects of violence against women; the following case is more subtle than others. This fatwa evidences the notion of liability, which holds that killing or poisoning one's husband in order to avoid committing *zina* after divorcing him exempts the wife from liability for *diya,* or blood money:

> Question: Zeyd says, "If I do this thing, may my wife be divorced three times." He then does it. His wife knows this, but is unable to prove it. Is Zeyd's wife a sinner because Zeyd is intimate with her?
>
> Answer: It is fornication *(zina).* It is essential that she does not [submit] voluntarily [to Zeyd's embrace]. She must give what she has and there must be a *khul'* divorce. If he tries to have intercourse [with her] and there is no other means of escape, it is licit according to the shari'a to add poison to his food. She would not commit a sin and there is no *diya.*[88]

The fatwa argues that the wife has the right, to the point of murder in self-defense, to defend herself against unwanted and unlawful sexual advances. This case involves a conditional divorce in which the husband vows to divorce his wife based on a particular action or event. She is legally divorced once the husband fulfills that condition, even if she is unable to prove it with witnesses. The moment that the condition was fulfilled, the divorce went into effect. The fatwa reinforces the seriousness of verbal threats of divorce. If the wife were to accept the ex-husband's sexual advances, she would be committing *zina*. According to the fatwa, poisoning her ex-husband in order to avoid committing *zina* is a form of self-defense. The wife has no liability for her ex-husband's death and is not required to pay the *diya*. In his study of Ottoman Anatolia, Haim Gerber argues that "killing in self-defense against sexual attack also went unpunishable [*sic*]— provided that the kadi interpreted it as a case of self-defense," the reason being that self-defense removed any liability from the victim who chose to fight back against her attacker.[89] Therefore, in this context, the fatwa above reaffirms the legal position in Islamic law that a woman can be voluntarily or involuntarily engaged in sexual intercourse and fight back against unwanted sexual advances by any means necessary, especially as they violate the shari'a. This case clearly illustrates a notion of consent for a voluntary act of adultery or involuntary intercourse (that is, rape) that is present in both Islamic law and Ottoman law.

Ebu's Su'ud's position is that a woman has the right to self-defense when under threat of *zina*. This stance has its basis in all schools of Islamic law. The Hanbalis require that one defend his or her life if under assault, even if it means killing the assailant. More specifically, if a woman is under sexual attack, she is required to fight back, for not doing so implies consent to the act.[90] In Ebu's Su'ud's fatwa, a woman is commended if she wards off an attacker, inadvertently killing him.

> Question: Zeyd enters Hind's house, and wants to take her by force. Hind, unable to repel Zeyd in any another way, injures him with an ax. Zeyd dies from the wound. What should happen to Hind?
> Answer: She has performed an act of holy war [*jihad*].[91]

In this passage, Ebu's Su'ud has demonstrated a case of sexual assault, which he calls "force" because there is no distinct vocabulary for rape in the shari'a and *kanunname*. Furthermore, the fatwa condones the murder of the assailant through self-defense by calling it jihad. In this fatwa, the parties are unmarried, but for scenarios with married couples involving spousal abuse, there is a juridical gap. An example of the problems that occur when the assailant is married to the woman under duress is found in a fatwa by Khayr ad-Din ibn Ahmad al-Ramli in which he argues that a woman must prove a triple divorce has taken place in order to have a right to self-defense. Judith Tucker attributes his position to the notion of *ta'a* (obedience) afforded a man by his wife, even though marital obligations forbid "intentional ill treatment" of a wife.[92]

Other forms of *zina,* such as rape, are discussed in the Ottoman legal sources. However, the literature available on rape in Islamic law presents a methodological issue, as some authors question the existence of rape as a criminal category. In his study of Ottoman law, Colin Imber argues that the concept of rape did not exist in Ottoman law. He writes, "Since the *kanunname* treats housebreaking with intent to commit *zina,* abduction and sexual molestation as criminal offences, one might logically expect to find a similar treatment of rape. Instead, the *kanun,* like the shari'a, ignores the subject altogether."[93] For Imber, the difficulty arises from the very definition of *zina,* which encompasses all forms of extralegal and extramarital sex except that of concubinage. The nonspecificity of the term *zina* has led scholars, like Imber, to question the existence of rape based on language. The *fiqh* deals with a number of different criminal acts, such as adultery, fornication, sodomy, bestiality, prostitution, and rape—all of which are listed as *zina* crimes. Needless to say, *zina* encompasses rape as well as other forms of extralegal relations, yet the argument that Islamic law did not have a concept of rape is based on the absence of an independent criminal category. What does exist is a concept of consensual and nonconsensual extramarital sexual relations as the defining difference between rape and adultery. A number of studies employing archival sources have found evidence that rape, as nonconsensual sexual intercourse, did in fact exist in Ottoman legal discourse.[94] Without a doubt, one also finds rape as a distinct subcategory of *zina* in Ottoman *kanunnames* and fatwas. Ebu's Su'ud's formulations delineate the boundary between rape and adultery, in that his opinions pay careful attention to illustrating consensual and nonconsensual sex acts.

Evidence supporting the existence of rape in Ottoman laws can be found in the language used to describe the crime in the *kanunnames* and fatwas. Some examples of Ottoman Turkish phrases used to convey gender violence are *çikup cebr ile,* meaning "abduction with force," and *nikâh itdiduruna ceber ile,* meaning "forced to marry"; both of these examples are common phrases that convey the meaning of forced sexual relations. The sources not only deal with the rape of women but also deal with the rape of men and boys, which is called *cebr ile luta idub* in one of Ebu's Su'ud's fatwas. The language conveys both the use of force and a context of nonconsensual sexual intercourse, which is the very definition of rape. There are several terms used for rape in Ottoman fatwas: one of them is *cebr ile tasarruf etmek,* which means to "know a woman carnally with force," yet *tasarruf* can also mean to *use* something, or take *possession* of something.[95] The *kanunnames* present an interesting avenue for examining legal development as they struggle to reconcile the reality of gender violence within the shari'a framework of *zina.*

Dealing with premodern law demands that the modern scholar cast aside biases concerning language. For example, scholars cannot expect to find categories of crime in premodern texts that match modern legal categories. It is only through a close examination of sources that we can gain insight into the way jurists understood sexual assault cases. Consider the earlier example of Abu Hanifa, who argues that sexual desire exists only on the part of the active party in sodomy, yet he is again ambiguous about whether the "active party" should be punished. On the other hand, in Ebu's Su'ud's Ottoman interpretation there is no such ambiguity, as he prescribes the execution of the offender who forcefully sodomizes:

> Question: If Zeyd—may God forbid it—were to commit sodomy by force with
> a minor, 'Amr, rupturing his anus, and to acknowledge this in the *kadi*'s
> [sic] court.
> Answer: The shari'a permits his execution. If it were not his habitual act it would
> not produce this result.[96]

Whether against a woman or in the above case against a boy, the jurist in this fatwa affirms his position that the forcible sodomy of a youth is rape. Here we can see that Ebu's Su'ud upheld his verdict on rape as a *zina* crime by executing the assailant.

Crimes of passion are also discussed in Ottoman fatwas. These crimes occur when a husband, father, or brother takes the life of his wife or daughter without legal liability. These cases result in the murder of an "adulterous" wife or daughter caught with another man in flagrante delicto, or sometimes less since women have been murdered based on unsubstantiated rumors. For some schools, the evidentiary requirements are less in such cases; for instance, the Maliki and Hanbali schools require only two witnesses, just in case a countercharge of homicide is issued against the husband or male relative who kills them in the act. Rudolph

Peters has argued that such crimes of passion, according to Islamic legal theory, are permissible in order to halt a crime in progress and to defend one's honor. Ebu's Su'ud's fatwas (and even some modern Middle Eastern legal codes) condone the practice of this form of murder.[97] The fatwa reads as follows:

> Question: Zeyd kills his wife Hind and 'Amr in the act of *zina* [in flagrante
> delicto] will there be retribution for Hind's and 'Amr's inheritors or taking
> the amount of blood money from Zeyd?
> Answer: It will not be. There will be no investigation. It is forbidden.[98]

This fatwa takes the position that killing a female relative in the act of *zina* does not require the perpetrator to pay *diya* either to the family of the slain wife or to her lover. The fatwa even forbids an investigation, which further emphasizes the law's refusal to consider the murder a criminal offense. The refusal of blood money in such cases is not unusual, as fifteenth-century jurist Ibn Bazzaz ruled that a husband could kill his wife "if she is submitting [to the lover]." A century later Ibn Nujaym wrote, "The principle in this matter is that it is licit for a person to kill a Muslim whom he sees committing fornication. He holds back only lest he should kill him without it being certain that he is, in fact, committing fornication." Ebu's Su'ud's fatwa above does not permit the killing of fornicators by just any party, as does Ibn Nujaym; only family members are allowed to do so in such cases. Ebu's Su'ud diverges from the jurist on another point, the issue of what constitutes in flagrante delicto. One of Ebu's Su'ud fatwas permits murdering a female relative, in this case a sister, found alone at home with an unrelated man and not necessarily engaged in illicit sexual intercourse:

> [Question:] Zeyd sees his sister, Hind, in a house with 'Amr, who is outside the
> prohibited degrees of marriage *(namahrem)*. He kills Hind and wounds
> 'Amr, who dies on the following day. Zeyd acknowledges that he killed
> Hind and 'Amr, and goes to another place. Now his paternal uncles are not
> guarantors for Zeyd, but 'Amr's brother, Bekr, brings a claim *(qawl)* and, in
> contravention of the law, forcibly and wrongfully takes two hundred gold
> coins from the aforenamed persons. When he returns, can Zeyd lawfully
> recover the entire sum from the person whom they paid it?
> Answer: Yes.[99]

As evidenced in this fatwa, Ebu's Su'ud treated women and men who were found alone as guilty of *zina*. In this case, the jurist loosened the strict criteria of witnessing outlined in the shari'a, whereby seeing the sex act was a requirement. For some, being in a house with an unrelated man was grounds enough for murder.

It is important to note that such crimes of passion were dealt with not only by Islamic law; examples from other contexts are telling of the perseverance of patriarchal attitudes that have perpetuated honor murder in the wider realm of world history. In Natalie Zemon Davis's examination of court registers from sixteenth-century France, she has argued that killing one's wife or daughter because of her sexual impropriety was pardonable murder. Comparatively, the evidentiary requirements could be just as loose, as accusation rather than witnessing of adultery could result in a pardon. Although I did not find any cases or oblique references to honor crime in the shari'a court records of Aleppo, historian Dror Ze'evi has found some hints of the practice in his study of Ottoman Palestine. There were no records of murder of female relatives in the Jerusalem court registers; however, a number of records involved accidental death of female relatives. Ze'evi explains that when such deaths occurred, court procedure demanded that an investigation take place with a team of experts. In the cases he examined, he discovered one concerning a woman named Banwa, who mysteriously fell off the roof of her family home; while falling, a rock was disturbed and fell on her head. Her father related the story to the judge, and an investigation took place in the village. The villagers corroborated the story, and the death was deemed accidental. Ze'evi writes, "Reports of this kind, about women who slid into wells, fell off roofs, or were buried by stone avalanches, are fairly numerous, certainly more so than similar cases involving men. This may suggest that women worked on roofs, near wells, or in small stone quarries more than men did, but it is more likely that these incidents represent attempts to avoid murder charges where questions of 'family honor' were concerned."[100] It is possible that the lack of such records in the Aleppo court records indicates that these cases fell outside the purview of the court, if they indeed happened at all.

In conclusion, there are marked differences between the shari'a and the Ottoman legal literature. First, Ottoman laws associate intent with guilt. A person who enters a house and does not commit a crime can still be rendered guilty if he simply had the intent to commit the crime. This point is especially noticeable in the law, whereby suspicion of *zina* can be assumed if a man and woman are alone. This issue is a major point of difference between the Ottoman *kanunname* and the shari'a, although admittedly there are traces of the law of intent in earlier Hanafi texts. As stated earlier, the *Hedaya* notes that "seeing" and "touching" can be construed as *zina*. I suggest that this standard may be a precursor to the more developed Ottoman interpretation of intent that later became a standard practice in modern law.

One must take into account the folk law and cultural perceptions of women in order to understand the way in which unchaperoned mixed-gender settings are perceived. A primary example is the hadith of the Prophet, "A man is not alone with a woman but that the devil makes a third."[101] This hadith means that a man and woman alone, regardless of their actions, are assumed to have the intent to commit *zina*. This hadith, which is also a frequently uttered popular perception in many parts of the Arab-Islamic world, contradicts the strict criteria for *zina* conviction found in Islamic juridical writings.

Second, there is a difference between Ottoman law and the shari'a concerning the idea of paying (monetarily) for punishment instead of receiving physical punishment, as in the case of *zina*. Why did the Ottomans opt for cash payment versus physical punishment for *diya*? This interpretation of the *diya* may have been particularly attractive to the Ottoman Empire because fine-based punishment provided a source of revenue—something the empire was always seeking. Dick Douwes has commented that "fiscalism dominated Ottoman political thinking."[102] He has further documented that the preoccupation with finances often put Ottoman authorities in conflict with the local population, who were fleeced by the demands of administrators and soldiers who extracted their pay from the masses but were on occasion prone to abuse.

Fining is a concept found in the shari'a, particularly the *diya* system. Some crimes retained the concept of *ta'zir*, yet a price was attached to each stroke in the *kanunnames*. Hanafi *fiqh* strictly prohibited dual punishment, yet Ottoman law, which followed the Hanafi school, applied lashing in combination with fining as a form of prescribed punishment. Heyd argues that those individuals executing punishment in the Ottoman Empire would even sometimes add strokes in order to receive more payment.[103] This point may further support the idea that the

Ottomans adopted fines over *hadd* execution for *zina* because it provided another source of revenue for the empire, at least during the time they were written.

On the other hand, in terms of the field of law and gender, only a handful of studies have begun to examine *zina* crime. What these preliminary works have demonstrated is that when sex crimes are mentioned in Ottoman law, stoning is not discussed as a punishment; Ebu's Su'ud's fatwa regarding prostitution does not appear to be the standard practice at court. Heyd writes: "Stoning to death *(recem)* [*rajam*], though prescribed in many Ottoman *fatwas* as the required penalty for certain cases of fornication, seems to have been inflicted only in very rare cases."[104] The fact that fining as punishment was advocated by the Ottomans reflects the notion that the law was a process of negotiation between local customary law *('urf)* and *fiqh,* since the *kanunnames* were intended to be based on the shari'a but did not always follow it by the letter. The *kanunname,* by distancing itself from the corporal punishments advocated in the shari'a, may have conformed more to the welfare of the community over which it ruled, opting for punishments acceptable and customary to the local residents whom it governed.

The importance of the *kanunnames* shifted throughout the period under study. As Süleyman, rightly or wrongly, personified imperial law with his moniker "lawgiver," the criminal codes would soon fall into obscurity. The last set of *kanunname* would be issued in the second quarter of the seventeenth century, and by the following century the criminal codes found within them fell into disuse altogether. The reasons involve the increase of local power by judges and muftis that characterized an overall shift in power from the centralized government to locals who administered the empire in its provinces. The military did not complain about the decline of the *kanunname,* because its abuses, usually in the form of excessive taxation and fines, remained increasingly unchecked by the judge and his court. This latitude offered opportunities for individuals who sought power in the countryside to compete more vigorously for resources and prestige. It is in the context of the waning Ottoman criminal law that the adjudication of criminal cases in the shari'a court becomes increasingly important.[105]

PART TWO

Law in Practice

3

People and Court

Policing Public Morality in the Streets of Aleppo

The shari'a represents the point of view of religious doctrine compiled by centuries of jurists in order to create guidelines for Muslim believers, whereas later Ottoman law combined some aspects of the shari'a along with imperial edicts into a series of codes to guide the administrators of the empire. Neither of these legal traditions represents the full picture of the everyday practice of law in court. Even though we may never be able to create a complete picture of the courts, we do have sources to aid our understanding of their daily function, namely, the shari'a court records. These sources can lend insight into everyday life in the Ottoman Empire and provide the best possible information concerning the administration of justice and policing of crime in the Ottoman period. The shari'a court records have been used to construct the following thematic chapters that examine various ways in which criminal cases of *zina* as well as related issues of public morality were treated in the shari'a courts. Before embarking on those themes, I will highlight some of the aspects of this source as well as recent debates concerning their use.

The shari'a court records are helpful in their documentation of Aleppine social hierarchies and class that in many cases factored into policing patterns throughout the city. It was common for cases of moral wrongdoing to be policed by entire city quarters, whereby residents would appear in court and testify against a criminal. Abdul Karim Rafeq has called this process "quarter solidarity" in his study of eighteenth-century Damascus.[1] City quarters had an intricate system of patronage that was characteristic of the early modern state wherein neighborhood strongmen both represented their communities and mediated disputes between residents. These strongmen, and other neighborhood representatives, worked together to police their own neighborhoods. Ottoman legal codes placed the responsibility of policing on the quarters themselves. However, I suggest that quarter solidarity may have also been a reaction to both the lack of security offered by the Ottoman police and its origins as a practice predating the Ottoman state. This tradition may have been left undisturbed by the Ottoman authorities owing to its effectiveness and incorporated into their system of rule. Quarter solidarity served as an early modern form of "neighborhood watch" and in many ways secured the city from unwanted crime. Furthermore, quarter solidarity was a key force used in the apprehension of criminals and the prosecution of criminal cases.

In his study of nineteenth-century Istanbul coffeehouses, Cengiz Kırlı points to the state-imposed concept of *kefalet* (standing surety or guarantee), which was used as an instrument of social control by the Ottoman authorities. It linked the actions of the individual to the larger community, placing responsibility on the collective. It made it so that "one's neighbor's business was one's own."[2] However, Kırlı describes the system as a series of links among individual, community, and state that allowed the Ottoman authorities to regulate the population with little administrative supervision. Yet the system itself allowed for some autonomy in the neighborhoods, as such participation and surveillance "was built into the legal culture."[3]

Not only were communities involved in such policing, but the guild system also played a major role. These networks of craft organizations intersected with several social and religious segments of Aleppine society. Organized by trade, the guilds were driven by a strong sense of ethics, as evidenced in their removal of members deemed lazy and immoral, their demotion of immoral guild representatives, and their witnessing of a member's piety and strong moral character at court. The guilds actively used the shari'a court in order to register their representatives with the Ottoman authorities, since guild representatives were responsible for delivering tax revenues to the state. In turn, the guilds exercised strong witnessing power and actively used the courts to document their affairs. The representation of several social classes in moral breaches, the policing of neighborhoods by residents, and the power of the guilds as yet another policing agent combine to represent the deeper social networks behind these cases at court. In both community and guild efforts in policing one's reputation and social titles, the latter an indication of social class, played an important role in convicting less powerful residents of wrongdoing.

THE SHARI'A COURT RECORD AND SOCIAL HISTORY

Historians have explored the uses of the shari'a court record as a source for social history for the past forty years. This exploration began in American and European academic circles in 1966 with the work of Jon Mandeville. Legal sources, and in particular the court record, would later become an important source in historical studies owing to the richness of details they provide for historians of the Ottoman Empire.[4] The court record is the only source that offers insight into the practice of law as well as valuable information on taxation, marriage, dowries, divorces, business transactions, religious endowments, crime, and state-society relations that are precious for the construction of social histories. Still, after four decades, we know little about the actual structure of the courts, the prison system, and the administration of punishment. Comparative histories of the courts examining differences and similarities in the practice of law are in their earliest stages.[5] Even more, historians, including myself, are still struggling with how to effectively use these sources, as they are fraught with methodological problems.

Recent scholarship has opened the shari'a court records to rigorous scrutiny.[6] Scholars have focused on the many methodological problems found in the study of court records to the point that one scholar has called it the study of "the *sijill* façade," as the only things that can be understood are the underlying motivations of the actors behind them.[7] This postmodern approach to the study of shari'a court records starkly contrasts the more factual, often statistical, or Annales-inspired, histories in the field. While reading these critiques, it is easy to feel a wave of disillusionment sweep through the field of Ottoman studies and Islamic law and society; however, I am not ready to dismiss all of the informational qualities of the source quite yet. Without it, the wheels of social history, which for the field have been turning for only about thirty years, would stop altogether. Even still, no one has completely disregarded the source but only called for caution while reading them and more critical readings for the future.

One concern expressed by historians is the selective nature of the information offered within shari'a court records. We are given no insights into the way the judge processed the information presented at court to derive his verdict.[8] How did the judge reason through the evidence presented at court? What sources of law did he use to produce a verdict? Such information is missing from the record unless explicit references are made. Furthermore, records show that criminals were convicted and punished by a judge *(qadi)* without any evidence to reveal whether the punishment was ever carried out. Historians have lamented that determining whether the punishment was carried out is almost impossible.[9] Chronicle accounts, read in conjunction with the court records, can provide supplementary details concerning punishment, but trying to find specific outcomes for a court record is sometimes problematic because the outcome was not always clear. For instance, *ta'zir* could be prescribed by the judge, but what did it entail? Was *ta'zir* fining or banishment? Usually in cases of physical punishment, the records provided more detail, noting that *ta'zir bi'l-darb* was prescribed by the judge; however, the number of floggings was not listed.[10]

The court record is not an actual account of the court proceedings. It is a rendering by a court scribe *(katib)* who often employed formal court language. Some authors have called it "nothing but a translation of a particular legal performance into a formal and immensely formulaic language."[11] There is evidence that accounts were not recorded during or immediately after the court proceedings. These accounts are sometimes not recorded in the *sijills* chronologically and are sometimes copied twice. Additional evidence includes the fact that paternal names were sometimes left blank in the record, which hints at a later recording long after the case had ended.[12]

The methodological problems in studying court records have resulted in critical analysis of the source by authors such as Bishara Doumani, who views them as literary texts in his own work on Ottoman Nablus. He argues that the court records were "self-conscious representations reflecting the agendas of particular individuals, groups and institutions." Another Ottoman historian, Dror Ze'evi, makes a similar argument on methodology, stating, "No source is a simple mirror. All sources are complex webs of meaning, in which a social 'reality,' a series of specific biases, contemporary codes and symbols, styles and tropes of writing, the interventions of copiers and editors, all blend inextricably to form a written source."[13] I agree that there are a number of unwritten forces at work and that various interests often underlie the records. However, in terms of the scope of this study, I have chosen a more legal reading of the court records that focuses on the adjudication process. From that legal standpoint, I concentrate on the composition of the case, the use of witnesses, and the verdict of the judge. Therefore, I do not treat the court records only as literary texts but instead try to search for agency within them, as well as underlying motivations and legal outcomes.

Natalie Zemon Davis in her study of sixteenth-century French Inquisition records, as well as other court registers, has examined narratives and testimony with such innovation that it has inspired social historians both within and outside of European history.[14] Although Davis has conducted brilliant analyses of testimony, as in the infamous case of Martin Guerre, some of the ways that this methodology has been interpreted by Middle East historians can be problematic for the study of the already marginalized, that is, non-Western and gender histories. It is certainly possible to question interpretations of an event; it is something else to place the event only in the realm of discourse. If that is the case, did the event ever happen at all? I concede that testimony in some cases could be fabricated by a witness or sculpted by the scribe, and in those cases the historian can rightly question the intent of the witnesses or scribe. But what holds true is that these cases were actual cases brought to court and documented and not unlike court records in other legal traditions whose authenticity as lived experience is rarely questioned. If the event is a case of rape, as in Aleppo cases referenced in chapter 5, are we to treat the vivid descriptions of rape sometimes offered by women before the *qadi* as a "representation" or a lived experience? This is not to say that one cannot look at intention and the crafting of narratives by women who have submitted rape charges in court. For example, I call into question why women waited until their sixth month of pregnancy to appear in court and testify that they were raped. Therefore, I strive to examine the social, legal, and political factors in the crafting of testimony without detracting from the agency of marginalized groups whose voices we may be hearing for the first time in the shari'a court records.

Historians who use court records, whether in the European or the Ottoman context, do ultimately encounter the perceived voices of those individuals in the textual record. First-person narratives sometimes appeared in Aleppo's court records. In a language that does not use quotation marks, grammatical markers indicate the shift to possible quotations, although some historians have cautioned against understanding these narratives as the "actual words of the litigants." Instead, what we see in the court record is "the translation of their voices into the official language of the legal system."[15] I began to understand some of these narratives as "voices" not just because of their first-person grammatical constructions but also because of their use of colloquialisms that encouraged me to believe these records are fragments of testimony. For example, in a case of spousal abuse, the battered wife's testimony is awkwardly documented in the scribe's hand in first person colloquial Arabic, and we hear the wife's voice when she says, "He hit me and said to me 'free me *(ibri'ini)* of your dowry *(mahruki)* until I divorce you *(itlaquki)*' and then later he said to me 'I added it up and your dowry is a burden.'"[16] In this case, we have the wife's rendering of a conversation with her husband, and the court eventually ruled in her favor. This type of phrase gives us a small sampling of the plaintiff's voice and works to document the speaker's agency, in this case a battered wife. Other examples include rape cases in which women and sometimes even rapists describe the rape in vivid detail in a first-person narrative.[17]

Use of shari'a court records for quantitative analysis has been rightly criticized by historians. Such analysis would not be conclusive because the records are incomplete; for example, several volumes of court records *(sijills)* are missing from the Syrian collection.[18] Furthermore, a number of cases were not documented because they were settled outside of court through informal arbitration *(sulh)* conducted by families and neighborhoods; as they are undocumented, their outcomes cannot be determined.[19] Therefore, such statistics tell us only about cases that made it to court, not the ones that were settled through other means. Recent research by Boğaç Ergene indicates that the court fees may have been too high for the lower classes to afford, as the courts of Çankırı and Kastamonu tended to charge more than the official price dictated in Ottoman manuals. Thus, the samples from court records may not be as representative of class as previously believed, making it difficult to claim that the records allow us to actually get at a "history from below."[20] For residents, the cost provides yet another motivation for seeking outside arbitration rather than a formal court appearance. The court record occasionally makes reference to arbitration, indicating the use of informal, undocumented legal processes conducted at the local level. There was an informal arbitration, and if it was ever ineffective, neighborhoods brought the case to court of their own volition.

Aside from the shari'a court and informal arbitration, the people had access to the *hakim al-'urf*, the governor of the city. He could not administer the shari'a but instead applied the laws of the state. In some cases, if an appearance in front of the *hakim al-'urf* did not produce the desired result on the part of the litigant, plaintiffs could seek another ruling in the shari'a court.[21] This appeal process provides further proof that there were alternative legal avenues operating outside the formal shari'a court system that was available to the community at large.

Despite our access to shari'a court records, more questions are generated by them than answered. What do we know about punishment in the courts? Was there a formal prison system? The Aleppo court records mention prisons; for example, the sultan's prison and the police prison were both mentioned in the records studied. The prisons were usually mentioned in cases of those individuals imprisoned for outstanding debts.[22] Alexander Russell's account of eighteenth-century Aleppo notes that corporal punishment was rarely practiced, but when it was, the crime was usually a capital offense. Foreign observers reported that murderers and rebels were hung for their crimes on posts in the marketplace. Where the convicts were executed, how they were executed, and by whom are questions not documented in the court records themselves. Some evidence is available through Russell's account, as he notes that executioners were often Armenian Christians yet observes that they were not very skilled in beheadings, stating that they were "performed in a very bungling manner, from the executioner's want of practice."[23]

It is not only the process of punishment that is absent from the Aleppo records, for the police are rarely mentioned. We know that the Ottoman governor had means of policing, as Herbert L. Bodman Jr. writes, "Every *wali* had at his disposal a force of cavalry to keep order in the province and of infantry to police the city. These troops, called *dalis* and *tufınkjis* respectively, were in the pay of the *wali* himself and their number varied according to his means and needs." Whereas the *tufınkjis* operated as an urban police force for the governor, the official police, subject to the *qadi,* were the *subaşı.* While examining breaches of sexual and public morality in this period, only four cases were found in which an Ottoman police officer *(subaşı)* appeared in court.[24] The reason may lie in Ottoman law, which deemed it the responsibility of residents to bring cases to the attention of the court. Regardless, Ottoman officials were responsible for actually apprehending and bringing criminals to trial.[25]

In our pursuit for greater understanding of the Ottoman legal process, a few authors have explored the dynamics of shari'a court procedure and structure.[26] At the center of the court sat the judge *(qadi),* whose position was an official Ottoman post. In theory, judges were to be trained and later dispatched from the Ottoman Porte to various courts throughout the provinces. They were to be rotated every year in an effort to maintain some neutrality between judges and local residents.[27] Abraham Marcus determined that ninety-nine judges passed through Aleppo in the eighteenth century.[28] This heavy rotation placed the judges at an advantage in terms of arbitration, as they did not have the same local loyalties as the litigants involved in the court cases; however, their cultural differences did incur disadvantages. The judges, being outsiders, were generally unfamiliar with local customs and laws. They relied on local expert witnesses (shahud al-hal), who advised the judge of local customs and traditions he would not otherwise know. The judge also had a large resource at his disposal: the preserved court records from previous judges. Part of the motivation to document the court proceedings may have been their use as a recorded memory of previous rulings that could serve as a guideline for the foreign, and temporary, Ottoman judge.

There were other staff available in the shariʿa court as a resource for plaintiffs and defendants. Through references in the court records, as well as the aforementioned studies, we know that the court had three deputies (na'ib) who were present in court to represent the three alternate schools of Islamic law. These positions were often held by local members of the ʿulama, who often enjoyed longer periods of tenure than the qadi.[29] The deputies complemented the school represented by the chief judge of the court and offered alternative interpretations of the law for plaintiffs and defendants to choose from. This flexibility could be strategically important in some cases. For example, the Hanafi school of law did not allow an abandoned wife to divorce her husband until she reached the ripe age of ninety years old, yet the Shafiʿi school did allow annulments in such cases. When these cases appeared, the Shafiʿi na'ib would step up and grant an annulment.[30]

The volumes (sijills) of court records usually, but not always, list on their first page the name of the judge who is presiding over the court and the name of the court.[31] Although some features of the court are well known, little is known about the courts and staff who worked within them. For instance, we know little about the court scribes who recorded judgments and whose penmanship preserved important details of court cases. There is some evidence in biographical dictionaries that suggests scribes were from ʿulama families, as the position of scribe was often granted at the beginning of one's career; however, details on court scribes are rarely mentioned in Syrian records.[32]

Aside from these court positions, the position of mufti was separate from the court structure, yet it was connected in many ways to court procedure. The mufti, unlike the judge, was often a local member of the 'ulama who was appointed by his cohort. There was typically one position for each of the four schools of Islamic law.[33] The mufti was linked to the court through his fatwas that could be used by parties to support their cases before the qadi. In such cases, the mufti's role vis-à-vis the court was important, but not part of the actual court structure.

From the literature recently produced using the shari'a court records, differences in the ways courts operated from one locality to the next are beginning to appear. The ways in which the courts operated and were utilized by local populations varied. One observation is that urban populations had a tendency to utilize the courts for the registration of marriages. Cities such as Jerusalem and Cairo are frequently cited by historians for their vast amount of marriage contracts stored in the volumes of the shari'a courts.[34] For example, Judith Tucker in her comparative study of records from three shari'a courts observed that marriage contracts were recorded more regularly in the courts of Jerusalem than in Nablus and Damascus.[35] Such variations reflect the diversity of the usually cited monolith, "the shari'a court." It is clear that there is no monolithic shari'a court, and not all courts can be measured by the same yardstick.

The Syrian archives possess shari'a court records found in the cities of Aleppo, Damascus, Homs, and Hama.[36] The Aleppo court, usually referred to in the singular, contains records for five courts in all. Four of the shari'a courts practiced Hanafi law, and one administered Shafi'i law. The largest court was the Mahkamat al-Kubra, the city's major court where the Hanafi judge presided. "The Mahkamat al-Kubra was situated between Suwayqat 'Ali and Bab al-Nasr in front of the Mihmandar Mosque which was also called the Mosque of the Court or the Mosque of the Judge."[37] Since the Mahkamat al-Kubra was the major Hanafi court in Aleppo, before which the majority of criminal matters appeared, its records have been used in this study. The second court in Aleppo was the Shafi'iyya court. As important as the Hanafi court, the Shafi'iyya court was located in the Suq al-Sabbaghin, north of Khan al-Wazir. These two courts operated through the nineteenth century until the Tanzimat (1840–71) reforms, when the nizami court and a separate mahkamah shar'iyya were established in 1871. This process effectively dismantled the shari'a court into several courts with varying jurisdictions. From that point forward, the shari'a court held jurisdiction only over personal-status issues such as marriage and divorce, whereas the *nizami* court managed criminal matters. After the reforms, mixed courts managed cases regarding foreigners whereby they were subject to their own laws, and the commercial courts adjudicated issues under their jurisdiction. There is a difference between Syria and other places such as Egypt and Anatolia. For instance, Egypt had *zaptiyya* courts, created during the Tanzimat specifically for matters of crime, and Istanbul has police records, whereas Aleppo had no similar police or criminal records.[38]

Although *nizami* courts were established in Aleppo and Damascus during the Tanzimat, the records have not been located for Aleppo at present. Syrian authorities claim many of these documents were destroyed by the French during the French mandate (1920–46).[39] Their loss is but one of the limitations with respect to Aleppo's archival sources. The shari'a court records are also not complete for the nineteenth century but provided the court records used in this study. I have used 1871, the beginning of the reform period, as a cutoff date for my examination because of these dramatic shifts in jurisdiction that took place at that time, exacerbating the missing *nizami* court records.

Some of the eighteenth-century cases used in this study were found in the Jabal Sam'an court of Aleppo, which practiced Hanafi law. Although the location of the Jabal Sam'an court has not been historically documented, today a court exists in Aleppo near the citadel by that very name.[40] Jabal Sam'an, and occasionally Salahiyya, records were used when gaps existed in the Kubra court records in order to maintain chronological consistency. Together, the Jabal Sam'an and the Kubra courts contained the most criminal cases. Other courts, such as the Banqusiyya and the Salahiyya, were of minor importance for the purposes of this study, since most of the cases contained within those records were contractual, mostly financial. Mahkamat al-Salahiyya was located in the Madrasa Salahiyya in Suwayqat 'Ali. Mahkamah al-Banqusiyya is believed to have been in the Banqusa quarter.[41] In sum, there were five courts operating in Aleppo in the Ottoman period, leaving scholars with many court records to choose from.

So how does one determine which court to study? Cases of public morality and crime in general (*zina*, theft, murder, and general disturbance of the peace through cursing or hitting) addressed in this study appeared predominately in two courts—the Kubra and Jabal Sam'an courts. For that reason and after several months of archival research, I decided to rely mostly on these two courts.

The Kubra court was Aleppo's major Hanafi court and contained cases from the city proper. Compared to the Shafi'iyya court or other minor courts in Aleppo, the Kubra court contained a greater variety of cases. The same holds true for Jabal Sam'an. Its cases were more diverse than the three remaining minor courts. Whereas the Kubra court tended to deal with cases only from the city of Aleppo, Jabal Sam'an dealt with cases from within the city and the surrounding villages, and sometimes cases as far away as the Anatolian Peninsula. The fact that the Jabal Sam'an court contains cases from the surrounding countryside adds diversity to the cases gathered and used in this study. I used three volumes of *sijills* from the Salahiyya court when records from the Kubra and Jabal Sam'an courts were unavailable. Because the *sijill* collections are not 100 percent complete, it would be statistically inaccurate to use this source to quantify the exact number of cases that appeared in the Aleppo courts. However, by studying selected *sijills,* a progression of cases through time becomes available to study the consistency of judgments and patterns of criminal activity.

The selection method for this study was to choose one volume *(sijill)* of court records for each decade from 1507 to 1866, stopping before 1871, as reforms took place that greatly changed the courts. *Sijill* 4 was used in this study and begins with the earliest date, 1507, which is about ten years before the Ottoman conquest of Aleppo. This *sijill* places some of the cases covered in this volume under Mamluk (1250–1516) rule in Syria, demonstrating continuity in the shari'a court system that predated the Ottomans. Sometimes a *sijill* contained several years of court records; other times a *sijill* was a compilation of several decades of records bound in one volume. Earlier court records are often mixed together in large bound volumes located in the Syrian archives. I used several of those volumes, as they cover a large span of time and not just a sample from a given decade. By reading one volume for each decade available, my research covered at least one year and sometimes as many as ten years of records per volume (table 3.1).

After reading thirty-three volumes of court registers and several hundred cases involving breaches of public morality, some of which were *zina*-related cases, a pattern of policing and crime began to appear. Certain social groups were engaged in policing crime in the city, whereas other groups appeared more actively criminal. We will examine these social groups and the roles they played in crime as it played out in the quarters of Aleppo.

TABLE 3.1

METHODOLOGY

Selection of Sijills *from the Shari'a Courts of Aleppo*

Sijill number	Dates Hijra	Christian Dates	Court
1	956–972	1549–1565	Not listed
2	956–1119	1549–1708	Mixed
3	954–1119	1547–1708	Mixed
4	913–1277	1507–1860	Mixed
5	990–990	1582–1582	Not listed
8	1002–1006	1593–1598	Jabal Sam'an
10	964–1065	1556–1655	Mixed
11	1026–1028	1617–1618	Not listed
14	1033–1036	1623–1626	Not listed
18	1041–1048	1631–1638	Not listed
22	1050–1050	1640–1641	Kubra
27	1067–1078	1656–1668	Salahiyya
28	1070–1074	1659–1664	Salahiyya
34	1089–1090	1678–1679	Kubra
36	1098–1099	1686–1688	Not listed
43	1027–1127	1617–1715	Mixed
45	1130–1131	1717–1719	Jabal Sam'an
50	1135–1137	1722–1725	Salahiyya
55	1147–1149	1734–1737	Not listed
64	1153–1155	1740–1742	Jabal Sam'an
85	1167–1169	1753–1756	Not listed
94	1175–1176	1761–1763	Kubra
113	1189–1191	1775–1777	Kubra
130	1200–1202	1785–1788	Kubra
143	1208–1209	1793–1795	Kubra
149	1215–1217	1800–1803	Kubra
153	1218–1218	1803–1804	Kubra
154	1218–1225	1803–1810	Not listed
208	1241–1241	1825–1826	Not listed
232	1252–1253	1837	Kubra
239	1257–1258	1841–1842	Kubra
261	1267–1268	1850–1852	Kubra
296	1282–1283	1865–1866	Kubra

Source: Based on *Dalil sijillat al-mahakim al-shar'iyya al-'uthmaniyya,* an archive catalog compiled by Brigitte Marino and Tomoki Okawara.

POLICING THE QUARTER IN OTTOMAN ALEPPO

> Offend even your *pasha* but not the people of your quarter.
> —Proverb from Aleppo, quoted in "Privacy in Eighteenth-
> Century Aleppo: The Limits of Cultural Ideals," by
> Abraham Marcus

The Aleppine proverb in the epigraph conveys the importance given to neighbors over all other authorities, even the Ottoman governor *(pasha)*, in the popular imagination. This emphasis on the local is a common feature of the criminal cases investigated in the shariʿa court. Nearly all the cases studied make an explicit reference to Aleppo's quarters *(harat* or *mahallat)*, identifying plaintiffs, defendants, and sometimes the crimes by quarter. According to eighteenth-century statistics, Aleppo had approximately eighty-two quarters within and surrounding its city walls. Twenty-eight quarters (one-third) lay within the fortified city, whereas fifty-four (two-thirds) ringed the outer walls. These quarters lay within a one-and-a-half-square-mile radius and varied in size, some larger than others in population and parameter (map 3.1).[42]

A common feature of these quarters was the characteristics they possessed based on the ethnic and religious composition of their residents. The Jewish population of Aleppo, as in other cities like Damascus, was found mostly, but not exclusively, in the northwestern quarters within the old city walls: Bahsita, al-Bandara, and al-Masabin. For example, historian Antoine Abdel Nour has placed the population of Jews in Bahsita at 90 percent of the total population of the quarter.[43] There were also high concentrations of Christians as early as the sixteenth century in the northwest part of the city, just outside the city walls in the quarter of Saliba al-Judayda (called simply Judayda today), outside of Bab al-Nasr.[44] Yet, importantly, a population of Muslims also lived among these communities of Jews and Christians.[45] Several studies have noted that non-Muslim communities were not completely segregated. Egyptian scholar Muhsin ʿAli Shuman notes that in Cairo there were predominately Jewish quarters, yet there were Muslims cohabitants. Najwa al-Qattan has found that the Christian quarters of Damascus, Bab Touma and Bab Sharqi, as well as the Jewish quarter, had Muslim residents and that Christians were found scattered throughout the city's predominately Muslim communities. Similarly, Cengiz Kırlı has observed that heterogeneity more than homogeneity characterized Istanbul's neighborhoods in the nineteenth century.[46]

KEY TO MAP 3.1

1. al-Abraj (L5)

2. al-A'jam (J9)

3. al-Akrad (H3)

4. Akyol (K2)

5. al-Almaji (J2)

6. Altunbogha (K8)

7. 'Antar (L3)

8. al-'Aqaba (E6)

9. al-'Aynayn (C5)

10. Bahsita (al-Yahud) (E4)

11. al-Ballat al-Fawqani (Akrad al-Ballat) (N7)

12. al-Ballat al-Tahtani (al-Qattana) (N8)

13. al-Bandara (G5)

14. al-Bastina (H2)

15. al-Bayyada (K6)

16. Chukurjuk (M5)

17. Chukur Qastal (al-'Aryan) (K4)

18. al-Dabbagha al-'Atiqa (F5)

19. Dakhil Bab al-Maqam (H11)

20. Dakhil Bab al-Nasr (G5)

21. Dakhil Bab al-Nayrab (J10)

22. Dakhil Bab Qinnasrin (E9)

23. al-Dallilin (N3)

24. al-Dudu (M7)

25. al-Farafira (H5)

26. al-Farra'in (N4)

27. al-Hajjaj (Jubb Qaraman, al-Bakraji) (M6)

28. Hamza Bey (M4)

29. al-Hawarina (K11)

30. al-Hazzaza (F1)

31. Ibn Nusayr (L6)

32. Ibn Ya'qub (al-Sighar) (M4)

33. al-Jallum al-Kubra (E8)

34. al-Jallum al-Sughra (E9)

35. Jami' 'Ubays (al-Maghazila) (G10)

36. al-Jubayla (K5)

37. Jubb Asad Allah (E6)

38. al-Kallasa (C10)

39. Karlik (O3)

40. al-Kattan (N11)

41. Khan al-Sabil (L5)

42. Kharabkhan (K3)

43. Kuchuk Kallasa (K3)

44. al-Ma'adi (H11)

45. al-Magha'ir (D13)

46. al-Malindi (M3)

47. al-Maqamat (G12)

48. al-Mar'ashi (J4)

49. al-Masabin (E6)

50. al-Mashariqa (A6)

51. al-Mawardi (J3)

52. Maydanjik (M11)

53. Muhammad Bey (al-Takashira) (M10)

54. al-Mushatiyya (N4)

55. Mustadim Bey (al-Mustadamiyya) (K6)

56. al-Nuhiyya (K2)

57. Oghlubey (al-Bab al-Ahmar) (K7)

58. Qadi 'Asker (N5)

59. Qal'at Halab (Citadel) (J7)

60. Qal'at al-Sharif (F10)

61. al-Qasila (K10)

62. al-Qawanisa (B5)

63. al-Safsafa (L9)

64. Sahat Biza (G9)

65. Sajilkhan al-Fawqani (Harun Dada) (N5)

66. Sajilkhan al-Tahtani (Aghajik) (N6)

67. al-Sakhkhana (L11)

68. Saliba al-Judayda (F3)

69. Shahin Bey (J5)

70. Shakir Agha (Shukr Agha) (N5)

71. al-Shamisatiyya (Qastal al-'Aqrab) (M3)

72. al-Shamma'in (C5)

73. al-Shari'atli (Qastal al-Harami) (J1)

74. al-Shaykh 'Arabi (M3)

75. al-Shaykh Yabraq (L2)

76. Suwayqat 'Ali (G6)

77. Suwayqat Hatim (F6)

78. Tall 'Aran (Sahat Hamad) (M9)

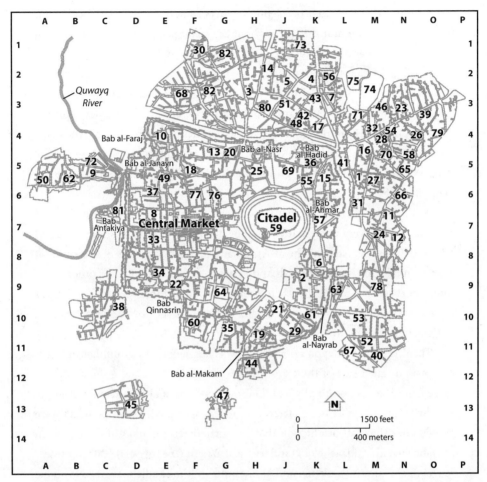

Map 3.1. Aleppo and its quarters. Modified by Joseph Stoll from a city plan of Aleppo in *The Middle East on the Eve of Modernity* by Abraham Marcus (New York: Columbia University Press, 1989); used by permission.

79. Tatarlar (O4)

80. Turab al-Ghuraba' (H3)

81. al-Warraqa (Jisr al-Salahif) (C6)

82. Kharij Bab al-Nasr (subdistricts G1, G2, and G3): 'Abd al-Hayy, 'Abd al-Rahim, al-Arba'in, al-'Atawi al-Kabir, al-'Atawi al-Saghir, Bali, Banqus (Bani Muhibb), al-Ghattas, Jisr al-Ka'ka al-Muballat, al-Mugharbiliyya, al-Qawwas, al-Qir, al-Shimali, al-Tabla, Tuma 'Abd al-'Aziz, Tuma Bishara, Tuma Hidaya

Disputes that appeared in Aleppo's courts sometimes reflect the cohabitation of religious communities throughout the city. Such cases are instructive in the way Muslims and non-Muslims negotiated the boundaries of morality, sometimes using the shari'a courts to mediate between the two. In November 1678 four residents bearing social titles from the neighborhood of al-Almaji filed a complaint against four Christians who lived in the same quarter. They reported that the Christians drank liquor and cursed at them in their quarter. They also produced two additional witnesses to their drunkenness, as required by the shari'a. The court found them guilty and administered an unspecified punishment (ta'zir).[47]

Aside from religious diversity, quarters reflected the ethnic diversity of Aleppo, as they were named after the non-Arab Muslim populations that had settled there earlier, such as the al-Akrad and al-A'jam quarters of the city that were originally inhabited by Kurds and Persians, respectively. On the other hand, some court records reveal that the ethnicity designated in a quarter's name was not a description of current residents but probably described earlier patterns of settlement by immigrants.

The diversity of Aleppo's population was augmented by a number of Turkmen who dwelled east of the city's outer walls. Other regional groups, such as those from Hawran, originally had their own quarter of al-Hawarina in Aleppo, but the composition of the quarter eventually diversified. Other quarters were named after the craft production that dominated certain areas of the city such al-Dabbagha al-'Atiqa (the old tannery), al-Farra'in (the furriers), Tatarlar (messengers), al-Dallilin (brokers), and al-Shamma'in (the candle makers). No single class, commoner ('amma) or elite (khassa), dominated any one quarter, although certain quarters were favored by the wealthy, such as the areas near the citadel, central areas, and markets.[48] Instead, quarters had a mixture of social classes within them, including members of the notable classes, 'ulama, craftsmen, merchants, and commoners.

Another important dynamic within Aleppo's quarters was the presence of Europeans in the city. On some occasions foreign nationals appeared in court to settle disputes. For example, in April 1742 two French citizens, who resided in the predominately Jewish neighborhood of Bahsita, came to court when one claimed to be injured by the other. Fantun walad Fantun stated that twenty days earlier, Yusuf walad Istifan La Funti had run over him with his horse.[49] The court record describes that "[the horse] stomped on him injuring his upper lip and the skin on his left hand."[50] Yusuf brought two titled witnesses with him. One of his witnesses held the title of hajji, which did not necessarily denote wealth but could enhance one's reputation as religious and trustworthy; the other witness held the title of *shaykh,* indicating a possible guild representative. The accuser brought no witnesses. Subsequently, Yusuf was found innocent. This case reveals that even European nationals knew the uses of powerful witnessing to win their cases. However, sometimes cases demonstrate tensions between foreign nationals and their neighbors. The seventeenth-century case of a foreign national named Paolo discussed in more detail in chapter 4 documents his removal from al-Jallum al-Kubra quarter based on suspicion of sexual immorality.[51]

The strategy of witnessing found in the French court case was not unique. Social hierarchies sometimes motivated the convictions dealt by the court, stacking the deck in favor of a plaintiff or a defendant, making them important in understanding the way in which court cases were structured and why some testimony was valued more than others. Although some social classes indicated connections with the Ottoman ruling class, many social positions date back to the preexisting Mamluk state. In the Ottoman Empire, the highest social class *(khassa)* was the ruling imperial class, consisting of various Turkish-speaking officials. The next highest social class was the *a'yan,* or notable class, consisting of merchants, the religious elite *('ulama),* scholars, teachers, and *shaykhs.*[52] The lowest social group was the *'amma,* or commoners, who were the trading and working members of the city, although sometimes the title *chalabi* was given to individuals employed in professional classes, including doctors and those engaged in important skilled trades such as goldsmiths and carpenters.[53] Professions that existed in this class included artisans, shopkeepers, retailers, and peddlers. However, at the bottom of the *'amma* hierarchy were the disreputable professions: servants, prostitutes, and entertainers.[54]

Social position was defined in the early modern state by three factors. First, an individual's position vis-à-vis the state determined his status. Namely, people who had a relationship with the imperial authorities or were granted Ottoman offices were able to elevate their rank in society. Second, a person's religious rank defined his position in society. Included in this category were members of the *'ulama* and *ashraf,* descendants of the Prophet Muhammad. It is important to note the politics of obtaining *ashraf* status, as one could become a member and obtain the appropriate title of *sharif* by claiming a female descendant who married a *sharif* in his lineage.[55] The *naqib al-ashraf* (head of the descendants of the Prophet Muhammad) was in charge of checking the validity of such claims; however, there is evidence that money could buy false lineage to aid those individuals with higher social aspirations.[56] Third, wealth determined one's rank. Sometimes these three factors overlapped, especially as Ottoman officials later exploited the powerful position of wealthy notable families in the provinces, bestowing them with official Ottoman government positions such as governor, mufti, *naqib al-ashraf,* and *amin al-fatwa* (chief of the fatwa). This phenomenon, called the "urban notables paradigm," was proposed by Albert Hourani and has been tested extensively in Middle East historiography.[57] The theory rightly argues that the *a'yan* were important in the process of administering the empire since they served as the middlemen between the highest class *(khassa)* and the lower class *('amma)*. As a class, the *a'yan* dated as far back as the ninth century and served an intermediary role "between imperial, often alien regimes and local society . . . ensur[ing] the stability of civil society in the face of chronic political instability between the Abbasid and the Ottoman Empires and in the later periods of Ottoman history."[58]

Such links with the Porte resulted in the increased power of local *a'yan* so much that by the eighteenth century, the wealth that used to be directed toward the Ottoman center in Istanbul was now in the hands of local urban notables, who sometimes served in a dual capacity as Ottoman administrators, particularly in the area of tax farming.[59] The increased number of public works, religious endowments *(waqf),* and widespread ownership of property in eighteenth-century Aleppo demonstrated the growing wealth of *a'yan* throughout the city during a period in which Aleppo was increasingly integrated into the world economy.

As these elites increased their own standing, they found themselves increasingly in conflict with the Ottoman Janissaries between the years 1760 and 1820 in a struggle for power. This political instability had serious repercussions, as the eighteenth century was ravaged by "revolts, factional strife, high food prices, heavy tax demands, and large scale extortion by the powerful."[60] In part, the Janissaries were successful in exerting their control over the city in the end. However, the Ottomans continued to struggle against Janissary efforts, and eventually the Egyptian occupation would break the Janissary hold on Aleppo for good.

Despite these struggles among the city's elites, a great majority of Aleppo's residents were from among the *'amma,* who constituted an estimated 65–75 percent of Aleppo's population.[61] Among them were individuals who were considered morally lacking and worked in dishonorable occupations, engaging in forbidden occupations such as slave dealers, money changers, and criers. The second category included people who were moral deviants: dancers and other entertainers, prostitutes (both male and female), wine sellers, and professional mourners. The third category of disreputable commoner included persons who were impure owing to a profession that included the handling of animals and animal wastes. "Barbers and surgeons were valued on other grounds, but butchers, tanners, donkey and dog handlers, hunters and waste scavengers were despised." Another class of undesirables was the torchbearers (al-masha'iliyya), hangmen, and executioners. This segment of the 'amma consisted of professions such as "the night watchmen, torchbearers who cleaned the latrines, removed refuse from the streets, and carried off bodies of dead animals[,] served as police, guards, executioners, and public criers[,] and paraded people condemned to public disgrace whose shame may have consisted in part in being handled by such men."[62] Often these jobs were carried out at nighttime and sometimes included police duties. Given their presence at night, they were also often active in the criminal underworld as thieves, gamblers, and sellers of hashish and wine. Slaves and servants of the sultan were also associated with criminals, drunks, and drug users, as they all belonged to the lowest social class.

The homeless and poverty-stricken were also among the lowest members of society. They included transient poor who immigrated to the city to panhandle as well as Sufi beggars. Bedouin were also seen as transient and, therefore, viewed as a socially threatening group. Furthermore, the homeless who lived on the street either out of poverty, illness, or handicap were considered the lowest of the low.

The class composition of Aleppo appears divided and segmented, yet all these strata form a cohesive social body because of their interrelationship with one another. The three major groups of khassa, a'yan, and 'amma were interdependent and lived in close proximity to each other within the same neighborhood. Amira El-Azhary Sonbol, in her recent work on Ottoman Egypt, urges historians of the Middle East to reconsider the use of the word elite when referring to khassa as well as other classes because "it gives the impression of absolutist control."[63] The khassa were not in complete control over the other classes of society since classes were interdependent in a complex system of patronage that linked them. A crucial link between classes was the aforementioned system of promotion for members of the *a'yan*. Other groups, such as the merchant classes, formed inter-mediaries among these three major categories.

Social hierarchies were important in framing the court cases under study. Particularly, in cases of public morality where en masse testimony was common, witnesses were documented according to social titles, listing the names of *sayyids* (members of the *ashraf*) first, then *shaykhs, aghas,* imams, and hajjis.[64] Accusa-tions of wrongdoing were not reserved for the socially marginal; corrupt *shaykhs* (religious and guild leaders), hajjis (Muslims who performed a pilgrimage), and *sayyids* were brought to court on several occasions for criminal activities.[65]

Social rank facilitated the policing and adjudication of moral breaches in several ways. The social standing of individual witnesses could make or break a court case, aiding the prosecution of public morality cases since criminal convic-tion was often guided by how many prestigious and titled community members were present as witnesses. Furthermore, social position was also noted in court records, as many offenders were also high-ranking in society as members of guilds, religious clergymen, or descendants of the Prophet Muhammad. Hajji, for example, was a title that in some way signified a pious status in the community, since the holder must have performed the pilgrimage, but did not necessarily sig-nify wealth because both the poor and the wealthy could perform pilgrimages.

In the *zina*-related crimes examined in this study, only 10 percent (12 out of 119 cases) involved defendants bearing social titles; all but 2 cases resulted in punishment. If we were to include cases in which defendants' names indicated fathers who bore social titles, the number of cases would increase to 37 percent (44 out of 119 cases). What these numbers indicate is that despite bearing social titles, individuals could still find themselves standing before the shari'a court and subjected to punishment. However, these numbers also indicate that the majority of defendants appearing before the court (90 percent) held no social title whatsoever, suggesting that the lower classes stood a higher chance of appear-ing in court. This number can be compared to Abraham Marcus's estimate cited above that 65–75 percent of the population fell in those lower classes, indicating that the *'amma* represented a disproportionate share of the *zina*-related cases examined in this study.[66]

How was it possible that the lower classes were disproportionately repre-sented in court? The criteria of evidence used these cases were brought en masse by neighbors who claimed defendants were "evildoers" or "harmful," but often the court record does not provide the criteria of evidence required by the shariʻa. Boğaç Ergene has argued that en masse testimony circumvented the rules of evidence, an aspect that leaves open the possibility for outright persecution of defendants by large groups of neighbors. Furthermore, untitled defendants brought to court by groups of titled plaintiffs often lost their cases. These cases may point to an underlying class conflict, though the cases would be equally effective if the plaintiffs had no titles whatsoever, so long as the defendants also lacked social standing.

The structure of city quarters served as a natural administrative unit for the Ottomans. Communities had long been led by quarter representatives *(shaykh al-hara* or *ʻarif al-hara),* usually nominated from among the leading quarter notables.[67] Some representatives were elected by ethnic groups to represent their interests to the Ottoman administration.[68] Part of their responsibilities included taking care of needed repairs or maintenance issues in their neighborhoods. They also gained respect in public gatherings and received governors and other Ottoman dignitaries. Ira Lapidus writes of the role of the quarter representative in policing neighborhoods during the Mamluk period: "Administrative responsibilities extended to police functions as well. Mamluk governors required the *shaykhs* of the quarters to enforce special ordinances, assist in the suppression of wine drinking, restrict circulation at night, regulate the opening and closing of shops, and enforce sanitary rules. They were also responsible for the prevention of crime, return of fugitives, and apprehension of criminals or payment of indemnities in unsolved cases."[69] Antoine Abdel Nour argues that this system of collective responsibility continued through the Ottoman period. The system of quarter representation was appropriated by the Ottomans through a network of clients and local elites. Criminal matters were handled by local strongmen instead of the appropriate Ottoman official. It is the co-optation of systems of local leadership that has led historians such as André Raymond to argue that "the Ottoman Empire must be regarded as a 'commonwealth' rather than as a highly centralized political entity."[70]

The lack of centralization is best demonstrated through the position of quarter representatives, whose duties were akin to the responsibilities of the police. Scholars have noted the presence of the quarter representatives in other parts of the empire.[71] This local network was a positive factor for defense. During raids by bandits and thieves, or during wartime, quarters would barricade themselves for protection from the onslaught.[72] In terms of policing, representatives and witnesses from a quarter could protect themselves and their neighborhoods from immoral and corrupt neighbors by showing solidarity in court.

The earliest Aleppo court records concerning *zina* and other moral breaches from the sixteenth century were brief. Often the scribe recorded only a few lines, and within them witnesses could be omitted altogether. Later records have very different witnessing patterns. Yet by the eighteenth century, long lists of residents appear at the beginning of a court record to testify against a resident in their quarter. This change in witnessing correlates with a weakening of the central administration of the empire, increased localism in the Ottoman provinces, and a loosening of its application of the Ottoman criminal code in the eighteenth century.[73]

Correlating with these eighteenth-century trends, quarter solidarity has been observed in the courts of Aleppo. We are left to question what motivated these communities to police themselves. Abraham Marcus's volume on eighteenth-century Aleppo was the most complete study to date when it was published in 1989. In his chapter on legal institutions, Marcus discusses public morality, and it is here that he presents his argument on "collective responsibility." He writes that "the concern with local security grew out of occasional thefts from homes as well as the offensive presence of prostitution, drinking, and other forms of vice. Behind it, however, was also another driving force: fear of the authorities. Ill equipped to police the residents closely the government resorted to a system of social control by which members of groups would police each other. It held each neighborhood and non-Muslim minority collectively responsible for the behavior of its members. Residents were expected to make local misdeeds known and find the offenders."[74] This argument places Ottoman coercion as the motivation for "collective responsibility." The *kanunname* of Süleyman "held individuals, urban neighborhoods, or whole villages liable for crimes committed on their property if they could not find the guilty party."[75] For example, it states, "If a person is a disturber of the peace [who] is always engaged in mischievous activities and [whom] the Muslims tell to his face that they do not consider him a law-abiding person, the [*qadi*] and the *subaşı* shall take no part [in the proceedings against him]. The person who is entrusted with [the infliction of capital or severe corporal] punishment and [the execution of] the [sultan's] order [to impose such penalty] shall punish [him]." So, when dealing with "mischievous activities," an ambiguous euphemism applied to issues of public morality, the Muslims, meaning the people, are in charge of apprehending the culprit, and the law of the sultan shall be applied. According to the *kanunname*, "the *ehl-i ʿörf* [executive officers of the court] . . . brought people to trial in *shariʿa* courts for sexual offenses, the drinking of wine, non-attendance at public prayer, market delicts, and similar crimes."[76] However, in the Aleppo court records studied here, the official Ottoman police apparatus was virtually absent in court cases concerning public morality. Instead, neighborhood residents often informally and formally warned neighbors who engaged in prostitution, drinking, or cursing or who ran brothels in their homes in order to escape a collective fine. Marcus sums up his argument, asserting that "the fear of official reprisals encouraged some covering up of misdeeds, but it also worked to a certain extent as an effective instrument of group control."[77]

Further support for the argument that Ottoman coercion motivated policing has been based on the Ottoman criminal codes that demand group punishment, in the form of a fine imposed on the neighborhood, if they did not report perpetrators. The criminal codes specifically address collective punishment with regard to the crimes of murder and theft. Ottoman criminal codes require community members to find the murderer if a dead body is found in their midst, or they will be collectively fined the blood money for the victim's family.[78] This order has its basis in Hanafi law that holds residents responsible for blood money in the case of unsolved homicides that occur within their communities.[79] Another criminal code requires that if a criminal hiding in a community is not found, the community will be required to pay the amount necessary to compensate the victim of his crime.[80] However, as demonstrated in the previous chapter, the Ottoman criminal codes often treat *zina* crime, as well as other moral breaches, on an individual basis rather than collectively. For example, the codes do not discuss community punishment for illegal consumption or distribution of alcohol in communities.[81] Furthermore, punishment for *zina* is punished on an individual basis and clearly separates *zina* acts from other types of crimes that would warrant communal punishment. In one instance it states, "If a person knows of [an act of] fornication [but] does not go to the [*qadi*] and tell him, no fine is [to be collected]. If he knows of a theft [but] does not tell [the *qadi*] a fine of 10 akçe shall be collected." Here a clear delineation is made between two circumstances, one moral and the other criminal, which subsequently separates communal responsibility.[82]

The code does require community policing when it states, "Furthermore, if the community of his (or her) [town-] quarter or of his (or her) village complains that a person is a criminal or a harlot and, saying 'He (or she) is not fit [to live with us],' rejects him (or her), and if that person has in fact a notoriously bad reputation among the people, he (or she) shall be banished, i.e., ejected from his (or her) quarter or village."[83] Here we can clearly see that the responsibility is placed on the community in policing these matters of public morality. However, the loose nature of the criminal behavior, in that it is based on reputation of wrongdoing, places the defining of what is immoral in the hands of the community. If, for example, someone had "a criminal past [töhmet-i sabıka]" or was engaging in what the community construed as "mischief," they could be punished as a troublemaker.[84]

Morality was not only something that concerned Ottoman officials. On the most basic social level, one's reputation affected the way he was perceived in the community and whether his testimony would be valid in court. Monitoring morality was, therefore, of concern to individuals, and built into both Ottoman codes and the practice of the communities on the ground. Leslie Peirce has found in her study of morality in Ottoman 'Ayntab that most major criminal cases were brought to the court's attention by local residents who assisted the authorities.[85]

The neighborhoods not only held the power to apprehend and expel undesirables in their midst. Another legal code in this series allows that same quarter to suspend banishment should the culprit repent and lead a more righteous life after the expulsion.[86] Thus, removal from city quarters was not viewed as a permanent action, but could be overturned in the future, should the resident show signs of improvement. Therefore, Ottoman law places the power of both condemnation and redemption squarely in the hands of the community.

In contrast to Marcus's argument suggesting Ottoman coercion was the motivating factor in community policing efforts is Abdul Karim Rafeq's explanations for the phenomenon in his article "Public Morality in 18th Century Damascus." Rafeq systematically outlines cases of moral breaches spanning a period of more than a thirty-six years in the Damascus court records. He argues, "Eighteenth-century Damascus was characterized by a weak administration, punctuated periodically by attempts at the enforcement of law and order." Moreover, he describes a city corrupted by profiteering Ottoman officials, governors, and notables; soaring food prices caused by hoarding; lawlessness of Ottoman troops;

lack of security owing to the decline in living standards of the poor; and a widening gap between rich and poor. All of these combined factors contributed to an unprecedented increase in crime, suicide, and theft, as well as crimes against the moral code. Therefore, "the solidarity of the quarter became important in defending the interests of its inhabitants, both morally and materially."[87] As for official reactions to the rise of crime, particularly in cases of prostitution, Rafeq writes that some governors often tried to appease the population who engaged in these acts. A motivation may have been placating the Ottoman local and irregular troops (as will be illustrated in chapter 5), who were patrons of prostitutes. Prostitutes were a crucial link between the ruling elite and the rebellious soldiery who made up their clientele. These examples depict a very different picture of Ottoman administration, an administration dealing with social and economic pressures, one that turned a blind eye to some crimes in order to placate an unruly soldiery. In this case, the phenomenon of group solidarity represents an attempt for the community to police itself in place of a weak administration— an argument that stands in stark contrast to those scholars who argue that coercion was the root cause of neighborhood policing.

Rafeq's assessment of Ottoman Damascus holds striking similarities to the function of neighborhood policing in Aleppo. Neighborhoods acted as groups of witnesses in several types of court cases, including business transactions, releasing debtors from prison, criminal cases, and cases involving breaches of public morality. Furthermore, each quarter had elected representatives who were responsible for the quarter's well-being. The representatives were to protect the residents, their property, and the moral order of their quarters. This tradition was one that existed prior to the Ottoman conquest of Syria, in the organization of youth, or *futuwwa*, bands of men organized within communities who ensured peaceful quarters. This tradition can also be seen in the local tradition of neighborhood strongmen, *qabaday*, who continue to arbitrate disputes and ensure neighborhood safety in Syria today.[88]

Although several authors have argued that coercion was the impetus for policing, the records surveyed for this study fail to provide adequate evidence of its importance as the major motivating factor in these cases. Travel narratives, such as the writings of Alexander Russell, describe this type of neighborhood surveillance as common in the eighteenth century. He argues that entire neighborhoods could be held liable for immoral acts, like *zina,* should the Ottoman authorities discover the crime.[89] However, the Aleppo courts never referenced the Ottoman criminal codes that contained this order. Therefore, it remains unclear whether Ottoman coercion was truly the motivation for community policing or quarter residents. Scholars have deduced that the Ottoman criminal code was systematically applied in the provinces based on the codes addressed above; however, the lack of reference to those codes in the *sijill* documents still leaves room for some doubt that fear of fines motivated communities to monitor immoral conduct in their quarters. The records make occasional references to fines, but a clear majority of cases fail to reference them at all.[90] This failure hints at a possible application of the *kanunname,* but is it the only reason the cases were brought to court? Neighborhoods appear to have had an established legal culture and used the court to authorize their actions. Community surveillance and policing have been documented in earlier studies of the Mamluk period.[91] The court served as notary, documenting the will of the neighborhood, and almost always agreed with the group judgment made prior to the appearance in court. This is not to say that the Ottomans did not use this system in order to find effective ways of policing the community, but this folk tradition of law seems to have been more diffuse than motivated simply by sheer imperial edict and fear alone. Moreover, the fact that communities were policing themselves may have been a cost-effective way for the Ottomans to manage the empire, and the Ottomans may have chosen to keep it intact rather than interfere with it. Its long-standing tradition as a practice that dated back to the Mamluk period may explain the Ottomans' lack of interference with grassroots policing and appropriation of the practice in its criminal codes.

Communal policing efforts also served an important legal strategy at court. Boğaç Ergene's study of Ottoman Çankırı and Kastamonu has highlighted what he calls "communal domination" in the court, citing mostly cases of immoral conduct in the court records. He calls this phenomenon "one of the most convincing indicators of the collective competency of the community in the use of the judicial process to advance its own interests." He posits that this type of witnessing en masse was the only way to ensure conviction, especially when the defendant was a titled, elite member of society. He argues that when community members appeared en masse, they always won their cases.[92] In Aleppo, as in the above Anatolian cases, it was common for only one or two members of the community to submit testimony before the court. The rest had their names recorded and provided the strength in numbers necessary for conviction while witnessing at court.

An important aspect of Ergene's argument is the way in which strict evidentiary requirements for most court cases were bypassed in what he calls a "strategy of substitution," especially when the usual evidence was not available. This tactic ensured the community's ability to punish undesirables with weak evidence. Conversely, the good reputation of the plaintiff could also used to ensure conviction over the defendant.[93] In many ways, the system was able to serve the rich and powerful, as they could use their reputations, if they were good, and their social titles to sway the judge. This point is not to be understood as falling into the *qadi* justice paradigm that has been pervasive in the field of Islamic law. Nor is it to be understood as Ottoman corruption. What is apparent is that the way the population was able to use the court reflected power struggles between social classes at the local level in Aleppo. Residents learned how to turn a case in their favor by using en masse testimony, and judges sometimes took sides in a given case.[94] Instead of looking at this system as an indication of corruption, or "*qadi* justice," Ergene calls the way the court conformed to multiple interests of the state and the community "operational flexibility."

Ergene's analysis does not include a theory of coercion, as have other Ottoman studies mentioned earlier; instead, he suggests that the court may have altered its procedure in order to accommodate the interests of the community. It did so by first ensuring that a powerful member of society could be challenged through group action. This strategy also had the potential reverse effect of allowing for the persecution of an individual by his or her neighbors through such witnessing. The second accommodation of the court was lowering the standards of evidence in some cases that threatened to harm the public good *(maslaha),* a concept founded in classical *fiqh* writings. The Ottoman term *fomenter of corruption (sa'i bi'l fasad)* indicated that a person was a threat to public order, and the *qadi* could punish the offender with a severe corporal punishment, employing the Ottoman laws, which demanded considerably less evidence, to preserve public order.[95] All things said and done, the public interest of the community was to be upheld first and foremost. Corruption was the opposite effect desired by jurists in the classical age, who were willing to bypass strict criteria of the law in order to preserve the best interests of the community. They had several means at their disposal, including concepts such as *maslaha/istislah* that focused on the public welfare, concepts discussed at more length in chapter 4. The Ottoman judges of Aleppo were certainly affected by this basic principle found in all four Islamic schools of thought, and it may have factored into the way the desires of the community were catered to by judges.

THE GUILDS AND PUBLIC MORALITY

Community surveillance was only one form of policing found in the shari'a courts. The guilds that formed the backbone of Aleppo's economy also played an important role in policing public morality. In Ottoman Aleppo, the guild system controlled the economy of the city, making it mandatory that skilled tradesmen work within their respective guilds. Guilds also controlled the price of goods in the market and made it easier for state authorities to locate taxable income. One would not think that guilds would have much to do with the criminal world or criminal cases in the shari'a courts, yet many of the cases that appeared in Aleppo's courts were cases dealing with guild members and their immoral behavior, which presents a system of policing parallel to the method of the city quarters.[96] This presence was in part owing to the way in which the *kefalet* system worked among the guilds, as it did in the neighborhoods.[97]

The Arabic term for guild, *ta'ifa,* is a term that can be used in many contexts, including descriptions of groups of non-Muslims, as in *ta'ifat al-yahud* (Jews). In other instances, it can be used to denote social groups, such as *ta'ifat al-nisa'* (women) and even *ta'ifat al-sarraqin* (thieves).[98] In the Ottoman context, the guild was "an autonomous group of craftsmen engaged in the production, servicing, and marketing of commodities."[99] The Ottoman government had a dual purpose in regulating the guilds: to manage the market affairs of the empire and to effectively levy taxes.

Approximately 157 guild organizations existed in Aleppo during the eighteenth century. They consisted of professions such as silk spinners, rope makers, bakers, butchers, and porters. According to Marcus, there were no guilds for many of the professions dominated by women, such as entertainers, prostitutes, dancers, wet nurses, and midwives.[100] However, during the course of this research, a document was found that references a guild of midwives in Aleppo. In the document registered in July 1642, four midwives appeared in court as expert witnesses in a case of virginity testing. The group of women midwives was led by *shaykha* Fatima bint shaykh Mustafa. *Shaykha* (or *shaykh* in its masculine form) was a title indicating the head of a guild, in this case a guild of midwives.[101] The women examined a girl named Karima bint Hajj Yusuf al-Mu'asirani and affirmed that she was indeed a virgin. Interestingly, Karima lived in the predominately Jewish quarter of Bahsita, which draws attention to the fact that Muslims and non-Muslims were living in the same quarters and not completely segregated from one another. Nonetheless, the case of the midwives' guild demonstrates that the influence of the organizations was far-reaching, expanding to include marginal members of society such as women, non-Muslim minorities, and the lower class *'amma*.

There is no evidence of a guild of prostitutes in Aleppo.[102] Some sources have recognized that guilds of prostitutes may have existed in Cairo, where the Ottoman traveler Evliya Çelebi observed guilds of prostitutes organized into two social classes.[103] Gabriel Baer's reconstruction of Cairo's guilds using a number of manuscripts depicts a hierarchy based on skill and moral aptitude of the work being performed. Guilds that performed work deemed immoral were on the lowest level of this hierarchy. Prostitutes ranked with the lowly professions "involved in entertainment such as snake charmers, jugglers, and hashish sellers."[104] Organizing even these lowly professions into guilds allowed the authorities to control these social groups. Cairo seems to be exceptionally well documented, as Khaled Fahmy has noted the names of prostitutes were kept along with the names of thieves and beggars by the governor in the eighteenth century.[105]

The guild hierarchy placed lower levels of the *'amma* (the masses) above guilds that were seen as immoral. Other higher-ranking *'amma* guilds included cooks, tobacconists, butchers, bakers, and entertainers, to name but a few. Among the higher classes of guilds were barbers, druggists, spice sellers, physicians, furriers, booksellers, and rice merchants.[106] Class differences among guild members also resulted from the slow infiltration of Janissaries into the guilds. In later years of the Ottoman Empire, Janissaries began to join the ranks of the guilds in order to profit from the tax exemptions they enjoyed through their imperial connections.[107] A similar phenomenon took place in Egypt when Janissaries and their sons began to dominate guilds at the turn of the eighteenth century.[108] As the Janissaries began to penetrate the guild system, they were eligible to become *shaykhs* and extort money from their fellow members.

A major function of the guilds was to serve their members by minimizing the amount of competition in the marketplace, creating a stable source of income for their members. Although the guilds were autonomous and monopolized on their respective trades, they were restricted only by interference from state economic policies, especially in cases of famine and price-gouging. "The guilds system operated outside government, but not independent of it." According to the normative histories of the Ottoman Empire that outline the way in which the guilds were supervised, the *muhtasib,* or inspector of markets and public morals, monitored guild activity. The *muhtasib* was in charge of both regulating the selling price of goods in the marketplace and regulating public morality in the public interest. He could punish those individuals who transgressed norms by drinking, fornicating, and general evildoing. Examples of wrongdoing punishable by the *muhtasib* included selling goods at high prices, not delivering goods promised to customers, and "public bath attendants who do not use separate razors, towels, etc. for Muslims and infidels." The *mustasib* was not bound by the shari'a but instead was connected to the secular authority. In such cases, he could bypass the criteria for punishment established in the shari'a. He was not allowed, for instance, to hear evidence or "even authorized to give judicial decisions *(hukm).*" The shari'a court does not reference the office of the *muhtasib* in guild cases. Abraham Marcus suspects that the office fell into disuse prior to the eighteenth century, as the duties of the *muhtasib* were increasingly fulfilled by the guilds.[109]

The importance of the guilds is reflected in the election of their own leader *(bash)* responsible for collection of taxes owed the state by members. These supervisors appear often in the court records, as they were registered in the courts upon assuming the responsibility. When registered, the guild supervisors were often praised for their high moral character, a prerequisite for the position.[110] In a case from February 1662, a guild of rope makers *(ta'ifat al-habbalin)* testified on behalf of their new spokesman, Hajj 'Aqil ibn Mahmud. They described Hajj 'Aqil as being "a pious *(dayyin)* and morally upright *(mustaqim)* man." Some guilds had stronger moral and religious guidelines than other lower-ranking guilds, such as the guilds for immoral occupations. Guild supervisors had indefinite terms, and in order to remove one from office, according to Amnon Cohen, issues such as old age, illness, improper behavior, or complaints had to be used as a cause for removal.[111]

Generally speaking, cases like the one above reflect that most guilds had a strong work ethic to uphold that was visible in certain cases brought to court in order to remove unethical members. Marcus argues that the guilds used the courts because they lacked a "police apparatus" that could serve to enforce the rules of the guild. He writes, "Disciplinary action against members also rested with the authorities. Members of a trade occasionally took troublesome colleagues to the judge, who imposed a punishment or fine. No member could be expelled from his guild without the court's approval. Such extreme measures against colleagues did occur, but quite infrequently." Marcus continues, noting that between the years 1746 and 1770, forty-eight cases of expulsion from guilds appeared in court. The cases ranged from "violation of guild rules and abuse of public trust to professional incompetence and cursing of the *shaykh*." Several examples of cases of expulsion are documented in the court registers. In June 1776, Hajj ʿAbd al-Qadir ibn Hajj Hussein was brought to court by the guild of rope makers because "he always strives to breach matters of our profession violating our laws." In yet another case of expulsion from June 1786, the guild of printers *(ta'ifat al-basmajiah)* brought a member of its guild to court, Sayyid ʿAbd al-Razzaq ibn Muhammad. Guild members complained that "he works in our profession and he always brings about our harm in his unfounded complaints to the judges."[112] The guild revoked his membership because of his mischievous behavior.

Although the guild rules are difficult to discern, they did have a strict guideline of moral conduct for their members. Many cases brought to court were not so much criminal violations as they were moral breaches among the members and violations of guild laws. This strictness implies that guilds had a moralistic or, arguably, even a religious heritage. Scholars have pointed out two possible origins for the guild system. The first was the *futuwwa* associations that existed in the early modern period. The *futuwwa* were not organized according to profession but were bands of organized youth. The second possible origin of guilds is that they descended from Sufi orders, which would help explain why monitoring the moral standards of its members was important. Rafeq has argued for the possible connection between Islamic mysticism and the guilds, which may explain its strong moral character. The earliest accounts of Sufi orders found in Ibn Battuta's writings from the fourteenth century mention brotherhoods *(akhiyya)* of craftsmen who held meetings in Sufi lodges *(zawiya)*.[113] Although little information exists about the history and inner workings of the guilds with respect to religion, this fourteenth-century reference draws a strong connection between the guilds and Sufi orders. The guilds would gather and perform ceremonies *(shadd)* in their lodges. They would also begin their meetings reciting the *fatiha,* the opening prayer from the Qur'an, a practice that further affirms the religious foundation of the guild system. These brotherhoods valued piety, chivalry, and craftsmanship in their brand of Sufism. It is possible that the ideals of discipline and perfection in work were seen as attributes guild members could strive for, but in harmony with Sufi aesthetics.

Therefore, it is not surprising that the guild members who failed to perform their work adequately were reprimanded in court. In April 1679, four men bearing the title hajji and one member of the *ashraf,* along with several other guards from the guild of Moroccan guards *(ta'ifat al-mugharba al-haras)* appeared in court in order to expel Hajj 'Ali ibn Mubarak (described in the document as *asmar,* or dark-skinned) from their guild. They complained that Hajj 'Ali and his friend Hajj Mabruk, who was not present in court, were lazy in guarding the market. Their fellow guards argued that their laziness harmed the well-being of the marketplace.[114]

Although the guilds were organized around religious principles within the heterodox Sufi tradition, they were tolerant toward Christians and Jews. In turn, guilds valued their members' abilities and moral integrity regardless of religious denomination.[115] Some guilds were mixed with both Muslim and non-Muslim members, whereas others remained religiously, ethnically, and sometimes regionally segregated. André Raymond cites the example of guilds specific for the Christians of Damascus that he located in Ottoman Cairo. Even segregated guilds tended to use the powers of the courts to record their actions. In a case from March 1755, a group of thirteen witnesses from the guild of Sasun bakers *(ta'ifat al-susani al-khabbazin)* appeared in court to remove Markar walad Arakil as the guild representative, claiming he was a liar, harmful to others, an evildoer, and "vicious tongued." These early migrant *ta'ifas* were from the region of Sasun located in Anatolia near Lake Van and most likely Armenian, as the name Markar walad Arakil indicates.[116] The guild, one of Sasun bakers, reflects the subdivisions of guilds by both religion and region in this case.

It is difficult to say why these cases were brought to court, but it is evident from the court registers that the guilds brought cases to court either for reprimand or to obtain a notarized document from the court signifying a change in leadership. Guilds often appeared in court to notarize officer changes when a new person was appointed as the supervisor of a guild. Usually, these records described the moral uprightness of the new guild representative. A record from April 1736 reports that *Shaykh* Nasr ibn Hajj Muhammad, the former spokesman for the guild of carpenters *(ta'ifat al-najjarin)*, was "just" *('adl)* in his dealing with their matters. Hajj Salah ibn Hajj Muhammad was selected as his replacement by the guild and is noted as being "religious" and "morally upright." In yet another case, this one from August 1662, the guild of grocers *(ta'ifat al-sammanin)* appeared in court to appoint the current guild head, Ahmad 'Iz al-Din, as the new *bazar bashi*.[117] The guild testified that Ahmad was morally upright *(mustaqim)*. All of these cases constitute examples of the relationship between the guild and public morality as it was monitored in the city of Aleppo. The guild served a police function among its membership, bringing cases to court and providing testimony en masse, as in other breaches of morality. The courts upheld the values dictated by guilds when they expelled members and replaced undesirable leaders.

Through the examples of quarter solidarity and guilds, the informal grassroots mechanisms for policing moral breaches become clearer. People used the court to exercise the will of their communities, whether local neighborhoods or professional craftsmen. The court, so long as proper witnesses were available, endorsed the will of those communities. Sometimes legal procedure conformed to those local interests, allowing communities to expel undesirables based on circumstantial evidence and loosely defined moral breaches. Ottoman law, in many instances, placed the onus on the community in these matters, a continuation of a practice held by earlier empires. The *kefalet* system was effective for the empire, and little energy was expended, as neighbors and guilds apprehended mischievous members of the community and brought them to court. The court, in this sense, served to document the will of the community in these cases. These trends apparent in the archival record are a common feature of the crimes of public and sexual morality that are investigated in the next chapters.

4

Prostitutes, Soldiers, and the People

Monitoring Morality Through Customary Law

Private dwellings sometimes functioned as sites of sexual and moral vice. Residents accused of facilitating prostitution were brought to court by their indignant neighbors, who petitioned the court to remove corrupt individuals from their neighborhoods. Despite the moral outrage of such neighbors, justice was often noncorporal. The shari'a court records show that Aleppo's prostitutes, as well as other violators of societal norms concerning sexuality, did not receive the draconian punishments mandated in Islamic juridical writings. Instead, their punishment was to be banned from living in the neighborhood where the crime took place, although they were free to live in any other of the eighty neighborhoods within the city. These court orders for removal could not be reversed later without the consent of the neighbors.[1]

How was it possible for the courts to impose a punishment so different from the doctrinal prescriptions found in the shari'a? This question is best answered by an examination of some of the principles found in the shari'a, especially the concepts of *istihsan* and *istislah,* which allowed jurists to circumvent doctrinal law and opt for customary law in these cases. These legal procedures offered the courts flexibility in their application of the shari'a, allowing them to take into account the standards and norms of specific communities. The court records document the application of a more local interpretation of the law in the courts; however, it was also Islamic legal theory that made that variation possible.

THE EUPHEMISM

Although Islamic juridical writings define the categories and boundaries of the law in great detail, Aleppo's court records are incredibly vague on the matter.

94

The court records are reluctant to use explicit or even standard juridical language found in the shari'a to describe the crime of *zina*. Instead, euphemisms are used to describe a number of crimes, particularly moral violations. Court records often use a number of formulaic expressions that exalt the judge or certain members of society that appear in court. This feature is common in court records throughout the empire, reflecting the fact that the court was managed by an Ottoman official, namely, the judge *(qadi)*, and the record was written by an official Ottoman scribe.[2] On the other hand, such euphemistic formulas are also used to describe other types of criminal conduct.

It is not clear who created these euphemisms, the people who brought the cases to court or the court itself. As stated earlier, Michel Foucault pointed to the origins of defining the normal from the abnormal, or the moral from the immoral, in "social practices of control and supervision [surveillance]." Certainly, Aleppo's neighborhoods had a popular conception of what was acceptable from what was unacceptable behavior. It is unclear, though, owing to the official nature of the court records that often use formulaic expressions to convey the context of the case, where the language representing the crimes originated. If we were to use a Foucaultian approach, we should lend some agency in the framing of the cases to the neighborhoods, as such definitions of deviancy originate in the power dynamics within communities. A good example of the way power is deployed at a local level can be found in Kathleen M. Brown's study of power, race, and gender in colonial Virginia wherein she examines some of the labels affixed to women, such as "good wife," "nasty wench," or "witch." These various labels indicated the status of women at the local level; thus, a "good wife" garnered great respect, as marriage had the ability to elevate the status of women. However, if neighbors referred to a woman as a "nasty wench" or a "witch," it had serious ramifications in terms of a woman's reputation, especially at her witchcraft trial.[3] In either case, these examples indicate that neighbors wielded a great deal of power in terms of defining deviancy in their own language. That possibility is certainly true for residents of Aleppo's neighborhoods whose ability to exercise their collective will is evident in the court records.

In the cases located in Aleppo, neighbors often filed complaints that they were being harmed by residents. In many cases, the records used the euphemistic expression *li-yandafi' dararuhum*, which describes the community as "warding off their evil or harm."[4] Plenty of examples of euphemisms are found in the courts' vague terminology describing women and men as "harmful to neighbors" *(yu'thi al-jiran)* and committing "acts of indecency" *(af'al shani'a)* or "morally repugnant deeds" *(af'al qabiha).* Cases involving breaches of public morality not necessarily sexual in nature resulted in expulsion just the same. These euphemisms give the reader very little information about the actual acts that took place to warrant such accusations. Occasionally, supplemental phrases can provide enough information to the reader so as to understand that the accused had cursed, harassed, or threatened residents or tried to pick up women in the streets. Through my selection process, I chose to exclude all cases that were too vague to discern the type of crime that had been committed. Therefore, hundreds of cases were examined in which euphemisms like "harmful" were used, including assault, cursing, as well as the revoking of guild membership. Yet, on other occasions, these euphemisms peppered court cases that were clearly describing sexual violations. I chose to include in my database court cases that provided details indicating more clearly that the charge was sexual transgression. Often, euphemisms describing the man or woman as an "evildoer" *(ashrar),* mischievous *(ashqiya'),* or "off the straight path" *('ala ghayr al-tariq al-mustaqim)* were used; all are vague and sometimes used interchangeably with non-*zina* cases.[5] These euphemisms, at first glance, may seem as though they should be dismissed because the legal category of crime has been blurred with euphemism. Instead, upon closer reading, it becomes clear, through context and comparative readings with other court cases, that the crime committed was indeed *zina* according to the shari'a.

Euphemisms are found in numerous cases of sexual indiscretion; for example, the procurement of prostitution is couched in language describing the crime as "gathering" *(yujama'u)* men and women together in inappropriate ways. This language is often coupled with more explicit language detailing the sexual nature of the assembly, namely, that it was for the purpose of evildoing and fornication *(fisq/fujur).*[6] Abdul Karim Rafeq explains that the Damascus records also used euphemisms to describe similar sexual offenses: "The court records in cases of prostitution deal with them rather kindly by first repeating the general cliché about evil doings and bad character, and then they elaborate that the accused are facilitating the association of strangers, both men and women, who are unrelated." All the cases in which brothels were discovered and the procurers apprehended were framed with the same euphemism—the offenders were described as "gathering *strange* men and women in their home." In the context of the court record, describing people as *ajanab* means that they were "strangers."[7] Although the Arabic term today is often used to connote "foreigners," in this instance the term described that the men and women in question were unmarried or unrelated within acceptable degrees of association. In this situation, a cousin would be considered a "stranger" because it is acceptable for marriage to take place between a woman and her first cousin—a practice found among both Muslims and Christians throughout the Middle East. On the other hand, a woman's brother and uncle would not be considered "strangers" since they are forbidden to marry under the law. These same degrees of relationship hold true for veiling; it is acceptable for a woman to walk unveiled in front of immediate family members, which includes a brother or an uncle but excludes a marriageable cousin.

Why did the court use euphemisms? Why not make direct accusations of *zina* using the language of the shari'a? There are several possibilities as to why euphemisms were used in Aleppo and Damascus. The first theory has been proposed by Rafeq, who suggests that in Damascus, family and quarter privacy was of so much concern that a euphemism might have been used to conceal the horrible details of a crime from the public. In this case, the euphemisms emanate from the neighborhoods rather than from the official court apparatus. This theory certainly holds true, as society has some hand in defining categories of deviancy and as neighbors were a large part of the court cases. In terms of the law, though, I would like to suggest another possibility as to why the court used euphemisms. From the perspective of law, using a nonlegal term greatly changes the possible outcome of a case. Scholar of Islamic law Rudolph Peters has argued that "testimony to unlawful sexual intercourse *(zina)* must use this technical term and not just any word meaning sexual intercourse." Testimony must explicitly describe, in the language of the law, the unlawfulness of the act committed, and exculpatory circumstantial evidence is not admissible where retaliatory punishment is requested (although the Maliki school accepts it). This strict evidentiary requirement is owing to the category of the crime *(hadd)* as the most severe and sometimes warranting the death penalty. On the other hand, Hanafi jurisprudence does allow circumstantial evidence to be admitted when determining the reputation of the individual in question.[8] In the long run, that person will not be subjected to *hadd* punishment based on such evidence, yet he or she could be punished at the judge's discretion *(ta'zir)*. Such legal rulings aid our understanding of the Aleppo court cases. The creation of a criminal category of "evildoer" allows the legal authorities to deviate from standard prescriptions of punishment advocated in the juridical writings. Therefore, a crime such as *zina*, warranting one of the worst punishments in Islamic law, stoning to death, can be completely avoided by not calling the crime *zina* at all.

This use of language also has the effect of loosening the criteria of evidence in cases of moral breaches, which is best demonstrated in the use of these categories in what Boğaç Ergene calls a "strategy of substitution." When the rules of evidence were not enough to result in a shari'a conviction, they could be circumvented by judges by invoking the authority of the state *(siyaset)*. This evasion is demonstrated in some breaches of public morality where the term *sa'i bi'l fasad* was used, a legal category that has a direct correlation with a category used by the Ottoman authorities to describe "fomenters of corruption in the world" but in its original usage described the *hadd* crime of highway robbery.[9] How this system translated into Ottoman justice was that such offenses, if they threatened the moral order, could be punished even by execution if needed.[10] Because such punishment was discretionary, it allowed for the rules of evidence to be circumvented, the admission of circumstantial evidence, and punishment to be administered to troublemakers, as it was in Aleppo. In most cases, as demonstrated below, defendants were charged based on circumstantial evidence, such as being alone with a woman or having a bad reputation with his neighbors, which placed his punishment squarely in the hands of the judge, who could punish him at his discretion.[11]

In fact, in the records examined in this study, the term *zina* was used in only ten cases to describe crimes, and in only three of them was there consensual sex. The term *zina* was not used in the few cases of illicit sex with men or young boys *(ghulman)* that appeared before the court. The record used no euphemism to describe the crime committed; the term *al-louti* literally described the offender as a sodomizer in the three cases, two of which resulted in punishment. The lack of court cases concerning homosexual sex acts may be attributed to two factors. The first is the lack of consensus among jurists as to whether homosexuality constituted *zina*. The second explanation could be the popularity of the practice, which, although frowned upon, was pervasive socially. Rafeq comments, "The love *(hawa* or *hama)* of boys *(ghulman)* among men was widespread and socially accepted at the time as witness several biographical notices of eminent people *(a'yan)*."[12]

Corporal punishments were rare for all cases of sexual indiscretion, as punishment often took the form of banishment from one's quarter, and to a lesser extent from the city. If physical punishment was administered in these cases, it was because more than one crime was committed; for example, when the second crime was cursing, the punishment of flogging was administered.[13] The euphemism and its function in legal practice may explain why there are no cases of stoning or even flogging for *zina* in Aleppo during the Ottoman period.

Calling these crimes by another name also served the purpose of loosening the criteria for prosecution. Accusing someone of "gathering strangers" in his or her home did not require the requisite number of witnesses discussed in the corpus of *fiqh* writings. Therefore, on several levels, euphemisms allowed for flexibility in the adjudication process. Plaintiffs did not have to be eyewitnesses to the actual act of *zina,* required by the shari'a. Instead, taking notice of the flow of undesirables to and from a neighbor's home could be sufficient grounds to initiate a court case. Judges were also afforded flexibility in that they were punishing defendants not for the actual crime of *zina* but for the new criminal categories created by the euphemism. This new categorization offered the judge flexibility in terms of his ruling, no longer bound by the shari'a, which called for flogging and stoning depending on the status of the person charged.

PROSTITUTION AND PATRONAGE

Prostitution is no stranger to Islamic history; some of the earliest references to the practice are found in the Qur'an. The Prophet Muhammad intervened in a dispute between two female slaves and a procurer named 'Abdallah ibn Ubayy. After hearing the case the Prophet received a revelation prohibiting the practice. In *Surat al-Nur* 24:33, the Qur'an states, "But force not your maids to prostitution when they desire chastity, in order that ye may make a gain in the goods of this life. But if anyone compels them, yet after such compulsion, is God Oft-Forgiving most Merciful (to them)." Prophetic traditions also describe another moment in which the Prophet was approached concerning the procuring of a female slave in order to provide funds for orphans; he once again received a revelation banning the practice.[14]

Prostitution was addressed yet again in 627 by the Prophet during the Battle of the Trench. The Prophet received complaints that while Medina was under siege, men were making sexual advances (ta'arrad) toward Muslim women, mistaking them for prostitutes. The objections prompted the verse on veiling that was meant to differentiate Muslim women from prostitutes.[15]

Distinguishing prostitutes from morally upright Muslim women appears to have persisted throughout the region. In Ottoman Aleppo, the court records describe some women as covered, and with or without a veil (hijab), indicating their morally virtuous classification.[16] Farther east, prostitutes in Safavid Iran, rather than being unveiled, identified themselves through their style of veiling, as they wore veils that were "shorter, thinner and less tight." Sometimes their clothing had seams that identified them as public women versus the more modest seamless clothing of reputable women.[17] There is some evidence that prostitution was practiced throughout Muslim empires, with various periods of tolerance and intolerance. In 934 the brothels of Baghdad were raided by Hanbali traditionalists who wanted to purge moral corruption from the city. In 1014 the Fatimid caliph al-Hakim prohibited women from walking publicly in an attempt to eliminate prostitution in Cairo.[18] Periodic backlashes against prostitutes occurred in Safavid Iran, as in the case of Shah Abbas I (r. 1588–1629), who banned prostitutes from sacred sites such as Ardabil, home of the shrine to the Safavid founder, Safi ad-Din. However, the ban proved ineffective.[19]

Some empires chose to profit from prostitution rather than ban the practice outright. For instance, in Andalusian Spain prostitutes "were called kharajiyyat, [meaning] those who pay the kharaj or property tax."[20] This moniker emphasized a prostitute's revenue potential as viewed by the Andalusian state. Under the reign of 'Adud al-Dawla (949–83), Persian prostitutes were taxed, as were Fatimid prostitutes, according to historian al-Maqrizi.[21] These taxes were collected formally by the official state tax collector (muhtassib). Safavid Iran also had its share of prostitutes, who were tolerated by the state so long as they were regulated and taxed. Two guilds of prostitutes existed in seventeenth-century Egypt indicating that, like other professions, they were likely taxed.[22]

There is, at best, scattered evidence of taxation of prostitutes in the Ottoman Empire. Existing evidence suggests that local governors had the discretion to either tax or prohibit the practice of prostitution within their cities at various times. For instance, there is evidence that one governor of Damascus, As'ad Pasha al-'Azm, collected taxes from eighteenth-century Damascene prostitutes, yet no taxes were levied in Ottoman Istanbul.[23] Prostitutes in Egypt were steadily taxed until Muhammad 'Ali outlawed the profession in 1834.[24] How-ever, the Aleppo court records did not record taxation on prostitution. The court records refer to guilds *(ta'ifas)* and guild members in the text systematically, yet do not reference an existing guild when prostitutes appear in court. It could be argued that prostitution was one of the few areas of work in Aleppo that did not demand guild membership. This factor may have been one of the attrac-tions of entering the vice trade, since it allowed one to avoid regulation through the guilds and subsequent taxation by Ottoman officials. Guilds were divided according to profession and then sometimes subdivided once again. Jewish and Christian bakers had their own guilds separate from the Muslim bakers' guild. With the details available concerning the guilds, it would be difficult for a guild of prostitutes to exist without it being referenced like other guilds in the documents. In that every legal profession was part of the guild structure, it fol-lows that residents may have policed their neighborhoods against prostitution because, among other reasons, it was a form of tax evasion that may have caused resentment among taxpaying guildsmen.[25]

An important distinction between premodern and modern prostitution is regulation. During the Ottoman period, there was no government regulation of prostitution in Aleppo as in other cities. The records indicate that prostitutes were not banished to certain quarters, and were not registered or subjected to government scrutiny. In other parts of the empire, prostitution was regulated through guilds and taxation; however, such regulation cannot be compared to modern European methods such as the British model adopted by the Egyptians in the 1860s, inspired by the Contagious Diseases Acts.[26] The French also imple-mented a similar model in Morocco, Algeria, and Tunisia whereby they encour-aged military brothels organized in specific quarters under medical supervision.[27] Prostitutes in later years were then relegated to certain quarters, inspected peri-odically for venereal diseases, and quarantined if they failed inspections. Regula-tion on this scale did not occur in Ottoman Aleppo but may have been eventually brought to Syria during the period of the French mandate (1920–46), which is currently an unexplored area for future research.

One of the few sources for understanding everyday life of the socially marginal in Ottoman Syria is the chronicle of al-Budayri, a Damascene barber who docu-mented the daily events of Damascus in his chronicle called *Hawadith Dimashq al-Yawmiyya.* As a literate member of his class, he offers a unique popular account of Damascene life in the eighteenth century—there is no equivalent chronicle for Aleppo.[28] His profession enabled him to meet a wide cross-section of society: members of the religious establishment, guildsmen, and even the local storyteller.[29] We are able to gain some insight into the social and political issues in the Syrian provinces in the eighteenth century through al-Budayri's chronicle.

Al-Budayri describes the Damascus of his day as being characterized by disorder and high inflation, problems that resulted, in his opinion, from the governor's incompetence. Although in some places al-Budayri praises the governor's public works in the city, Dana Sajdi has illuminated the way in which As'ad Pasha al-'Azm was addressed as "Lady Sa'diyya," emasculating the ruler as a commentary on his political rule.[30] This reversal of acceptable gender roles coincides with moral transgressions and soaring prices in the city's markets. Prostitutes were described by the chronicler as having a very public presence, smoking in public, and drinking coffee.[31] "The people have despaired of the lack of means and the increase in prices. The women have become loose (bahat) and prostitutes, whom they call 'whores (shlikkat),' are roaming in the alleyways and markets day and night." The "looseness of women" in a public space is coupled with statements of emasculation of men, described as the "melting of men," which, according to Sajdi, "translates into the narrowing of the space of one of the few privileges that his social position accords him, namely his patriarchal authority." Therefore, part of the alarm for the literate barber of modest heritage is the loss of the only power he has in light of the social chaos before him. The chaotic times went unchecked by Damascene notables, whom the barber blames for ignoring the problems that plagued the city. In one instance, a man who discovered his philandering brother-in-law reported it to the notables, who disregarded the matter. According to al-Budayri, he went to the mosque and prayed. Afterward, he climbed to the top of the minaret and shouted, "Oh, Community of Islam, dying is easier than pimping with the state in this age," then jumped off the minaret, committing suicide. In this statement, Sajdi argues, al-Budayri viewed the neglect and persistence of disorder as reducing commoners to what she calls "metaphorical pimping and prostitution."[32]

The barber documents prostitutes as public personae; they "staged public celebrations and walked unveiled while chanting and dancing" in celebration of the "fulfillment of a vow made by one of them to celebrate the recovery of her boyfriend from his illness."[33] They would often gather near markets and caravansaries, where traders from all over the empire and abroad would congregate to sell their merchandise.[34] These transient caravan traders served as some of the clientele of prostitutes in places such as Syria and Safavid Iran. For example, Rudi Matthee notes that the red-light district in Isfahan was directly behind the premises of the Dutch East India Company, which had "seven caravanserais, called the caravanserais of the unveiled." These regional examples indicate that the flesh trade may have catered to the international trading community. Both Isfahan and Aleppo benefited from the influx of foreign merchants because they were situated along the silk road, and for Aleppo such communities were found throughout its approximately sixty caravansaries *(khans),* centrally located in the city.[35]

Al-Budayri's chronicle also documents the patterns of prostitute patronage. There appears to have been a hierarchy in terms of their clientele. Prostitutes, usually thought of as a marginal social group, sometimes appeared in celebrations and on special occasions with Ottoman officials. Fathi al-Daftari, the Ottoman treasurer of Damascus, invited prostitutes to attend his daughter's wedding in 1743. In an ostentatious display, which al-Budayri subsequently condemns, al-Daftari hosted different social groups from Damascus for a lengthy seven-day celebration and assigned the seventh day to the prostitutes and even provided them with gifts.[36] "On the last day of the wedding, they went too far *(badda'u).* In doing so, their intention was to promote bad behavior *(qillat al-adab),* and they publicly performed vulgar acts, and behaved with excessive corruption and morality."[37] These examples reveal the public visibility of prostitutes and their linkages with patrons in government circles.

Examples of government patronage were not the only evidence of linkage between prostitutes and powerful social classes. The bottom rung of patrons included the troops, particularly rebellious military officers, some of them called irregular troops *(levend),* and some of whom were implicated in prostitution cases.[38] Increased rebelliousness among the troops, especially local conflicts in eighteenth-century Aleppo, went hand-in-hand with the increased presence of prostitution and other sexual violation cases evidenced in the shari'a court (tables 4.1 and 4.2).[39] Therefore, it is worth pausing on the topic of Ottoman soldiers to further illuminate the connections between them and the prostitutes discussed in this chapter.

One of the main characteristics of the "classical" Ottoman Empire was its elite soldier corps, the Janissaries, who constituted the backbone of the empire's supremacy. The Ottoman military relied in its formative years, the fourteenth

TABLE 4.1

PROSTITUTION AND *ZINA*-TYPE CASES BY CENTURY[51]

Sijill number	Dates Hijra	Christian Dates	Number of cases found
1	956–972	1549–1565	3
2	956–1119	1549–1708	1
3	954–1119	1547–1708	1
4	913–1277	1507–1860	0
5	990–990	1582–1582	0
8	1002–1006	1593–1598	1
10	964–1065	1556–1655	1
11	1026–1028	1617–1618	1
14	1033–1036	1623–1626	1
18	1041–1048	1631–1638	0
22	1050–1050	1640–1641	0
27	1067–1078	1656–1668	2
28	1070–1074	1659–1664	8
34	1089–1090	1678–1679	4
36	1098–1099	1686–1688	4
43	1027–1127	1617–1715	1
45	1130–1131	1717–1719	10
50	1135–1137	1722–1725	0
55	1147–1149	1734–1737	15
64	1153–1155	1740–1742	4
85	1167–1169	1753–1756	6
94	1175–1176	1761–1763	5
113	1189–1191	1775–1777	10
130	1200–1202	1785–1788	2
143	1208–1209	1793–1795	0
149	1215–1217	1800–1803	2
153	1218–1218	1803–1804	2
154	1218–1225	1803–1810	3
208	1241–1241	1825–1826	9
232	1252–1253	1837	6
239	1257–1258	1841–1842	5
261	1267–1268	1850–1852	4
296	1282–1283	1865–1866	4

Source: Based on *Dalil sijillat al-mahakim al-shar'iyya al-'uthmaniyya,* an archive catalog compiled by Brigitte Marino and Tomoki Okawara.

TABLE 4.2

TOTAL NUMBERS OF PROSTITUTION
AND *ZINA*-TYPE CASES BY CENTURY

Century	Total number of cases
Sixteenth	3
Seventeenth	25
Eighteenth	60
Nineteenth	36

century, on an institution called *devşirme* (collection) by which young boys were abducted, converted to Islam, and adopted by the empire into military service. The boys were given the best possible training and education in the Palace School in Istanbul, intended to create utmost loyalty to the state.[40] Much has been written about the *devşirme* system. Some have argued that the origins of the institution can be found in the one-fifth tribute of prisoners of war (from *Dar al-harb*) afforded the state in Islamic law.[41] However, other scholars have questioned the legality of the practice, as Muslim rulers were obliged to protect non-Muslim subjects *(dhimmis)*, not forcibly enslave and convert them.[42] The practice of "slave soldiery" whereby a young boy was removed from his family and placed in a position of dependence on the ruler was not an Ottoman invention. It had been practiced by other empires as early as the ninth century.

An annual abduction of Christian and Muslim boys from the Balkans and Christian boys of Anatolia continued, although gradually it decreased by the late sixteenth century. By the seventeenth century the corps was so saturated with local Muslim recruits that it was no longer necessary to continue to exact children through the *devşirme*. Despite the disciplined soldiery of the empire's early years, it is apparent that there were two classes of Janissaries in Aleppo by the seventeenth century, between whom there was a sharp distinction: those soldiers who had undergone the strict traditional training and the locally recruited, free-born Muslims. The imperial troops were referred to as the *qapi-qul* and were sometimes at odd with the central Ottoman authorities, but more often at odds with the local forces stationed in the city.[43] Several court cases indicate that local irregular troops were regularly involved in crime in Aleppo, in particular soldiers among the *levend*.

Who were the *levend*? The earliest references to the *levend* are found among Venetians who called eastern Mediterranean sailors employed on their ships "Levantinos." These sailors were replaced in the late sixteenth century by the Ottoman Navy, and "many of those disbanded turned to brigandage, while others became employed as private troops." By the seventeenth and eighteenth centuries, the court records of Aleppo make frequent references to the *levend*. Often called irregular troops, the *levend* were later to become Ottoman cavalry auxiliaries. Upon their arrival in Syria, it was said that they "did fear neither death nor ruin." The *arna'ut* (Albanians) and the *levend* were both recruited from the Balkans and seemed to appear with Ahmad Pasha al-Jazzar, who ruled Haifa from 1775 to 1804. It has been suspected that since Ahmad Pasha was Bosnian, he recruited his compatriots as cavalrymen among his troops. Additionally, it has been suspected that troops like the *levend* may have been organized by clan or common place of birth. In contrast to other studies, Abdul Karim Rafeq has noted that in eighteenth-century Damascus, the *levend* were often of Kurdish origin.[44] Regardless of ethnicity, the *levend* had a reputation for unruly conduct.

Eighteenth-century French traveler Constantine François Volney described the *levend* in his account of Syria as equipped with "short sabers, pistols, muskets and lances," resembling the Mamluks, except they were not nearly as orderly and distinguished as the latter. They were an undisciplined group, according to Volney; their clothes were ragged, they rode horses of different sizes, and their armaments were rusty. They resembled bandits more than soldiers and also behaved like bandits by "exercising the trade of robbers."[45]

Needless to say, the reputation of the *levend* as criminals always held true. Volney, based on his travels through Syria, remarked that all "the villages would tremble at every *lawend* [sic] who appears." Villagers feared the *levend* because they would enter villages and seize residents' property. Volney describes a typical *levend* soldier: "He is a real robber under the name of soldier; he enters as a conqueror, and commands as a master: dogs, rabble, bread, coffee, tobacco; I must have barley, I must have meat. If he casts his eyes on any poultry, he kills them."[46] Another account, this time from Damascus, described the *levend* as terrorizing the city and countryside:

> When news of the advance of Muhammad Abu'l-Dhahab arrived in Damascus, the lawand [sic], who were defending the city, terrorized the countryside,

pretending they were protecting the villagers, and confiscated much money from them. The villagers flocked into Damascus to take refuge, not so much for fear of the troops of Abu'l-Dhahab as of their own protectors. Again, when the vanguard of the troops defending Damascus was defeated by Abu'l-Dhahab in early June 1771, the fugitive soldiers plundered and ravaged the suburban quarters of the city. The inhabitants resorted to force to restrain them.[47]

Many of these descriptions emphasize the unruliness of the *levend* and the victimization of residents. They also claim that villagers were never able to seek any retribution for the abuses heaped upon them by the *levend*. However, some of those claims are contradicted by cases where villagers brought the *levend* to court for their crimes and they were duly convicted.

One such case involved an assault charge against a *levend* found in the Aleppo court records. A soldier, Muhammad ibn al-Baktash, struck and killed a man by the name of Muhammad ibn Hajj Rajab ibn Muhammad in a village near Idlib. The soldier struck Muhammad with a metal spear on the waist so severely that he died two days later. The family of the victim appeared in September 1621 with a fatwa from Abu Sa'ud, the mufti of Aleppo, suggesting that punishment be the death penalty.[48]

There were other instances of *levend* raids resulting in violence, but villagers were quick to use the powers of the court and did not hesitate to bring criminal soldiers to justice. These cases exemplify a pattern found in several parts of the Ottoman Empire in which villagers would prosecute corrupt officials. In *Palestinian Peasants and Ottoman Officials,* Amy Singer documents several cases in which villagers successfully brought suits against Ottoman officials. She argues that the empire punished officials who mistreated peasants by overtaxing and, in some cases, physically abusing them. These cases were often successful because the court did not hesitate to punish officials who crossed the line. However, it is important to note that corruption existed even among court officials. This point has been the topic of recent scholarship that has challenged the notion that corruption was rare in the empire.[49]

Other crimes committed by *levend* soldiers included sexual attacks recorded in the court registers.[50] There is also reason to believe that the *levend* were associated with some of the lower classes of the *'amma,* including prostitutes. In a case from April 1736, a group of procurers and prostitutes, Fatma bint Hadhr, her daughter 'Abra, and Mustafa ibn 'Abdallah, an unrelated male, were brought to court for prostitution in two houses on Zuqaq al-'Atawi al-Saghir, outside of Bab al-Nasr. Their accusers claimed they receive "strange men from among the fornicators and the *levend* to their home to fornicate."[51]

Soldiers were often linked to crimes like prostitution, as in one case when two soldiers battled each other to win a prostitute's favor.[52] Soldiers on a prolonged tour of duty sought access to local women in Aleppo so much that the term *levend* became a pejorative term that described their association with women for hire, as demonstrated in the next case. Association with the *levend* could be so damaging to a woman's reputation that in February 1736 a woman named Tayiba claimed she miscarried when Myriam bint 'Abd al-Rahman defamed her, saying, "You have known *levend*."[53] This statement implied that Tayiba had intimate relations with these soldiers, noted for their "bad-boy" image and association with Aleppine prostitutes. Accusations such as this one were the same as calling a woman a prostitute. This case corroborates that the word *levend* began to take on multiple meanings in Ottoman society. In the case of Tayiba's slander, she and her husband were not able to prove that Myriam was responsible for the miscarriage, and she was found innocent.

Court cases from seventeenth-century Kayseri further suggest that there was a common association between Janissaries and immorality outside Aleppo. One such case involved two women, Mihriban and Fatma, who were apprehended after sitting and drinking with Janissaries at the house of a *dhimmi* (non-Muslim). That this immoral activity took place in the house of an a non-Muslim further adds to the impropriety. Overall, the case offers further insight into the popular perceptions of the *levend*. Ronald C. Jennings writes that they operated as "large gangs of trained professional soldiers, either demobilized or openly rebellious, who lived off the countryside as predators on the local people."[54] This reputation followed the Janissaries to the degree that al-Budayri, while describing the oppressive actions of the soldiers and failure to assist the commoners who have suffered at their hands, refers to them as *zurbawat,* a term from the Turkish word *zorba,* meaning "bullies," or possibly from the Greek, meaning "rebel."[55] Such depictions complement the Aleppo cases above, showing how these soldiers had the ability to disrupt the countryside. These descriptions of the *levend* conflict with the characterization of the elite Janissary of the early Ottoman period, known for strict discipline and obedience to the state, demonstrating both the oppressive and the morally corrupt reputations they sometimes had in the local community.

There is some evidence that the military connection with prostitution had a persuasive effect on rulers who showed some reluctance to ban it outright. Al-Budayri reports that by the mid-eighteenth century Damascene governor As'ad Pasha al-'Azm was under pressure to put an end to the bold and defiant presence of prostitutes in the streets of Damascus, yet he did nothing, for fear of angering his troops.[56] This failure to act was not an uncommon pattern in history, as Muslim rulers sometimes catered to their troops by tolerating prostitution. The tenth-century Buyid ruler 'Adud al-Dawla created a brothel for his troops in order to "protect his subjects against the passions of his unmarried soldiers." He also taxed the brothels for revenue. Furthermore, the Safavids designated prostitutes who would attend to the royal troops while they were on campaign.[57] The perceived threat to society posed by unruly soldiers is paralleled by representations of unruly prostitutes.

Al-Budayri in his entry for 1744 begins by lamenting the general decline in morality, noted in an increase in the number of suicides and prostitutes in the city of Damascus.[58] He then describes an incident with a prostitute named Salmun who attacked a local judge in the month of Muharram of that year:

> It came to pass, that a prostitute *(min banat al-khata')* named Salmun was quarrelsome in the street; she was drunk, with a visible face (unveiled) and held a knife in her hand. A group with the *qadi* shouted at her, "Turn away from the street." In front of this judge she laughed, yelled, and attacked the judge with the knife, and they separated her from him. Then the *qadi* gathered the governor *(wali)* and tax collector *(mutasallim)* and related to them his situation with this whore, and they told him that this was one of the prostitutes and her name was Salmun and most of the people were infatuated with her . . . and the mufti issued a *fatwa* calling for her death. . . . [T]hey investigated her and she was killed.[59]

Salmun was executed not for being a prostitute but for her attack on the judge, an Ottoman official. Al-Budayri provides the case of Salmun as yet another example of the chaos and disorder of the eighteenth century. The case had consequences in the lives of prostitutes living in the city when the governor decided to take action against them soon afterward.

After the incident with Salmun above, there was a government crackdown on prostitutes, and some began to leave Damascus, whereas others formed an encampment on the outskirts of the city. "Governor As'ad Pasha al-'Azm is reported to have said when approached to either banish the prostitutes, assign a fixed place for them or simply look into their affairs that he was reluctant to do anything of the sort lest they appeal to God against him." This remark, according to Rafeq, is in reference to a popular belief that "prostitutes bear the guilt of mankind [and therefore] God out of sympathy to them accepts their appeals." Following this incident, bans were issued on prostitutes but were not able to break the strong links prostitutes had with Ottoman officials and soldiers, which meant they were ineffective in the long term. Rafeq writes that "the ban on prostitutes was not maintained for long, and they were reported in three consecutive years [1747–49] as strolling the streets of Damascus and gathering in marketplaces." The attempt to suppress prostitution in Damascus after Salmun's near-knifing of a local judge seems to have been ineffectual and underscores the perseverance of prostitution despite periodic government crackdowns. Eventually, in 1749, the Damascus governor banished prostitutes from the city. Khaled Fahmy has argued that similar bans were ineffective in Egypt where, at the insistence of the 'ulama, Muhammad 'Ali declared public dancing and prostitution illegal in 1834. There were efforts at periodic bans on vices such as liquor and prostitutes, particularly in areas that housed troops, and eventually dancers and prostitutes were banished from Cairo to Upper Egypt until the 1860s.[60]

With regard to prostitution in Aleppo during the period under study, the data collected from the sixteenth to the nineteenth centuries from the shari'a court records reveal several patterns. First, the rise in crime, including prostitution, in cities such as Aleppo and Damascus in the eighteenth century correlates with a peak of economic hardship and social disorder (see table 4.1). Second, the women who appeared as prostitutes were most likely women from lower social classes. These women often lacked social titles in their names, and had only their fathers' names to indicate their lineage. That is not to say that prostitution was exclusively a lower-class phenomenon, but prostitutes unable to forge links with high-ranking patrons may have been the ones who appeared in court. In some of the nineteenth-century records the lineage of the prostitute is provided, whereby the record lists the father's name and his profession. In several cases, it is apparent that the fathers lacked social titles and worked in humble professions as butchers, saddle makers, gunsmiths, consignors of goods, and perfumers.[61] Four prostitutes in the records have the lineage "bint 'Abdallah," meaning "daughter of 'Abdallah," which indicates that they may have been of slave origin, manumitted slaves, or converts to Islam. Similarly, the data provided in appendix 1, three men prosecuted for sexual indiscretions also had the "ibn 'Abdallah," or "son of 'Abdallah," moniker. Other documents are more explicit in providing information about the actual conversion.[62] Many of the prostitutes who appeared in court were foreign, as evidenced by the court scribes' choice to include this information in the nineteenth century. Women from as far away as Hama, Damascus, Latakiya, Antakya, Marash, 'Ayntab, Birecik, Adana, and Kilis appeared in Aleppo's shari'a court and repented for their past wrongdoings.[63] Although these women noted places of residence in Damascus, their names describe them as hailing from other cities, many of them in Anatolia. We can only wonder what brought these women to the large urban metropolis, far from the small country towns from which they hailed. One must consider their vulnerability once separated from their family networks, and the potential for neighbors to use their numbers to remove them from their quarter. This notion presents an even bleaker picture of these women as vulnerable former slaves and foreigners trying to survive on their own, without family networks to support them. Yet even when family links were available, they did not always offer a life free of prostitution, a subject discussed further below.

There are also methodological issues worth discussing before analyzing the data. It is important to concede that these cases may be completely fabricated and circumstantial. In other words, neighbors could have conducted witch hunts to remove undesirable neighbors from their midst. What we are left with are formulaic statements in the court register that do not tell us the full context of the cases. It has certainly been demonstrated that with the correct lineup of witnesses and little evidence, conviction was definitely possible.

Another issue for the user is the way the records read, as they are extremely formulaic. Court documents always provide the name, title, and residential quarter of the offender. One is also able to distinguish a married woman from an unmarried one based on the use of the term *bint* (girl) for an unmarried woman and the term *mar'a* (woman) for a married woman. These terms are laden with cultural meanings. For instance, a *mar'a* has been either married or lost her hymen; therefore, all prostitutes are referred to as women in the court records.

Ethnicity and religion are usually pointed out by the court scribe, although there is usually no information about the offender's social class, educational level, and appearance. Such omissions mean that there will always be unanswered questions for historians. The reasons a woman might have turned to prostitution are not revealed in these sources. Furthermore, there are no diaries of prostitutes where one could learn more about the thoughts and ideas of these women or their economic motivations, average income, and social attitudes toward them. Until detailed sources are discovered, the information contained in the court records and some chronicles will be our only guide through these uncharted areas of social history.

Sometimes the court records describe the procurement of prostitution in public spaces. For instance, bathhouses were a site of concern for bath keepers who attempted to bar some members of their guild from procuring within them. Another instance of more public procurement of prostitution occurred in Damascus, when a cook used his restaurant as a front for a brothel. Sayyid Muhammad al-Hamawi, who happened to be of *sharif* status, was "accused of facilitating the intermingling of men and women in his restaurant, allegedly with bad intent."[64] Coffeehouses were another place of prostitution, but exclusively male prostitution, where the entertainers, dancing boys and coffee servers, would solicit patrons. Gardens were sometimes mentioned by the courts as spaces in which moral transgressions took place. Yet despite the appearance of these public spaces in the court records, the most common space for prostitution was the common household rather than a public brothel. In fact, there is no evidence of the existence of a public brothel in Aleppo in this period. This point may explain why the cases of prostitution brought throughout the court were from all over the city, as patrons often frequented the homes of prostitutes rather than public brothels (map 4.1).

The spatial representation of the court cases located in the archives suggests that cases were brought to the court from all over the city; therefore, adopting a quantitative approach does not enhance our understanding. There were no specific areas that would indicate a red-light district, for instance. This use of private homes on the part of prostitutes and procurers may be the reason the crime was dispersed throughout the city. More frequent incidents of crime occurred around the outskirts of the walled city, which correlates with cheaper real estate than in the central citadel area and to the northeast suburb of Saliba Judayda, which were more

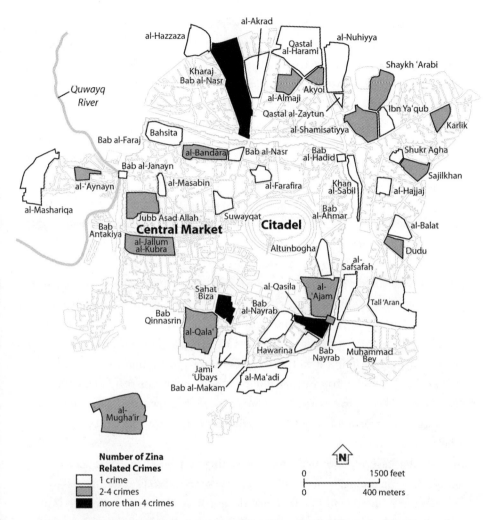

al-Akrad

al-Hazzaza

Qastal
al-Harami

al-Nuhiyya

Shaykh 'Arabi

Kharaj
Bab al-Nasr

Akyol

al-Almaji

*Quwayq
River*

Qastal al-Zaytun

Ibn Ya'qub

al-Shamisatiyya

Karlik

Bahsita

Bab al-Faraj

al-Bandara

Bab al-Nasr

Bab
al-Hadid

Shukr Agha

Bab al-Janayn

Sajilkhan

al-'Aynayn

al-Masabin

al-Farafira

Khan
al-Sabil

al-Hajjaj

al-Mashariqa

Bab
al-Ahmar

Jubb Asad Allah

Suwayqat

Central Market

Citadel

al-Balat

Bab
Antakiya

al-Jallum
al-Kubra

Altunbogha

Dudu

al-
Safsafah

Sahat
Biza

al-Qasila

al-
'Ajam

Tall 'Aran

Bab
Qinnasrin

Bab
al-Nayrab

al-Qala'

Hawarina

Bab
Nayrab

Muhammad
Bey

Jami'
'Ubays

al-Ma'adi

Bab al-Makam

al-
Mugha'ir

**Number of Zina
Related Crimes**

☐ 1 crime
▨ 2-4 crimes
■ more than 4 crimes

N

0   1500 feet

0   400 meters

Map 4.1. Spatial representation of *zina*-type crimes committed in Aleppo in the period under study. Modified by Joseph Stoll from a city plan of Aleppo in *The Middle East on the Eve of Modernity* by Abraham Marcus (New York: Columbia University Press, 1989); used by permission.

affluent.[65] Major clusters of activity can be noted in three areas: Kharij Bab al-Nasr, al-Qasila, and Sahat Biza. The southeastern gate of the city at Bab Nayrab and the Banqusa district to the northeast, as it housed the military garrisons, were zones of Janissary influence.[66] The Banqusa region also held one of the major markets of the city and was an important northeastern suburb that was mostly tribal, containing Turkoman, Kurdish, Bedouin, and peasant residents, many of whom had only recently settled in the urban environs and were connected with the caravan trade. It has been argued that the Janissaries were composed of similar ethnic groupings as the residents of the quarter, which could explain the coresidency.[67] This region was also known as a place of dissent, a place of rebelliousness, as Janissaries would organize in the *agha* coffeehouse *(qahawat al-agha)* a *"rendez-vous* of this unruly corps."[68] That these clusters appeared in areas of two major markets in the city and the housing of foreign merchants and foreign military personnel does match some of the data from scholars who have found connections between these two social groups and prostitution in other contexts.[69]

As stated in chapter 3, a quantitative analysis of the records is not always the most telling, especially as only 121 definitive *zina*-related cases were located throughout the period under study, not a great number given the fact that more than three centuries were examined. However, these court records do provide valuable information about the way prostitution was treated in the shari'a courts. Two types of prostitution cases were found in Aleppo's court records. The first type that appeared before the court was in the case of reformed prostitutes. In these "testimonials," prostitutes confessed that they had once strayed but were now returning to moral life. The second type of prostitution case was documented in criminal court cases and reflected the phenomenon of quarter policing discussed earlier. In these cases, neighbors policed their own quarters, bringing a prostitute or a procurer to court in order to remove a problem or a nuisance from their neighborhood.

In the case of reformed prostitutes, they appeared in court and confessed to wrongdoing, which conjures up Christian notions of forgiveness and redemption. Doctrines of Islamic law do not have the same notion. Islamic law, especially in cases of *zina,* viewed confession as testifying against oneself, which could eventually lead to conviction. If one were to follow Islamic legal prescriptions to the letter, the confession of prostitution should have led to an immediate conviction of *zina.* On the other hand, these women appeared in court, confessed to wrongdoing, and vowed to pursue a change of lifestyle of their own accord. This appearance could be in accordance with the Qur'an 5:33–34, which states: "The punishment of those who wage war against Allah and His Messenger, and strive with might and main for mischief through the land is: execution, or crucifixion, or the cutting off of hands and feet from opposite sides, or exile from the land: that is their disgrace in this world, and a heavy punishment is theirs in the Hereafter; Except for those who repent before they fall into your power: in that case, know that Allah is Oft-forgiving, Most Merciful."

Yet such confessions were also the basis of several hadiths in which individuals who committed *zina* were subsequently stoned to death, as in the case of Ma'iz and al-Ghamidiyya. In such tightly knit societies, a good reputation secured one's position in a guild, one's ability to provide trustworthy testimony, and one's social rank. In this context, the confessional may have been an attempt to remove the social stigma a woman might have had for her past transgressions. The confessional may have also served as a precaution against any future suits that may be brought against her for her previous lifestyle.

Cases of reformed prostitutes appeared in the Aleppo court records from the seventeenth century onward, but by the nineteenth century testimonials were the only type of prostitution cases recorded by the courts.[70] A total of forty-eight cases were found during the course of this research. The cases are usually simple, containing a formulaic statement that announces that the woman was once a prostitute but has since repented and changed her ways. Almost all the women who appeared in these cases were Muslim women: only four of the forty-eight women documented were non-Muslims, all of them Christian women. Only one testimonial was registered by a prostitute of Druze origin.

The records were almost identical in wording. A sample document from March 29, 1762, reads:

> The woman Myriam bint 'Abdallah appeared in the shari'a court, saying in her statement that she was from among the young girls who perpetrate things causing God Almighty's anger. Now she has repented [*qad tabat*] to God, expressing she has returned toward God's forgiveness in her statement. The order was given by the high judge that God forgive the woman Myriam all the known sins, and she petitioned after identifying [her witnesses] 'Abdallah bin Muhammad and 'Ali bin Hussayn, who were completely identified. This document was composed preserving her account on the third of Ramadan, 1175.[71]

What was the purpose of this record? Leslie Peirce has found similar documents of repentance (Arabic: *tawba*, Ottoman: *tövbe*) recorded in the 'Ayntab court. She argues that the records reflect the narrative strategy of the women who appeared in court. Who adopted the discourse of remorse and repentance in order to avoid punishment and, more important, reinstate their good reputations? Peirce argues that in sixteenth-century Ottoman 'Ayntab, preserving one's reputation was important, as it made one's testimony in court viable, but it also served a protective function. If one had a negative mark *(töhmet)*, one could be easily targeted for accusation of wrongdoing, even based on mere suspicion, and punished.[72]

Peirce's argument is supported by occasions in which confessionals were recorded and sealed with marriage contracts in the Aleppo court records. The fact that marriage contracts were sometimes attached to the confession emphasizes the social importance of these records and the ability of the confession to transform a former prostitute's social standing. For example, in March 1664 a woman named Khadija bint Shaykh Salah confessed that she was "from among the women who perpetrate sins," a euphemism for prostitution, and "is sincerely repentant." Interestingly, on the same record she was married to Mustafa ibn 'Ali, who offered her a typical dowry for that period, 10 *ghrush*. Another case was recorded in August 1786, when Sharaf bint Hajj Mustafa ibn 'Abdallah also repented in a similar manner and then married Hajj Isma'il ibn Qasim with 10 *ghrush* as her dowry. The most exceptional case occurred a century later, when in April 1851 one reformed prostitute, Fatima bint Ahmad al-Sarraj, appeared in court, confessing that she was no longer a prostitute. She then married Hasan ibn Muhammad al-Balubi with a 1,250 *ghrush* dowry, with 50 *ghrush* up front as the preliminary dowry.[73] Fatima left the larger part of the dowry (1,200 *ghrush*) as her final dowry *(mahr mu'akhkhar)*, which would be given to her upon the dissolution of the marriage. Larger sums were sometimes requested by wives in their marriage contracts as a shield against the husband's unilateral right to proclaim divorce. In this case, Fatima's strategy may have been to protect herself against the likelihood of a divorce by requesting such a large sum as a final dowry. Her ability to do so demonstrates not only her savvy with regard to the law but also her ability to exercise this right despite her troublesome past. Although these cases were rare—only four testimonials containing marriage certificates were found in all—they indicate that women were able to use the court to remove some of the stigma caused by their past life and begin anew.

The importance of such documents is supported by the findings of urban historian Cem Behar, who has conducted a thorough study of the Kasap İlyas quarter in Istanbul, using a number of sources that include Ottoman court registers, *waqf* documents, and personal interviews with residents of the quarter. Behar also used *mukhtar* notebooks, the documents produced by the neighborhood representative who served in an official capacity over minor legal and social matters of the community. Inside these notebooks, Behar has found "letters of introduction" used by the *mukhtar* to guarantee not only the identity of a community member but also "his very personality, his morals, respectability and character." Behar notes that sometimes such documents were produced by the shari'a courts in order to legitimate the testimony of a particular individual witnessing in court. Importantly, "every time some resident of Kasap İlyas moved to another Istanbul neighborhood he rightfully asked for a note of introduction addressed to the *mukhtar* of his new *mahalle,* and stating that in his previous *mahalle,* he had been well-behaved and 'respectable.'"[74] It is possible that the court served the same protective function through the registry of these confessionals.

The reason these testimonials are so unique is that confession to *zina* in Islamic legal doctrine does not result in redemption. As discussed in chapter 2, hadiths on the issue of *zina* are explicit about the way in which confession works toward incrimination. This point is especially true when confession is done in a sequence of four, whereby it serves as the four witnesses necessary for a *zina* conviction, as outlined in chapter 1. When confession was submitted, it was not enough to dismiss the crime, but one confession was also not enough in the Hanafi interpretation to convict someone of *zina.* Three more confessions would have been necessary, as one confession equaled only one witness, not the four required by the shari'a.

These testimonials reveal a unique pattern of behavior among former prostitutes and their use of the shari'a court, namely, they were able to use the court to confess to their wrongdoing without being punished. The two cases above have marriage contracts attached to them, which suggests that the women were able to redeem themselves through confession in court and put their past transgressions behind them. The fact that the women registered these records in the shari'a court only strengthens the notion that the court was the place that residents viewed as optimal for registering such confessions. It is possible that by registering the confession in court, a former prostitute could stave off any future lawsuits that might be raised in the future. Nonetheless, these cases reveal that the court was a place where the intimate details of the community were heard and where the news of a lifestyle change of a former prostitute would certainly travel to the surrounding community and possibly clear her reputation.[75]

In the second type of prostitution case, entire neighborhoods brought a prostitute or a procurer to court in order to remove her from the quarter. Myriam bint Yusuf and her mother, Yara, described in the record as being Christian, were brought to Aleppo's Salahiyya court by a mix of residents from their quarter, Jubb Asad Allah. The witnesses in the court record included a number of Muslim male witnesses, followed by a list of Christian couples, including the names of wives along with their husbands. The women were charged with "gathering strange men in their homes," a common euphemism used by the court to describe prostitution. The women were described as being "off the straight path." The residents petitioned for their expulsion from the neighborhood, and it was summarily granted by the court.[76]

In the formulas of the courts, procurement for prostitution was described as the "gathering" or "mixing" of strange men and women in one's home. Several of the cases that appeared before the court involved procuring by couples or family members, as in the case of a couple that was ousted in the neighborhood of al-Bandara. In December 1781, Sayyid Ahmad ibn al-Hajj Muhammad and his wife, Khadija bint Bakri, were kicked out of al-Bandara for their disgraceful (shini'a) behavior of gathering women with Muslim and Christian men in their home. The record, composed in the first-person plural from the perspective of the neighbors, states that "the two pimps procured men and women in their house of residence in our neighborhood" and "performed evil and sin, and they gather non-Muslim men in their home with strange women and harm us that way with their words and deeds. We are harmed by them and their disgraceful behavior." One of the women who worked as a prostitute in their home, a Christian named Myriam, testified against the couple in court.[77] Although Christians were subject to punishment for zina, along with other crimes, Myriam remained unpunished in this case. Instead, the two Muslim procurers were punished. In this case, the law focused on pimps, punishing them for coercing prostitutes into their line of work. Oftentimes, prostitutes walked away from these cases unpunished, and sometimes they even testified against their pimps in the court records, as in the case of Myriam.

All the criminal cases of prostitution brought to the shari'a court documented private homes as the space where the pimp or madam conducted business. Many of these procurers were couples or family members. The particulars of these cases are not documented: the court records do not tell us who performed which services that were being purchased, who served as procurer, and the circumstances that led individuals to turn to prostitution. The families who were sometimes brought to court could have been providing the space for prostitution, as on occasion prostitutes outside the family are mentioned and may have serviced the customers. There is also the possibility that female relatives were procured, a notion that challenges prevalent notions of the traditional patriarchal Arab and Muslim family structure and its emphasis on morality and family honor.

The records reveal a family dynamic in the creation of crime, be it prostitution or other violations, in Ottoman Aleppo.[78] These crimes are worth noting because in many cases they were mixed-gendered and involved several members of the same immediate family. In March 1687 a man by the name of 'Aqil ibn al-Hajj 'Uthman was brought to the shari'a court along with his sister, Hina, and his mother, Alif. The residents of the street of al-Shimali apprehended them because the family had been "gathering strange women and men in their home." The residents petitioned for the removal of the family on the basis that they were harmful to the neighborhood, and they were subsequently expelled.[79]

In January 1622 a married couple was brought to court when their neighbors in al-Ma'adi filed a complaint against them. Mustafa ibn Fathi and his wife, Fatima bint Musa, were removed from the quarter when eight hajjis from the quarter testified that they were "evildoers" and were operating a brothel, "gathering strange men and women in their home." Married couples were engaged in a number of undefined moral breaches that resulted in court cases. In December 1687 thirteen residents bearing social titles from the neighborhood of al-Jallum al-Kubra brought a married couple to court, claiming that they were "evildoers" and had "harmed the residents" of the neighborhood. 'Uthman Pasha ibn al-Hajj Mahmud appeared in court, though his wife, Amhan bint Abi Bakr, was absent. The couple was subsequently banished from the neighborhood.[80]

A September 1741 case involved two brothers, Hajj Muhammad ibn Rajab and Mustafa ibn Rajab, and an unrelated woman, Fatima bint Muhammad, who were brought to court for a brothel operation in al-Mugha'ir, outside Aleppo. The document reads that "they bring corrupt men and women prostitutes [*fawahish*] in their home." Also, the court record indicates that the witnesses came upon three men who were patrons from 'Azaz and two prostitutes from Antakiya, all of whom were apprehended in the home and brought to court. This case suggests that not only prostitutes but also patrons could be visitors from outside the city. The court ruled in this case that the residents of the house be removed. The record listed no punishment for the patrons or the prostitutes found at the residences.[81]

Prostitution cases were not the only ones to involve extended family. One case from March 1736 involved a man, Sayyid Hassan ibn Hamad, his wife, Khadija, and his mother-in-law, Ghantusa bint Hajj 'Abdallah, all of whom lived in the neighborhood of Muhammad Bey, outside of Bab al-Nayrab. Seventeen witnesses bearing various social titles from their neighborhood accused them of being "evildoers" and "vicious tongued," and for that they were removed from the neighborhood.[82]

Understanding why family members would engage in prostitution as a family unit demands an examination of several socioeconomic factors. Most of the cases found indicate that immediate family members were involved in crime together. From the fifty criminal cases of prostitution found, thirty-nine cases involved male intermediaries of some type. Astonishingly, 42 percent of the cases involved defendants who were related to each other, meaning family members were accused of conducting prostitution together. This discovery can be compared to Abdul Karim Rafeq's study of eighteenth-century Damascus, whereby he found that 67 percent of the prostitution cases that resulted in conviction involved family members. In such cases, the family relationship meant that married couples, siblings, and occasionally in-laws were implicated in the prostitution charges. Studies have shown that households in Ottoman Aleppo usually included only immediate family members. These families usually centered on one married couple and their unmarried children, and sometimes a married son. The expanded household was not a universal feature of the Ottoman Empire.[83] The fact that these immediate families, rather than extended families, were brought to court together further indicates their living arrangements.

What is the significance of family members being involved in these crimes together? Family connections in prostitution were not uncommon in Europe; for instance, in nineteenth-century France, husbands of prostitutes often ran cafés or lodging houses as fronts for prostitution. In the French case, it was an attempt to avoid the tedious bureaucracy attached to state-regulated prostitution. Furthermore, prostitutes were often connected romantically to their pimps and madams.[84] Such examples suggest that relationships among procurers and prostitutes were not unique to Aleppo and Damascus.

Another issue that could have affected the high percentage of families involved in prostitution together concerns the traditional architecture of the houses in Aleppo's quarters. André Raymond argues that there were two styles of housing in the major Arab cities, individual and collective. Both styles of houses consisted of several rooms attached to a common courtyard (ill. 4.1). This trend was common for most Mediterranean housing and not exclusive to Muslim homes. There were also houses called *hawsh,* which literally means "courtyard." In these dwellings poorer residents would erect shacks around a common courtyard where they would live in crowded conditions. The district of Qarliq, which is located in northeast Aleppo, was made up primarily of this type of collective dwelling. Some of these collective houses were caravansaries where merchants and sometimes military personnel lived.[85]

In both types of housing, very little privacy was available to the inhabitants. Surrounding family members and neighbors would certainly know what was taking place within the house or courtyard wall. Both types of housing had only one door for residents and guests to use. It is possible that since the majority of documented prostitution cases operated within private homes, the nature of this space demanded the cooperation of relatives. This factor may explain why a number of cases consisted of defendants with family ties. For example, in the decade-by-decade sample of *sijills* (court registers) from the Aleppo courts from 1549 to 1892, a total number of forty-five cases were clearly descriptions of procurement for prostitution. These cases do not include the testimonial documents registered by prostitutes, nor do they include cases of sexual immorality that do not specifically describe procuring. This sample does not include a number of cases in which family members perpetrated other crimes together, such as breaking and entering, cursing, and unspecified breaches of public morality, which were vaguely described as "evildoing" or "harmful" in the records. Some of the documents that list "evildoing" are very likely *zina*-type cases, but they have been disregarded in this sample. Instead, only cases explicitly describing the perpetrators as engaged in procurement for prostitution by inviting male and female strangers to their homes were used in this study. The data also reveal that an overwhelming number of Muslim women and men were apprehended for prostitution (table 4.3). We cannot prove that Muslims were more involved in the flesh

4.1. Typical courtyard from an elite home. Library of Congress, Prints and Photographs Division, G. Eric and Edith Matson Photograph Collection, LC-DIG-matpc-03558.

trade, but simply that they were policed and adjudicated more often (Muslims formed about 75 percent of the city's population and constituted 93 percent of the prostitution cases found in this study). Muslim women may have been targeted more generally by communities than non-Muslim women. Furthermore, the data available in table 4.4 suggest that men and mixed-gender groups were more involved in procuring than female-only operations. There may be a number of explanations for this phenomenon.

In eleven out of fifty criminal cases of prostitution, as opposed to testimonials, women engaged in prostitution without male intermediaries, as in an October 1687 case in which two women were apprehended, Farah bint al-Hajj

TABLE 4.3

BREAKDOWN OF PROSTITUTION CASES BY RELIGION

Case type	Muslim	Christian	Jewish	Druze
Court cases	43	2	0	0
Testimonials	48	3	0	1
Total	91	5	0	1

Note: Only 97 of 98 cases listed religion.

TABLE 4.4

BREAKDOWN OF ZINA-TYPE AND PROSTITUTION CASES

Case type	Total number of zina-related cases	Prostitution cases only	Male	Female	Mixed gender
Court cases	70	43	34	11	19
Testimonials	48	48	0	48	0
Total	118	98	34	59	19

Note: Data for some cases were incomplete, which explains the discrepancies in the totals in some categories, one of the many methodological problems that arise when quantifying court records.

Mustafa and Kohar bint 'Attallah. The women were removed from the neighborhood of Shukr Agha for running a brothel in Farah's home. The record added that Kohar also lived there and is "off the straight path." In another case of two sisters, Fatima and Khadija bint 'Abd al-Karim, their neighbors from al-Akrad quarters accused them of prostitution. The February 1777 case stated that Fatima and Khadija were receiving men in their "home by night and day without fear [of punishment]," and they were subsequently removed from the quarter.[86]

Were families actually involved in these crimes together? Or did the entire family's reputation suffer if one member was involved in criminal activity? Reputations were important in the small neighborhoods of Aleppo and could easily be damaged through gossip and slander. When neighbors appeared in court en masse, they almost always won their cases. There truly was power in numbers when it came to the court, the power to redeem and the power to convict. Group action on the part of neighbors was a powerful tool in obtaining an order for removal, but it left room for corruption. If neighbors had problems with residents in their quarter, producing a group of neighbors and a few witnesses could result in the desired decision. Boğaç Ergene casts doubt on similar cases he found in Ottoman Çankırı and Kastamonu, noting the lack of evidence proving moral wrongdoing in these cases.[87] Instead, weak evidence amounting largely to gossip was accepted by the court and resulted in the removal of undesirables from city quarters. One case from the Aleppo court records from December 1676 reveals the potential for corruption in the system in such cases. A man named Paolo, described as a foreigner *(afranji)*, was brought to court by his landlord, Muhammad Agha ibn Qasim Basha, and other witnesses from the neighborhood of al-Jallum al-Kubra. The dispute concerned his rent. Paolo had rented the same place for thirteen years, paying only 10 *ghrush* a year. When the landlord attempted to raise the rent in court by judicial decree, Paolo came to court, equipped with a *berat,* and was able to block it. The same day Paolo was brought to court again, but this time by ten men, one of whom was an imam of al-Jallum al-Kubra named Shaykh 'Uthman. His landlord was not one of the witnesses in this second case. They charged him with immoral conduct, accusing him of "gathering strangers" in the apartment and drinking liquor. The record also echoes concerns of the landlord from the previous court case over the defendant's tampering with the construction of the apartment and damaging it. For harming the neighborhood, Paolo was removed from the quarter.[88] This case presents the possibilities with regards to manipulation of the law. When Muhammad Agha was unable to remove his unwanted renter from the house by raising the rent, the neighbors, possibly through his urging, were able to get him removed by charging him with immoral conduct. The potential for the persecution of undesirables by their neighbors was great, as these cases appeared back-to-back and the evidence presented was weak and anecdotal.

On the other hand, it is possible that cases involving breaches of public morality were sincere rather than just neighbors using the system so as to achieve an end. Neighbors may have been showing sincere concern in these cases and trying to purge their quarters of morally corrupt residents. If we look at all these cases as witch hunts against those residents perceived as deviant, we detract from the agency of the neighborhoods revealed in the policing process itself. However, neighbors did have the potential to bully undesirables in their midst by using the court to their advantage. This point is best demonstrated in a document from May 26, 1762, that describes the plaintiffs as approaching the *hakim al-'urf,* that is, the governor of the city who had the right to rule independently of the shariʿa, for a ruling prior to their appearance in court.[89] The full text of the record reads:

Sayyid Mustafa Chalabi ibn Ibrahim Agha Nawaʾizade, Sayyid Nasri ibn Sayyid Nasri, Sayyid Mustafa ibn Sayyid Nasri, Shaykh Mustafa Efendi ibn Shaykh Hijazi, Hasan Chalabi ibn Hajj Asad, Sadiq Agha ibn Hajj Ismaʿil Agha, Hajj Muhammad ibn Hajj Ahmad and his son Sayyid Ahmad and Shaykh Salah ibn Hajj Qasam, and his son Sayyid ʿAbd al-Karim, Muhammad ʿAli Chalabi al-Harakji ibn Hajj Muhammad, Sayyid Bakri ibn Hajj Muhammad, Mustafa ibn Muhammad, ʿAbd al-Qadir ibn Hajj ʿAbd al-Aziz, Hajj Ahmad ibn Hajj Hussayn, and Sayyid Hijazi ibn Hajj Ismaʿil, a group from among the people of Altunbogha quarter in Aleppo protected by God, appeared before the shariʿa court. With them Sayyid Bakri ibn Hajj Muhammad known [by the nickname] "Abi Ras" and his mother, Khanum bint Hajj bint Hajj ʿAli ibn Hajj Muhammad, appeared; all of them are residents in the same quarter.[90] They said in their report against them that [Sayyid Bakri and Khanum] perpetrated a crime with strange men in their home of residence in the aforementioned quarter. And they perpetrated it also with strange women. They commit acts that merit Almighty God's wrath, and several times we tried to prevent them [from committing] these despicable acts. They did not stop and do not refrain from it. They do not refrain from this [activity]. Some people from the quarter complained to the governor [hakim al-ʿurf] in this town [balad], and they were fined a sum of money [durahim] because the informant complained against them. They endured their morally repugnant deeds until now, as yesterday night [laylat inbarha] we seized two male strangers in their house and unveiled women strangers were with them. They are evildoers, with loose tongues [salitat al-lisan] and harmful in their words and deeds. We do not want them to live in our quarter after today to ward off their evil [li-yandafiʿ dararuhum] and out of fear of the honorable judge's blame. We petition from the judge, with the evidence of the informant, to remove [them] from the house in question and to rid us of our opposition in this residential matter altogether. The petition was complete. The woman Khanum confirmed in front of the informants that last night in her home two men and with them strange unveiled women sat with them. The judge ordered that the investigator carry out his duty in his capacity by sealing the door of the house with clay, and he notified Sayyid Bakri and his mother, Khanum, and expelled them from the home. They are not to live among the informants in their quarter after today because of the despicable descriptions mentioned before. [The judge] ordered their punishment [*ta'zir*], decreed and recorded on the fourth of Dhu'l-Qa'da in the year 1175.

This case begins with a series of witnesses, the most important bearing social titles at the beginning. As compared to other court cases, this one contains a long list of persons bearing the social title *sayyid,* and some with the title *chalabi,* which could be owing to the fact that the defendant also bore a social title, indicating he was from the *ashraf* class. The accusations fit the previously mentioned formulas or euphemisms concerning the mixed company of strange men and women in the same residence. Important, in terms of the legal process, is the fact that the witnesses relate, in the first-person plural, that they had previously attempted to prosecute Sayyid Bakri and his mother, Khanum. The witnesses were not able to obtain the desired results with the governor; in fact, he punished the residents by fining them in accordance with the *kanunname* previously discussed that holds neighbors responsible for criminals in their midst. The residents then turned to the shari'a court to seek a different ruling. This case reflects a phenomenon found in other parts of the empire, that is, residents sometimes shopped for the legal ruling they desired by repeatedly bringing the same cases to different courts.[91] This depiction is indeed a critique of previous assumptions of Ottoman justice that were often idealistic and instead offers a realistic picture of the way in which people used the courts, and worked to sway cases in their favor. One can imagine the frustration of the community after being fined for crimes they were trying to bring to the attention of the governor; in this case, the community's sense of justice was served by removing the undesired elements from the neighborhood in the shari'a court.

The extended record above also describes punishment in much more detail than other records. It describes not only the removal from the neighborhood but also the way in which property was treated after that punishment was administered, namely, the loss of property. The vivid description of the sealing of the door of their home by the authorities offers some insight into the property losses that could be incurred by owners should they be removed. So although the relative punishment, banishment from the neighborhood versus death, is light, the financial losses could be quite devastating to those individuals convicted of *zina*-related offenses.

One way to rectify the power that resided in the hands of neighbors is by recognizing that some of the accused had recourse in the courts. In May 1718,

Shaykh Muhammad ibn Hajj Murad, from the neighborhood of al-Safsafah, was brought to court by an amazing forty-six witnesses from several of Aleppo's neighborhoods. They stated in the record that Shaykh Muhammad was a devout man "living on the straight path [*sakin al-turiq al-mustaqim*]," meaning he has no bad record. The volume of witnesses on his behalf greatly overtook the accusations of four men who had slandered the *shaykh,* as the record relates a long string of pejorative terms in the court record that the four men accused Shaykh Muhammad of: being a fornicator, a facilitator of prostitution, a sodomizer, and a pimp *(bi'inu fasiq fajir luti dayyuth).* With the powerful testimony of four witnesses, requisite in Islamic law, the four men were given discretionary punishment *(ta'zir)* for their crime of slander. Therefore, through *ta'zir,* the court applied the punishment for the *hadd* crime of *qadhf,* wrongful accusation of *zina.* In one case Darwish Ahmad ibn Ibrahim Pasha was brought to court in July 1718 along with his two sons, Hajj 'Abdul Karim and Hajj Mustafa, by their neighbors in Akyol. The weighty titles of this group, which included the father's title, *darwish,* indicating he was a member of a Sufi brotherhood, were not enough to protect them from a series of nine witnesses, all bearing titles, who testified that these men were evildoers and harmful to the residents of their neighborhood. The neighborhood petitioned that the family be removed from the quarter. In this case, the father stood up and took an oath in front of the court, stating, "After today if there is any harm from his sons to the people of the neighborhood it will be in our dreams." Through this statement, Darwish Ahmad ibn Ibrahim Pasha vowed to protect the community and control his sons, which in turn saved his family from being removed from the neighborhood. This case is unusual because the father was able to speak on behalf of the family, giving his assurance that no further violations would occur. His ability to do so based on his reputation and titles indicated his status in the community, which may have saved his sons from punishment, as the court record does not state that the neighbors' petition was accepted. However, not all cases fared so well. In July 1762 another father, Hajj 'Ali ibn Mustafa, was brought to court with his two sons, Salah and Mustafa. They were charged with disrupting the neighborhood with their "shameful deeds," "foul words," and "vicious tongues." For their breaches of public morality, the court ordered that they be removed from the neighborhood.[92]

Prostitutes were not the only targets of neighbors' fury; on some occasions, their male patrons were apprehended. Men were sometimes accused of lewd sex acts in the court records, as in the case of Taha ibn Bilal, who was brought to court by his neighbors in Sahat Biza. His neighbors complained, "He is a drinker of liquor and a corrupt fornicator in that he picks up women and young boys [ghilman] for sex and immorality." He was punished by flogging, which was most likely because of the additional crime of drinking, as flogging was not usually administered for sexual violations alone. Another man, Sayyid Ahmad ibn Hajj Muhammad al-Dawalibi from the al-Hawarina quarter, was brought to court by thirteen of his neighbors. According to their testimony, Sayyid Ahmad had a poor reputation in the neighborhood, as he went to places where entertainers and singers gathered. He owned a house in their neighborhood and established two shops that manufactured garments. Between those two shops, the record explains, men of ill-repute and other "suspicious persons" gathered and passed the time horsing around. They also "approached women who were passing by on the street while exiting the shops, saying despicable things to them, defiling their honor [ta'rruduhum li'l-nisa' al-marrat min al-zuqaq al-lathin akhrajtu ila al-dukanan bi-aqwal qabiha yilhaqhuna biha manqasat fi 'aradahum]."[93] Despite the fact that more men were involved in these acts, Sayyid Ahmad was targeted in this court case and subsequently removed from the quarter.

One case recounts charges against a man who was a patron of prostitutes. In June 1776, Taha ibn Ahmad from al-'Aynayn (outside of Bab al-Janayn) was brought to court for gathering women in his home. Four witnesses bearing titles testified against him, saying that "women whores [zawani] talk to him, and he brings them to his house and gathers them there without veils [hijab]." The residents argued that they were harmed by his actions and sought to avoid any future punishment against them because of his actions. This case suggests that the residents feared repercussions for the criminal activities in their neighborhoods, as the Ottoman authorities would make neighborhoods pay fines if they harbored criminals in their midst.[94] This record is one of the rare instances in which such punishment is invoked as a cause for removal; however, the Ottoman codes are not referenced in the court record.

What all these records indicate is that when cases of prostitution were brought to the shari'a courts, a consistent form of punishment was administered—removal from the city quarter of residence. This punishment not only was nonviolent but made it so that the convicted prostitute or pimp could relocate and set up residence in another quarter only a few feet away. In his history of Ottoman Aleppo, Abraham Marcus writes that "prostitutes and pimps, highest on the list of local offenders, provided services too much in demand to be eliminated. Pushed out of one district they reappeared in another."[95] Therefore, it is important to bear in mind that the punishments did not prevent prostitutes and pimps from continuing their work; it only removed them from one locality giving them the possibility to set up in another.

For Aleppo, banishment from one's neighborhood was the dominant form of punishment in prostitution cases. But was the same true for other parts of the Ottoman Empire? An examination of the present state of studies in the Ottoman Empire can aid our understanding of how prostitution, and the crime of *zina* more broadly, was treated in various localities.

PUNISHMENT IN PRACTICE: COMPARING LOCAL PRACTICE OF LAW IN THE OTTOMAN EMPIRE

Although no book-length studies have been dedicated to *zina* crimes exclusively, scattered cases documented by researchers in the field suggest how these crimes were treated in many of the courts in the Ottoman Empire. Of the shari'a court cases available to date, scholars have found no conclusive evidence that stoning was prescribed by the courts as a regular punishment for *zina* crimes. There is one exception, the court case cited earlier that occurred in seventeenth-century Istanbul in which a married Muslim woman was accused of *zina* with a Jewish man. This case occurred during the height of a Muslim revivalist movement called the Kadızâdeli movement that was supported by Sultan Mehmed IV (r. 1648–87) and led by his personal preacher, Vânî Mehmet Efendi. The purpose of the movement was to "strip the Islam practiced in Istanbul of innovations that they believed ran counter to the practices of the first Muslim community," including Sufi rituals.[96] It was in that context that the discovery of an illicit relationship between a Muslim woman and her *dhimmi* lover resulted in her being stoned to death, whereas the Jewish lover "converted to Islam and was executed by sword."[97]

With respect to evidence of *zina* punishment in Ottoman Anatolia, two studies have confirmed that punishment was usually a fine in conjunction with flogging, mostly in the form of bastinado. Uriel Heyd describes the administering of bastinado: "The culprit was laid on the ground and his feet were immobilised between a stout pole of board (*falaka*) and a rope passed through two holes at its ends. Two men lifted the pole so that only the offender's shoulders touched the ground. Two others then inflicted strokes on the bare soles (and other parts of the body) with long pliant sticks about one finger thick."[98] Haim Gerber corroborates Heyd's claim that the bastinado was the dominant punishment in Anatolia, mentioning in his study of Bursa that prostitution was evident from the court records, and "in all cases women were condemned to bastinado." Alexander Russell's account of eighteenth-century Aleppo comments that bastinado was a common punishment for several crimes committed in the city, but did not specify which crimes warranted the beating. He notes that a specific number of strokes were specified in the sentence, and usually the bastinado was performed either in the presence of a judge or within hearing distance. When it was performed on women, they were usually beaten on their backsides.[99]

In the imperial center of Istanbul, Yvonne Seng cites a *zina* case that occurred in the neighborhood of Üsküdar in the sixteenth century. A woman by the name of Zühal bint Hamza appeared in court for prostitution and was flogged for immoral behavior. Seng adds that male associates were sometimes punished by the courts. Similar flogging has been documented by Dror Ze'evi, including a seventeenth-century case from Jerusalem in which two men locked a married woman inside a room as she ventured out of the house in search of her husband one evening. The court, without stating it explicitly, assumed that the two men intended to commit some sort of criminal sex acts with the woman. They were punished with whipping and "forced to follow a town crier (*dallal*) who denounced their sordid, vile deeds, to deter others from following their example."[100]

These examples from Anatolia all demonstrate the implementation of forms of punishment other than the juridical mandate of punishment by stoning found in shari'a doctrine. Furthermore, Seng's findings compare to what was found in Kayseri, where adulteresses and prostitutes were not killed for their crimes but were maintained in the home because of their value to the household economic unit. Women were crucial to the family economy and worked to generate income in several capacities. Along the silk routes, many women worked in cottage industries, spinning thread and working in other areas of silk production and manufacture. Ronald C. Jennings's study supports the notion that "the homework-mother (social-economic) role of women in Kayseri society was more important than sexual virginity and chastity."[101] He suggests that this point may explain why lighter punishments were administered in order to preserve the socioeconomic balance of Anatolian society.

Although the Anatolian method of punishment appeared to be bastinado, Marcus's study of eighteenth century Aleppo found that banishment from the city quarter was the dominant punishment for prostitution, and, as has been mentioned, banishment as practiced in Aleppo took the form of expulsion from a particular neighborhood more than banishment from the city.[102] However, even as banishment was frequently practiced, some jurists, such as al-Marginani, warned against this form of punishment. The *Hedaya* states, "Banishment with respect to a loose woman in the way of punishment, is not lawful; but yet if the magistrate should find it advisable, he may banish her for the space of one year, or less, but this banishment if in the way of *ta'zir*, or discretionary correction, as banishment in some cases operates as a warning, wherefore it is committed to the Kazee or the Imam." The *Hedaya* argues that this form of punishment was used as a warning for some offenders, but it appears to have been a standard punishment in Syria, as the court records demonstrate. Russell notes that there were two different kinds of banishment practiced in Aleppo. There was expulsion of undesirables from certain quarters or expulsion from the entire city. Instances of banishment from the city included the cases of Musa ibn 'Ali al-Musari'a, expelled from the city for harassing passersby and threatening to harm them with a knife; Ahmad ibn Murad, who was described as committing "indecent acts harmful to people [*mudirr al-nas b'il-af'al*]" of his quarter; and the Christian woman Sara bint Hana from Bab al-Nasr, who was described simply as "harmful," proving that even the vaguest charge by one's neighbors could result in serious punishment.[103]

Russell commented on similar expulsions in his writings, noting they could be initiated either by local governors or by residents, which may indicate the difference in terms of severity. Russell includes a short description of the procedure used when one was banished from the city: "The person is at once torn from his family, is escorted some miles on his way by the Bashaw's officer, and then left to pursue his journey. The Island of Cyprus, and the maritime towns of Syria are the usual places of Banishment."[104] Although our state of knowledge about the practice of banishment is scant, in Aleppo it appears to have been practiced more often as removal from the quarter rather than as outright exile from the city. This notion is supported by Abdul Karim Rafeq's findings for Damascus in which removal from the quarter was the primary punishment for crimes of immorality, including the crime of *zina*, in the Ottoman period.

Leslie Peirce's study of Ottoman 'Ayntab discusses *zina* law in the Ottoman Empire. In particular, she writes that although the grand mufti Ebu's Su'ud advocated stoning for married adulterers, he also left room for negotiation on the part of judges. Judges had flexibility in these cases and could impose *'urfi* punishments, such as fining. Peirce argues, "The mufti's approval was useful, for the state's efforts to 'fiscalize' punishment by imposing fines in place of corporal punishment was critical to preserving the option of violent punishment as its own instrument. Violence was to be identified with *siyaset*, those corporal and capital punishments that the sultan retained in his personal disciplinary arsenal."[105]

Upon studying the shari'a court records, one notes that the most violent punishments in court records were reserved for crimes against the state. The 'Ayntab records demonstrate a shift from the corporal punishments advocated in the shari'a to the nonviolent punishment of fining for *zina* crimes. Peirce offers a persuasive argument as to why this shift in legal practice took place, namely, that the state preferred to reserve this severe form of punishment for special cases. Islamic legal theory provides other explanations for the commutation of the strict punishment found in shari'a evident in the local practice of law.

Istihsan and Istislah: Flexibility and Divergence in Islamic Law

How can the strict formulations of the shari'a conform to local interpretations of the law? The answer to that question can best be found in the principles of *istihsan* (preferred result) and *istislah* (public interest). When jurists made decisions about the law, they had several resources at their disposal. Haim Gerber has pointed out four resources: jurisprudence *(usul)*, doctrinal law found in legal writings *(mutun)*, the mufti and his fatwas, and the shari'a courts.[106] In the third area, the mufti, we see the process of legal debate open to the use of legal reasoning *(ijtihad)* to formulate the law. It is within this area that we find the greatest variation. However, aside from *ijtihad*, another important area of legal reasoning is *istihsan*, by which Islamic law reaches conformity with the rules of everyday life and the general interest of the community. The implementation of *istihsan* is a deviation from the strict word of the law, which is something objected to by many jurists and religious purists. Some of the controversies lie with the debates concerning the use of opinion *(ra'y)* in legal writings. According to Joseph Schacht, *istihsan* developed since the "strict application of analogy would have led to undesirable results" in some cases. All four legal schools sometimes used such controversial maneuvers in their writings. For instance, the Maliki school showed preference for *istislah* and juridical practice *('amal)*, which has a long tradition in Morocco, that sought to bring the customary practice of law in alignment with the shari'a. The Shafi'is and the Hanbali traditionalists also used *istislah* on occasion, even though Hanbalis, in theory, were reluctant to use any laws not found in doctrine.[107]

Interestingly, traditional Orientalist scholars often held positions on *istislah* and *istihsan* that were very similar to the views of the traditionalists. One major reason was the focus of both on doctrine found in the Qur'an, hadiths, and *fiqh*, rather than looking at sources that reflect the actual practice of the law, such as fatwas, which frequently emanated from the experience of the community at large and court records (which reflect the practices of law in the courts). Schacht argues with respect to *istislah* and *istihsan*:

> This principle, both in theory and in its actual application, occupies too subordinate a position for it to be able to influence positive law to any considerable degree. However much consideration of fairness and appropriateness entered the decisions of the earliest lawyers, in the fully developed system the principle of *istihsan* (and *istislah*) is confined to very narrow limits and never supersedes the recognized rules of the material sources (Koran and *sunna*), their recognized interpretations by early authorities, and the unavoidable conclusions to be drawn from them; it often amounts merely to making a choice between the several opinions held by ancient authorities, that is to say, *ikhityar* (preference).[108]

Despite this opinion, documentation provided by the voluminous fatwas issued by muftis demonstrates the continuous use of *istihsan* in legal deliberations.[109]

Current scholarship on Islamic law and society has documented customary legal practices that deviated from Islamic legal doctrine. Lawrence Rosen views it as the convergence of custom and religion: "Custom and law are not completely discrete categories—institutionalized entities that compete for identity and legitimacy—but are, in many instances, conceptually merged. The "merging" of custom and law links what Rosen calls "the formal" with "the informal" and, in turn, creates a complete body of law. "For the law on the books or in the court to fully assert that local practice not only completes Islam but covers most of its domain is too threatening to be acknowledged directly, yet to fail to contain the local is to risk undermining one of the law's own sources of legitimacy, its power of inclusion."[110] An example of merging custom and law can be found in the use of *mudaraba* (silent partnership) as a surrogate for charging interest that has been permitted through *istihsan* on the grounds of custom, despite its resemblance, perhaps even equivalence, to usury, something forbidden by the shari'a. This type of financial agreement is one in which the investor would receive two-thirds of the profit, whereas the merchant would receive only one-third; any losses in the venture were to be assumed by the investor. Through this type of economic exchange, Muslim merchants were able to circumvent the restrictions placed on interest found within Islamic law, and at the same time attract the capital needed for trading ventures. The investor was able to obtain great amounts of capital in successful ventures owing to the large rate of profit incurred through *mudaraba* transactions.[111] Here is yet another example of compromises in legal practice in which loopholes have been found that accommodate local custom.

There is another closely related legal principle found in Islamic juridical writings that can aid in our understanding of local variations in the law. *Istislah* is described by al-Ghazali (1058–1111) as "God's purpose *(maqsad,* pl. *maqasid)* in revealing the divine law, and more concretely, that this intention was to preserve for humankind the fine essential elements of their well-being, namely their religion, life intellect, offspring and property."[112] The main goal of this legal technique is to avert any harm that could be caused to the community. The use of *istislah* by the judge or jurist was part of the debate concerning "the closing of the gates of *ijtihad*." This division resulted in the appearance of two distinct schools, the Ash'ari and the Mu'tazili schools of theology. The Ash'ari's, founded by Abu al-Hasan al-Ash'ari (873–936), maintained the authority of divine law and argued that decisions made outside the revealed law using rational argumentation were not acceptable.[113] On the other hand, the eighth-century Mu'tazilis argued that humans could distinguish the good from the bad through the use of reason. This debate lasted for three centuries until it came to a halt when both schools were able to put differences aside and create a legal foundation in which reason could be used within certain limits. Thus, all four schools of Islamic legal thought accepted the Qur'an, the Sunna, consensus *(ijma'),* and legal analogy *(qiyas)* as sources of law. Yet "when revising or disregarding established and accepted rulings, jurists had to refer to subsidiary legal principles, such as juristic preference *(istihsan)* and custom *('urf)*." Still, both of these concepts were associated with one another, especially for those jurists who supported the primacy of the shari'a. Al-Ghazali deliberated on this issue, as everyday social problems sometimes existed outside the realm of divine law and still needed to be addressed by the Muslim community.[114] In such cases, he argued, *istislah* could be used to address cases that were not previously dealt with or to change law in particular situations.

Al-Ghazali was able to circumvent the controversial nature of *istislah* by placing it epistemologically under the category of analogy. In this sense, he looked for examples in which the laws of the Qur'an might be put aside for the greater interest of the community. One example includes the prohibition of killing innocent believers in the Qur'an. However, this prohibition could be overturned if killing innocents would preserve the Muslim community as a whole.[115]

Lawrence Rosen has examined the practice of *istislah* in Morocco, whereby judges ruled using either juridical writings or public utility. On the surface, it would appear to be a device wherein a judge could circumvent all but the most clear-cut of Qur'anic propositions to implement an approach he regarded as desirable.[116] However, Rosen is quick to point out that these decisions were based not on the whim of a judge but on a number of social and legal considerations. An example of *istislah* used by Rosen is a case of forcing a man to marry a woman he has "molested" rather than punishing him in a way that would subject him to the "shame of a criminal accusation."[117] This practice is also common in modern Egypt, where the state has encouraged rapists to marry the women they rape in order to resolve these legal issues without lengthy court cases.

Another more historical instance of *istislah* occurred in the lifetime of Ibn Taymiyya (1265–1328), the famous Hanbali jurist who lived in the Mamluk period (1250–1517). The case concerned the influx of Turks, many of whom converted to Islam yet continued non-Muslim practices. "Ibn al-Kayem [*sic*] related that his teacher ibn Taimiah [*sic*] passed a group of Tatars drinking wine. His disciples wanted to forbid them from doing so, but ibn Taimiah did not allow this, his reasoning being that God prohibited wine because it distracts from prayer and devotional rituals, but in the cases of the Tatars wine distracts them from murder, loot and rape." This variation on the law exemplifies the flexibility of shari'a in everyday experience. Drunken Tatars were less likely to harm the Muslim community; therefore, it served the public interest to not interfere with the practice. Rosen's work on law in modern Morocco demonstrates similar systems of flexibility, focusing on *'amal* literature, collections of actual juridical practice, "which often did not correspond with the preferred opinion of scholars." *'Amal* literature allowed the law to be mutable in specific circumstances.[118] Through such mechanisms, the law was able to adapt and conform to particular circumstances in a given community.

This explanation of the concepts of *istislah* and *istihsan* provide insight into the ability of Islamic law to accommodate the interests of a local community. In Ottoman Aleppo, judges were able to bypass the vast corpus of *fiqh* within which they were trained to treat *zina* cases by means of *istislah* and *istihsan*, and thus conform to the legal culture found in the communities in which they lived.

The differences between the theory and practice of law with respect to *zina* crime may have developed as a response to the way prostitution was linked to the wider society. First, prostitutes were often linked to Ottoman soldiers, the influx of foreigners who may have been involved in international trade, and other government officials. Furthermore, in the case of As'ad Pasha al-'Azm, there is evidence that he collected taxes from prostitutes, a phenomenon also found in earlier periods of Islamic history. Governors may have eventually given up on banning prostitution for the political benefits of appeasing troops, who were often associated with prostitutes. Second, prostitution, even as a cultural taboo, does not appear to have been considered so great a crime as to warrant such a violent punishment as stoning. Neighbors did not seek the death penalty in these cases, only the removal of these women from their quarters. Abdul Karim Rafeq argues that the residents viewed prostitutes with pity rather than as suitable objects of revenge.[119] This point may offer some explanation for the difference between the doctrine and practice of law in the courts with respect to prostitution.

Legal doctrine, when brought down to the social level, did not fit the best interests of the community. In turn, we find a level of cultural accommodation in the law. Judges disregarded the criteria for conviction found in the shari'a, which included four eyewitnesses to the actual act of fornication. Instead, judges conformed to the legal culture of their environment. Neighbors were able to testify that they witnessed unrelated men and women entering the home. In these cases, suspicion of wrongdoing was enough for conviction, so long as proper numbers of respectable and socially titled witnesses were lined up to testify. Determining what crime was committed, and what acts in particular, is difficult to discern through the legal metaphors used by the courts. Neighbors determined the acceptability of their neighbors' behavior. Having unrelated men and women in one's home on a fairly regular basis was enough to support claims of deviant behavior, creating the conditions for the persecution of undesirables in these neighborhoods. It also had the potential for the loss of property, as doors were sealed up by the court and residents forced to move.

Furthermore, when judges applied the law, they did not apply the violent corporal punishments for *zina* advocated in the juridical writings they studied as students of the law. Unmarried prostitutes were not flogged; married prostitutes were not stoned to death. Instead, a local variation of punishment, namely, banishment, in the form of removal from one's neighborhood, was the norm. There are also several other possibilities for the lack of corporal punishment in these cases. One factor could be the relationship that prostitutes had with Ottoman troops. There is also evidence found in chronicles such as al-Budayri's that some prostitutes had strong links with Ottoman officials. These powerful links of patronage could have bred a culture of acceptance of prostitution, within certain limits. Instead of advocating flogging or stoning, neighbors took the position of toleration toward prostitutes so long as they did not work or live in their neighborhoods.

Most important for our understanding of the policing of prostitution, we see the court validating the decisions being made by the community. These cases were formulated according to criteria of evidence determined by customs of the community. The communities policed their neighborhoods, bringing deviants to court and prosecuting them there. Through the court documents we can see the validation of the community's collective will. In this way, communities engaged the court in a way that challenges conventional wisdom regarding state-society relations in the Ottoman Empire. Furthermore, the judge, rather than being the arm of Oriental despotism making arbitrary decisions regarding the law, generally negotiated between the shari'a and the legal culture of the community, and more often than not the community's legal standards and interests tended to prevail at court.

5

In Harm's Way

Domestic Violence and Rape
in the Shariʿa Courts of Aleppo

Issues of gender violence, whether rape or spousal abuse, are of ongoing concern to gender historians. Rules of evidence in such cases can mount against the victims, making it difficult for them to prove their cases. Islamic law operates, like other legal systems, such that cases must be proven in court in order to ensure that the victim receives compensation or retribution. This burden of evidence has made rape particularly problematic in almost all legal traditions. Rape cases from the shariʿa court records allow for an examination of the way in which rape was treated in the practice of law as compared to the doctrinal formulations of law found in theoretical writings of Islamic jurisprudence. Through the study of gender violence in cases from Aleppo, women's access to the law can be better understood. Women sometimes appeared in court in cases of rape and domestic violence in order to seek retribution. Although several domestic violence cases were successful and women were able to obtain immediate divorces from their husbands, the same did not hold true for rape cases. Not all rape cases appeared in court; however, when they did, they were complicated by the rules of evidence, particularly the lack of witnesses and a lack of oath-taking by the victims that could have substantially strengthened testimony in court. These factors hindered the success of rape prosecutions.

The concept of spousal abuse in American and European law is a fairly new one and cannot be easily translated into legal categories in Islamic law. In many cultures, beating one's wife was deemed acceptable, culturally and sometimes legally. In Islamic law, in both Islamic juridical writings and in the shariʿa court records of Aleppo, injuring anyone, whether friend or foe, wife or stranger, was in violation of the law. Cases appeared in the court records in which wives testified to abuse and won their court cases. Importantly, the success rate of domestic violence prosecutions was significantly higher than the success rate of rape prosecutions.

DOMESTIC VIOLENCE

A common assumption is that Islamic law is a system of law that undermines women's rights, particularly the rights of wives against abusive husbands.[1] Although many studies overstate the role of Islamic law in the oppression of women, problems do exist in the contemporary practice of law. Muslim feminists have protested the inability of Islamic law today to ensure the safety of women in marriage. In fact, according to one scholar, rapists in Pakistan have claimed they were married to their victims, as marital rape, like spousal abuse, has not been clarified in the present laws of Pakistan.[2]

One possibility for this misunderstanding and the underlying problems of women's rights may lie in a controversial verse of the Qur'an that many interpret as advocating spousal abuse. The verse addresses the problem of disobedient (*nashiza*) wives. The reason for this distinction between obedience (*ta'a*) and disobedience (*nushuz*) is owing to the fact that the Muslim marriage contract is based on a mutual understanding between husbands and wives: a wife owes her husband obedience and faithfulness; in return, the husband provides maintenance.[3] It is in the context of the Muslim marriage contract that the *Surat al-Nisa'* (Verse on Women) states, "As to those women on whose part ye fear disloyalty and ill-conduct, admonish them (first), (next), refuse to share their beds, (and last) beat them (lightly); but if they return to obedience, seek not against them means (of annoyance)" (4:34). Whereas the translator of this edition of the Qur'an, 'Abd Allah Yusuf 'Ali, interprets this verse as calling men to "beat them (lightly)," the verse in fact simply states in the original Arabic *idrabuhunna*, meaning "beat them" in the imperative and conjugated in the feminine plural form of the verb, without qualification. Yusuf 'Ali's parenthetical insertion of "lightly" into his translation is owing to popular interpretation by Muslim writers of *tafsir* (Qur'anic interpretation), where the matter is settled. Ibn Kathir (1300–1371), a well-known interpreter of the Qur'an, cautions men to refrain from severely reprimanding their wives, urging them to in these cases "hit them nonviolently *(ghayr mubrah)."* Although it may appear contradictory to call for a nonviolent beating of one's wife, other jurists concur and continually describe the type of hitting that is permissible in these cases. For example, al-Tabari in his interpretation of this verse has documented a tradition of the Prophet Muhammad in which he was asked specifically about chapter 4, verse 34, and its common interpretation as a "nonviolent hitting." It is there that the Prophet reportedly said a husband was not allowed to beat his wife with anything larger than a *siwak,* a kind of toothbrush or large toothpick, or something similar to it.[4] This description is intended to convey the idea that this beating was to be nothing more than a slap on the wrist. Therefore, hitting one's wife was supposed to be symbolic of her disobedience, but in no way harmful to her physically.

The verse provides grades of punishment for unruly wives. First, she is to be rebuked, but if she persists in being disobedient, separate living or sleeping arrangements should be made. The assumption underlying the second step is that she is being denied sexual access to her husband as part of her punishment, which also indicates the importance of a woman's sexual desire in a healthy marriage. The third and final level in punishing a disobedient wife is to beat her, but not so as to cause any permanent injury. The final sentence in the verse warns men not to seek the opportunity to beat their wives simply because they have the power to do so.

With respect to jurists, they addressed the issue of domestic violence through the concept of *darar* (harm). *Darar* is broadly defined as any type of harmful behavior toward a wife that can include the failure of a husband to provide the obligatory provisions (food, clothing, and shelter) for his wife. According to Islamic law, the husband has the responsibility of providing maintenance *(nafaqa)* for his wife. This provision ensures that the wife does not have to spend her own money to maintain the home—the financial burden is exclusively on the husband. Furthermore, *darar* is expanded to include cases of a husband's absence from the home, inability to fulfill his wife's sexual needs, or mistreating a wife's family members, all of which could result in dissolution of the marriage for failure to fulfill the marriage contract. "The most important proof needed was to show that the husband had broken the marriage contract or that the marriage caused the woman harm."[5] *Darar* also includes physical abuse against one's spouse. The laws concerning *darar* state that if a husband harmed his wife, she could have the marriage annulled. So if a husband was to take a literal interpretation of the

Qur'anic verse stated above and freely beat his wife, he would still be committing *darar* and his wife would be entitled to an annulment.

The problem with *darar* is that is also falls into conflict with yet another principle, a wife's obedience *(ta'a)*, to which a man is entitled in marriage. Gender historians have shown how *ta'a* in social practice comes into conflict with the injunctions against *darar*. Judith Tucker has illustrated through fatwas from Ottoman Palestine and Syria that disobedient *(nashiza)* wives were in fact forfeiting their rights to spousal support *(nafaqa)*. However, forfeiture was the only punishment that jurists approved of in such cases. On the other hand, in some late Ottoman contexts such as Egypt and Tunisia, disobedient wives could be reprimanded physically through confinement. Amira El-Azhary Sonbol has documented the use of *bayt al-ta'a,* forced confinement, in Ottoman Egypt, which was by no means restricted to Muslim women, as Coptic women were sometimes subjected to it by their husbands. Similarly, Dalenda Largueche has examined records for a similar system in Tunisia called the *dar juwad,* used to confine disobedient wives, daughters, and even in some cases mothers-in-law. These systems of control are but examples of the kinds of effects that *ta'a* has had on the legal system.[6]

Those examples aside, much of the juridical literature was consistently on the side of the wife or victim in spousal abuse cases. A good place to find the discourse of jurists is in fatwa literature. Khayr ad-Din ibn Ahmad al-Ramli (1585–1671), a prolific mufti from the Palestinian town of Ramla, wrote extensive fatwas on marital issues during his lifetime. In his compilation *Kitab al-fatawa al-kubra li naf' al-barriya,* he addresses the issue of spousal abuse with this fatwa:

> Question: There is an evil man who harms his wife, hits her without right and
>> rebukes her without cause. He swore many times to divorce her until she
>> proved that a thrice divorce [a final and irrevocable divorce] had taken effect.
> Answer: He is forbidden to do that, and he is rebuked and enjoined from her. If
>> she has proved that a thrice divorce has taken place, it is permissible for her
>> to kill him, according to many of the *'ulama* [jurists] if he is not prevented
>> [from approaching her] except by killing.[7]

In the case of Khayr ad-Din's fatwa, a thrice, or triple, divorce occurs when a man states three times that he has divorced his wife. This type of divorce is called irrevocable because he cannot legally reunite with his wife unless certain conditions are met. Those conditions are complicated in that she must wait out her mandatory period, called 'iddah, after the divorce. In addition, she must remarry another man, in what it called a tahlil marriage, with the intent to stay married to him and consummate that marriage. If and when she divorces the second husband, she will then be eligible to remarry the first husband.[8] What Khayr ad-Din has illustrated is the way in which threats of divorce and physical abuse can result in an irrevocable triple divorce.

Importantly, in this fatwa Khayr ad-Din permits murdering the man should he try to continue sexual relations with his ex-wife. Similar to earlier Ottoman discussions documented in chapter 2, the mufti based in Ottoman Palestine also found it the wife's right to prevent her husband from committing sinful acts, which in this case would be committing zina with her. This type of extreme case scenario in a fatwa is not unusual. The sixteenth-century shaykhul-islam Ebu's Su'ud issued a similar fatwa condoning the murder of an ex-husband who attempts to resume sexual relations with his ex-wife.[9] Comparatively, the findings of these Muslim jurists were not greatly different from the rulings of jurists in other contexts. Natalie Zemon Davis has found sixteenth-century French wives who claimed spousal abuse and later killed their husbands who were left unpunished. This exoneration was in part owing to the construction of effective narrative strategies that repeatedly played up their victimization, despair, and emotional distress at the time of the murder.[10]

However, in terms of Islamic law, Khayr ad-Din's fatwa demonstrates a common pattern among jurists that condone the use of force against abusive husbands if necessary. His other writings on this matter reflect a consistent discourse among muftis, indicating that husbands did have a legal obligation to treat their wives kindly. For instance, he notes that if a husband knocked out three of his wife's teeth, he would be legally obligated at a minimum to financially compensate his wife for her injury.[11] Compensation of this sort is standard in cases of physical injury.

Ottoman fatwas composed by Ebu's Su'ud include the following decision on spousal abuse:

> Question: Zeyd hurts his wife Hind in many ways. If the qadi knows about it, is he able to separate Hind from Zeyd?
> Answer: He is able to prevent his hurting her by whatever means possible.[12]

Noting the judge's responsibility in preventing spousal abuse, this fatwa demonstrates the proactive role of the judge in managing the well-being of the community under his jurisdiction, including protecting abused women.

Muslim jurists continued to discuss the issue to the degree that they outlined punishments for abusive husbands. Such punishments can be found in the writings of nineteenth-century Syrian jurist Ibn 'Abidin. In his *Radd al-muhtar 'ala al-durr al-mukhtar,* under the section titled "Excessive Hitting," he addresses the issue of spousal abuse. He states if a man hits his wife excessively and "breaks bone," "burns skin," or "blackens" (meaning to bruise her skin) and "does so without justification *ta'zir* is mandatory."[13] What form *ta'zir* would take is not stated in this section, but it is clear that a husband is not to go unpunished for beating his wife and causing her bodily harm.

The best evidence for the treatment of spousal abuse cases in Islamic law is found in the shari'a courts themselves. It is important to state that these cases were infrequent. Historians using shari'a court records have often speculated that many issues were resolved out of court, especially matters of such a personal and private nature as domestic abuse. However, some Aleppine women who were physically battered or emotionally abused by their husbands sought recourse in the courts. Several of them were granted divorces and were usually placed with their immediate families for their personal safety. One case from May 1687 was brought to court by Fatima bint Hajj 'Ali from the neighborhood of al-Malindi in Aleppo. She testified that her husband, Qasim ibn Hajj 'Ali, was abusing her. He had hit her with a stick to the point that blood was drawn. In fact, she claimed that he frequently harmed her. In her defense, Fatima brought along five witnesses who testified that Qasim was a man who had lost faith (literally, "stopped praying"), and they added that he was addicted to alcohol. They also claimed that Qasim made alcohol in his house, in violation of several moral and legal regulations on the production of alcohol. The court reprimanded the abusive and alcoholic husband, ordering that he be given *ta'zir.*[14] It is hard to say whether physical punishment was advocated for the spousal abuse or the alcohol in this case, as it was common for judges to prescribe *ta'zir* in cases of drunkenness. From the other cases found in the shari'a courts, abusive husbands were not given *ta'zir;* therefore, in this case Qasim was likely given the punishment for his distilling of alcohol or drinking, as it was forbidden for Muslims to do so.

A much later spousal abuse case appeared in August 1884. In this complicated case, 'A'isha ibn Qasim ibn Ahmad from the quarter of Muhammad Bey
came to court to testify against her husband, Ahmad Khatush ibn Muhammad
ibn Bakri. They had been married for eight years, during which her husband
constantly beat her. The document reads that her husband "hits her hard" and
"promises to kill her." She eventually fled to her parents' house and lived with
them. She came to court in order to collect spousal and child support (nafaqa) for
the two children she bore with Ahmad. The court granted that she be paid three
ghrush per day for food, drink, and housing.[15]

Sometimes women appeared in court with fatwas to support their allegations
of abuse. In February 1724, Haskiya bint 'Ali filed a complaint against her husband, Ahmad ibn Yusuf, from the village of al-Dana, west of the city of Aleppo.
She claimed that two months earlier her husband had hit her with a stick ('asa).
In Haskiya's case, she had protected herself in the marriage contract by stipulat-
ing that if her husband hit her, it would be the same as acquiescing to a triple
(irrevocable) divorce. The record states that Ahmad ibn Yusuf had hit her before
and had beaten her again with a stick on her head. This time she came to court to
demand her divorce, bringing a series of 'udul (expert witnesses) from the quarter of al-Abraj. In addition, she brought a fatwa issued by Abu Sa'ud, the mufti of
Aleppo, to support her claim. The fatwa as quoted in the court record read:

> Question: Zeyd vowed by a triple divorce that he would not hit his wife, then he
>   hit her with a stick on her head; did a triple divorce occur?
> Answer: Yes, it did occur and God is all-knowing.[16]

Using this fatwa greatly strengthened her suit, and Haskiya was granted a divorce
by the judge. Moreover, it appears from this record that Haskiya was well versed
in the law, not only by her use of a fatwa to support her case but also by her ini-
tial stipulations in her marriage contract. She had protected herself initially by
invoking her right to create stipulations (shurut) in her marriage contract—a right
that any Muslim woman had when contracting a marriage. When her husband
violated the terms of his marriage contract by hitting her, he immediately nul-
lified the agreement. Haskiya's marriage contract offered her protection against
an abusive husband, which is a testament to some of the safeguards provided to
women in Islamic law. These safeguards were available to all women if they chose

to use them; however, for a woman to request such stipulations, she had to have some knowledge of the rights afforded to her in her marriage contract.

RAPE

As previously stated, some authors have questioned the existence of rape as a legal category in Islamic law.[17] This rejection is attributed to the way in which rape is classified under the umbrella of *zina* law that encompasses a disparate group of crimes as broad as prostitution, procuring prostitution, adultery, sodomy, bestiality, and incest. Legal manuals sometimes included discussions of rape under the categories of personal injury *(jirah)*, highway robbery, and war against the state.[18]

Before discussing rape in Ottoman Aleppo, it is important to first address a methodological concern, namely, the problem of language. Often, issues of language were the cornerstone of Orientalist scholarship, but looking at language is necessary to debate the misconception that rape does not exist in Islamic law. Historians have doubted that Islam addressed any notion of rape because for centuries it had no specific terminology for rape in its vocabulary. The Aleppo court uses the term *zina* to describe the crime, a term that has historically been understood by scholars to mean "fornication" or "adultery," not "rape." Examples of this use of the term can be seen in a case that appeared in November 1621 when Fatima bint Hussein, from the neighborhood of al-Qasila, was removed from her quarter when she admitted to committing *zina* with 'Abdul Karim ibn Muhammad, who was also present in court. She confessed that she was pregnant with his child.[19] In this case, *zina* meant consensual intercourse and was a crime of fornication rather than rape.

One must carefully read the records in order to discern whether the case was consensual *zina* or nonconsensual *zina*, that is, rape. Juridical manuals used the term *mustakraha*, placed under the discussion on *zina*, but clearly nonconsensual sexual intercourse under duress.[20] The terminology used to describe rape in the Aleppo court records is usually the phrase "he had *zina* with me forcefully [*zina bi kurhan*]."[21] By taking a strict reading of the source devoid of context, one would think at first glance that these cases are not about rape. However, if one notices the passive voice in the rendering, he is the active agent in the *zina* act, not the plaintiff. Therefore, when it comes to the criminal act, it is being directed squarely toward the man who forcibly committed *zina* with an unwilling partner.[22] Other terms appeared in the courts to describe rape cases. One such term that appeared as early as the seventeenth century was *ghasb*—meaning "to usurp" something. This term gets to the heart of even earlier legal traditions in ancient Mesopotamia such as the Code of Hammurabi that viewed rape as a usurpation of a father's or husband's property, akin to theft. The earlier term *ghasb* evolved into the modern term *ightisab,* which still has the term *ghasb* at its root, but in this form means "to usurp what belongs to another."[23] *Ightisab,* a term laden with ancient notions of honor and male propriety over a woman's sexuality, is the term used today in the Arab world to describe rape. Another modern term for rape is *hatk al-'ird,* which refers to the "violation of honor" of a woman and her family through the act. By the twentieth century *zina* was removed from the juridical vocabulary, and *ightisab* and *hatk al-'ird,* both terms indicating shame on the victim and her family, became the dominant language for rape.

Jurists debated whether rape constituted *zina* owing to the lack of consent and desire on the part of the victim, who did not engage in a criminal act.[24] Jurists were clear that the victim of such violence was not to be punished with the appropriate *hadd* punishment for *zina.*[25] However, some jurists prescribed *hadd* punishment for rapists, which often translated into fining or flogging in legal practice.[26] Khayr ad-Din issued a related fatwa on rape and abduction as his first entry under *hudud* crimes:

> Question: A peasant abducts the daughter of so-and-so. She is in another marriage contract, and he takes her virginity by force [*'azal bikaratuha kurhan*]. What [punishment] should be imposed upon him?
>
> Answer: If he does not appeal that there is *shubha,* which would cancel the *hadd* punishment for *zina,* and there is evidence against him, carry out the *hadd* punishment. If he claims *shubha,* avert the *hadd* punishment for it and for her the equivalent of the *mahr* because there must be no [sexual] penetration in the abode of Islam without a [marriage] contract.[27]

Al-Ramli's discussion clearly places rape in the category of *zina,* as he addresses the *zina* penalty for the offender. Furthermore, he invokes the earlier cited juridical problem of *shubha*; if the man perceived he was married to the girl, it would hinder the application of *hadd* punishment. Importantly, al-Ramli points to the punishment of compensation awarded to the victim that would be equivalent to the *mahr* of a virgin bride in this case. The girl in question was already committed in a marriage contract that was not yet consummated, explaining her virginity.

Aside from compensation as a penalty for rape, the punishment of flogging was also based on a case that appeared before the caliph 'Umar. The hadith from al-Bukhari reads, "And Safiya bint 'Ubayd said: A state-owned slave had sexual intercourse with a girl from among the *khums* [one-fifth of a share of war booty]. He had coerced her until he (ultimately) raped her. Therefore, 'Umar flogged him according to the *hadd* and banished him, but he did not flog the girl because she was forced."[28] In this instance, a specific reference to the *hadd* is made, indicating that the rapist was to be subjected to the appropriate *zina* punishment for his crime.

Rape in Ottoman Aleppo was complicated by the rules of evidence applied in the court, namely, whether there were witnesses. Rape victims were not always able to prove their cases if witnesses were not present. It is also important to note the problematic status of female testimony, as it has only half the value of a man's testimony and juridical manuals specifically require four male eyewitnesses to the act of *zina*. Furthermore, although oath-taking was always an option for powerful testimony in most cases, rape victims were not afforded that option, and their cases failed. Oath-taking would have surely strengthened their cases. However, as will soon be revealed, that option was not available to women who came to court with rape charges, explaining the difficulties of proving rape in the court cases below. This may also explain why so few women brought rape cases to court, as the chances of winning were slim to none.

That being said, by the sixteenth century, some Hanafi jurists eased the evidentiary requirements for *zina*, allowing circumstantial evidence into court in cases of prosecution. This fact is confirmed in the writings of al-Marginani, who argued that "whoredom being an act the nature of which most frequently excludes the possibility of positive proof, it is necessary that circumstantial evidence be admitted as sufficient to establish it, lest the door of correction might be shut." Leslie Peirce argues that the *kanunname* of Süleyman allowed for the admission of circumstantial evidence, rather than the requisite four witnesses. Examples can be found in cases in which unsubstantiated rumors of *zina* between an unmarried man and married woman barred them from future marriage, according to Ottoman law.[29]

All legal schools agree that women who have been raped are not to be punished. However, if the case is unproven, she could have a charge of *zina* raised against her. In the woman's defense, Rudolph Peters argues that the fact that she has accused the defendant of rape produces judicial doubt *(shubha)* that should prevent her from the fixed punishment for *zina*. However, there is still a possibility that the rape victim could be charged with defamation *(qadhf)*, which also carries a fixed penalty of eighty lashes. Under such accusations, if unproven, the alleged offender is typically safe, unless he has a poor reputation and has been previously suspected of criminal behavior *(töhmet)*. Peirce illustrates this point with an example from the 'Ayntab court in which an individual was accused of entering a woman's home and raping her. During the investigation the villagers attested to a similar situation in which the same man was accused of sexual assault. Based on that previous suspicion, the defendant was punished.[30]

In May 1687 two Christians, Helena bint 'Abd al-Nur from the neighborhood of al-Arba'in outside of Bab al-Nasr and Bulus walad Ishaq, were involved in a case of rape. The record tells that Bulus had entered Helena's home seven months earlier, and "he raped her, taking her virginity by force *('azal bikaratuha kurhan wa ghasban*]," then "penetrated her again twice." She testified that she became pregnant with his child. Bulus responded to her accusation by taking an oath and producing four witnesses from the neighborhood, including two Muslim character witnesses, one with the title of *shaykh* and the other hajji, who testified that Bulus had no record of wrongdoing. Ultimately, by drawing on two witnesses whose titles further strengthened his testimony, and his good reputation, Bulus was able to win the case.[31] Furthermore, Bulus's oath allowed his testimony to surpass the integrity of Helena's testimony, permitting him to avoid punishment. It appears in these cases that women knew the power of oaths, as in this case the defendant used it to his advantage in court. Even as taking an oath would increase their chances of winning court battles, women repeatedly did not take oaths, and their rape cases failed. This lack of oath-taking was owing in part to a variation found only in Hanafi jurisprudence that did not allow oaths to be used as evidence in *hadd* cases.[32] The only option available to the women, with that restriction, would be to sue for physical damages, wherein oaths could be taken to provide evidence in such cases.

However, even in cases where oath taking was an option, defendants sometimes refused to take oaths when challenged to do so. James Grehan has conducted an important investigation into the sociolegal uses of oaths in seventeenth- and eighteenth-century Damascus. He opens the article with a case of a husband, 'Abd al-Rahman ibn Ahmad, who was being sued by his former wife and brother-in-law, who insisted her final dowry (mu'akhkhar) was one hundred piastres, whereas the defendant insisted it was only fifty. Because of a lack of evidence, the judge requested he take an oath on the Qur'an, but the defendant refused. Grehan writes that "reluctance to take this kind of exculpatory oath was regarded as a tacit admission of guilt." Such oaths were taken upon a vow of apostasy that, in the most formal application of the shari'a, would require the death penalty if it were ever broken; however, Grehan notes that such punishment was rarely administered.[33]

A March 1719 case involved the kidnapping and rape of Warda bint 'Ajrif from the village of al-Maliha in the district (nahiya) of al-Jabul. This case was unique in that the rapist, Milhem ibn Isma'il, from the same village, appeared in court and confessed to kidnapping her. In the record we can hear his voice, marked by its first-person narrative, describing his attack. The record states that Milhem confessed by saying, "I committed zina with her forcefully, taking her virginity." For his confession, the court ordered that Milhem be given the hadd punishment but did not specify the exact form it should take. Amira El-Azhary Sonbol in her research on Ottoman Egypt found that rapists were given the hadd punishment of fines. She writes, "During the seventeenth-century, rapists received hudud sentences and were expected to pay compensation, the amounts of which were not given in any great detail. Eighteenth-century records, however, itemize the compensations decided upon by the courts for rape as for other crimes." Although evidence of itemized compensation has been found for Egypt, Aleppo records do not list compensation amounts. However, rape records are specific about whether the victim was a virgin at the time of the rape. Sonbol writes that in Ottoman Egypt, the standardization of diya paid in cases of bodily harm in rape ranged according to the age and virginity of the victim.[34] This range may be indicative of a higher diya paid in cases where the victim was a virgin, suggesting that it made a difference in compensation.

One case revealed that rape could occur within the extended family. In July 1621, Saliha bint Muhammad appeared in court and testified that she was raped (zina bi kurhan) by her cousin Ibrahim Chalabi ibn 'Abdi Efendi. She added that another cousin, Rabia, helped Ibrahim rape her by holding her down on the floor. Her explicit description of the rape included a description of the rape in her own words. Saliha stated in court, "[Rabia] put a handkerchief [*mahramah*] into my mouth, and my cousin [Ibrahim] raped me forcefully [*zina bi kurhan*] and took my virginity." These rare instances where first-person narratives appear in the record provide us with voices of the victims, despite the obvious sculpting of the court record by the scribe. In this case, Saliha's cousin Ibrahim denied her accusation of rape. Ultimately, this case was dismissed based on a lack of evidence because Saliha had no witnesses to testify on her behalf.[35]

Although Saliha lost her case, other rape victims sometimes used the court to their advantage. Boğaç A. Ergene documents a case from April 1699 of a woman named Emine who appeared in the court of Çankırı, stating that three men from her village of Ünüz had beaten and raped her six months earlier. The defendants denied the accusations, as in the case above. Instead, Emine appeared with seven witnesses who claimed they heard her screams and saw the defendants leave after the attack (with some articles of clothing they stole from her house). Upon her request, the court looked into the backgrounds of the men who allegedly attacked her, and fifteen witnesses attested to their poor reputations. The men were given an unspecified punishment.[36] Emine's success demonstrates that women were sometimes able to use en masse testimony and the court's occasional leniency with evidentiary requirements to their advantage (table 5.1).

There was one feature of the Aleppo cases that was unique; the majority of the plaintiffs that appeared in court cases involving rape were pregnant, and almost always six months along in their pregnancy.[37] The women were several months along in their pregnancies, well beyond their first trimester, and sometimes had already given birth out of wedlock by the time they appeared in court, as in the case of Sara bint Rizq Allah related below. Children born out of wedlock were often socially taboo, considered children of sin *(awlad al-zina)*.[38] Out-of-wedlock children always had low status in Islamic societies. Formal adoption was forbidden in Islamic law, yet families did sometimes take in orphans (motherless, fatherless, or abandoned children) informally. If a woman admitted to having an out-of-wedlock child, repercussions from the male members of her family were a real threat and even her child's status would be forever negatively affected by the *zina* crime committed by its mother. Furthermore, her social status could be reduced to that of a *zaniya* (fornicator). One Islamic injunction reads, "The offspring belongs to the owner of the bed, and the adulterer gets the stone."[39] This statement means that the child will always be connected to the *zina* offense, bearing the social repercussions of the act.

TABLE 5.1

RAPE CASES LOCATED IN THE ALEPPO COURT REGISTERS

Case	Name of plaintiff	Name of defendant	Secondary crime	Religion	Residence (Plaintiff)	Date	Punishment
1	Amhan bint ʿAmr (mother of unnamed victim)	Mamluk Yusuf		Muslim	Saljikhan	1679	Taʿzir
2	Helena bint ʿAbd al-Nur	Bulus walad Ishaq		Christian	al-Arbaʿin	1687	None
3	Sara bint Rizq Allah	Nerses walad ʿAbdallah (Armenian)		Christian	Zuqaq al-Qir, outside Bab al-Nasr	1687	None
4	Saliha bint Muhammad	Ibrahim Chalabi ibn ʿAbdi Efendi		Muslim	Not listed	1621	None
5	Hilala bint Kaʿdan	Unknown levend		Muslim	Village of Nayrab[a] (Aleppo)	1719	None
6	Warda bint ʿAjrif	Milhem ibn Ismaʿil	Kidnapping	Muslim	Village of al-Maliha[a] (district of Jabul, southeast of Aleppo)	1719	Hadd
7	Fatima bint Darwish (Kurd)	Ismaʿil ibn Yaʿqub (Kurd)		Muslim	Village of Matara[a] (outside Aleppo)	1741	None
8	Farha bint Saʿdi (Jewish)	Shahada walad Yusuf (Jewish, collector of avariz and ʿurfi tax)	Evildoer (her)	Jewish	Bahsita	1662	None
9	Qamr bint Maʿtuq (Armenian)	Basil walad Yusuf (Rum Orthodox)		Christian	al-Qawwas, outside Bab al-Nasr	1735	None

[a]Village listed as a place of residence, as opposed to a city quarter.

Despite the severity of these injunctions, Islamic law does contain a fail-safe to ensure options for legitimating out-of-wedlock children, namely, endorsement of the shotgun wedding. For centuries, jurists deliberated on the topic of unwed expectant mothers and advocated marriage to ensure a child's legitimacy in the eyes of the court. That being said, cultural taboos may wear heavy on a couple, but legally speaking, jurists were quite flexible in their definitions of legitimacy. For instance, the mufti al-Tamimi (d. 1725) from Nablus rendered a child legitimate so long as the parents of the child married one month before the child was born.[40] Ibn 'Abidin, on the other hand, writes that the couple must marry six months before the child is born if it is to be legitimate. This idea is confirmed in a fatwa that presents a scenario in which "a man was married to a woman who was pregnant from *zina*. He did not have sex with her until after she gave birth less than six months after the marriage. From the time they married, she claimed that she was pregnant from him and the child is his. He does not believe her. . . . There is no evidence either way concerning patrimony." Ibn 'Abidin answered, citing as part of his argument a fatwa from Ibn Nujaym that stated by marrying her six months earlier, the man has claimed the fetus as his, sufficient evidence to rule that he is the father.[41]

However, if someone made an accusation of *zina* before the child was born, the "shotgun" wedding would be impossible. Many interpreters of Islamic law extended the period of time for legitimacy well beyond the birth of the child, which contradicts existing *zina* law.[42] What these interpretations tell us is that jurists were still looking for a way to avoid the stone. They sought to remedy these social problems and integrate both the *zina* offender and the child into the community. This flexibility stands in stark contrast to earlier interpretations that called for the death penalty in such cases.

In these cases, women testified that they were raped; however, unable to use oaths to buttress their evidence, they were unable to prove their cases without witnesses. Peirce argues that even in cases where oaths were permitted by defendants, in the court of 'Ayntab women were rarely offered the option as compared to men. In other words, in cases where they were accused of a given crime, they were not given the opportunity to defend themselves against such accusations.[43]

The fact that all the cases were reported after the fact, and after significant time spent pregnant, leaves one to ask why these women did not report the cases sooner. Also, one might ask, was documenting a case of rape a way of protecting oneself as an unwed mother? The answer to these questions may never be known. But what is for certain is that these women were pregnant and were not able to prove that they were raped. The combination of these facts would have implied guilt of *zina;* however, the women went unpunished. There were cases in which women suffered repercussions for unproven accusations of rape. In Ottoman Egypt, a woman who suffered from a bad reputation and was unable to prove that she was raped was removed from her neighborhood for committing *zina.*[44] Furthermore, traveler Alexander Russell observed collective punishment of neighborhoods in cases of out-of-wedlock pregnancy in eighteenth-century Aleppo:

> It is not the parties alone that are interested in the concealment of an illicit amour. A bastard child is an affair of Turkish cognizance, and a whole neighborhood is liable to be laid under contribution, on the pretence that they might either have prevented the offence or have given earlier information to the magistrate. It is on this account not improbable, that the crime of procuring an abortion is more frequent, than among the Turks; and the breach of chastity is not heard of among the Christians so often as it really exists.[45]

This account should be read with caution because the above cases illustrate that both Christian and Muslim women were reporting their out-of-wedlock pregnancies in court. Furthermore, unlike cases of prostitution and procuring, the cases were brought to court by the women themselves, not at the behest of the community. Moreover, there is no evidence in the official court record that a fine of any sort was placed on the community for either the crime of *zina* as an illicit affair or the crime of rape. In these failed rape cases from Aleppo, none of the women were punished in such a way. Nor was an accusation of *zina* placed on the victims by the community or the accused rapist after the case was dismissed in court.

In addition to the cases from Aleppo, new studies, such as Leslie Peirce's on the city of 'Ayntab, have noted the presence of pregnant women in court who were reportedly raped. One of the theories she suggests is that these cases may have been a step toward realizing a marriage that was disapproved of by the family. In her study of the 1540–41 Ottoman court records of 'Ayntab, she was able to find *zina* cases that resulted in marriage. She found several *zina* confessions made by couples rather than individual confessions. One case was between a man named ʿAli who confessed that he had fornicated with the girl Emine, and two weeks later her father came to court to grant his consent to the marriage.[46] On the other hand, in the Aleppo court, individual women came to court on all occasions—with the exception of the above confession of Milhem in which the couple appeared in court but only one confessed. In rape cases, rather than in consensual *zina* cases, the bride could be coerced to marry her rapist rather than live with the social stigma attached to being a rape victim. For example, in modern Egypt, there have been cases of men abducting and raping women whom they are unable to marry either because she is unwilling or because her family disapproves of the match. In 1980 the state imposed the death penalty for cases of abduction-marriage in order to bar lower-class men from marrying upper-class women.[47] This modern example demonstrates the possibilities of rape being used to leverage an unwanted marriage upon the victim.

Some cases that appeared in the Aleppo court demonstrate the effects that these rapes had on the family and the way in which some husbands chose to deal with them. In August 1687, Sara bint Rizq Allah from Zuqaq al-Qir (outside Bab al-Nasr) brought a case against Nerses walad ʿAbdallah, who was not present in court. In this case, Sara accused Nerses of raping her ten months earlier while she slept in the courtyard of her house. Nerses had been living in the house with Sara and her husband. However, the record states that her husband was absent at the time of the rape. She said that she became pregnant from the rape and gave birth to a baby girl. Sara's husband appeared in court with her that day. No punishment was given to Nerses in this case; the record seems to have been registered to document the events as they happened.[48] This case may have also been recorded in order to document the parentage of the child. We can speculate that the husband may have wanted to distinguish this child from his own to protect the inheritance of his own progeny.

Levend soldiers, who among other things were also involved in a series of criminal activities that included extortion, theft, and murder, were also involved in physical attacks against women. One case exemplifies the abuses of the *levend* against women. Hilala bint Kaʿdan from the village of Nayrab appeared in court with her father, Kaʿdan ibn Najm, in the month of January 1719. Hilala told the court that six months earlier "a group of *levend* grabbed my father and hit him.

He was injured from them and their hard blows, and I cried." Then, she continued, one of the soldiers entered the house, "raped me, taking my virginity *(zina bi kurhan 'azal bakarati).*"[49] She added that she was pregnant from the rape. In this case, she was unable to identify her attacker but used her testimony in court to explain her out-of-wedlock pregnancy.

These cases expose several underlying themes to rape cases in the courts of Aleppo. First, women tried to prosecute their rapists in court. They told their stories openly, presumably in an attempt to obtain justice against their attackers. On some occasions they were successful; in the nine cases I located, two resulted in punishment of the offender. However, statistically, these data demonstrate problems with the adjudication of rape, as victim accusations rarely inspired confessions from their attackers. Second, women sometimes reported their rapes without prosecuting the rapists. In these cases, the rapists were either from out of town or unidentifiable. In several cases, women were pregnant, which increased the need to report the rapes in order to stave off any potential threat to them or the children once they were born. Women in several cases appeared in court, many months along in pregnancy, to testify to the rapes. The taboos placed on an unwed mother and out-of-wedlock child were so severe that indicating the child was the result of a rape might have lessened the blow it would otherwise bring to a woman or her family.

Leslie Peirce argues that being a victim of rape could have been a slightly better status to have than being seen as one who had committed willful and compliant *zina*. It also deflects the shame and dishonor associated with rape, as the dishonor will be borne by the rapists, more than the victims. She also argues that another reason for confessions of this sort may have been to escape retaliation in the form of so-called honor killings by relatives. Peirce states, "By allying themselves to [the court's] legal structure and culture, they may hope to escape a harsher local legal culture. The most extreme form of local practice concerning *zina* was the custom of honor killing: that is, the right of an individual to kill a female member of the family and her lover if they were caught in the sex act." As discussed earlier, the custom was embedded in the legal culture of the Ottomans, as evidenced by Ebu's Su'ud's fatwa endorsing the custom and dismissing any claims that may appear in court concerning such murders. The Aleppo court record is silent on the subject. However, as evidenced by Ebu's Su'ud's discussion, there could have been a reluctance of the court to adjudicate claims related to such crimes.[50] What is clear from the confessions to *zina,* whether *zina* as prostitution or *zina* as rape, is that women did confess in court without any reference to retaliation or honor murder.

Why were rape prosecutions so unsuccessful in these instances? Their overall lack of success may explain why such a small number of cases appeared in court in the first place. Families may have resorted to less official means to retaliate against rapists or conceal the shame of raped female relatives. These matters may have been dealt with using local intermediaries to negotiate between the parties. Peirce's explanation for the trouble with adjudicating rape cases has to do with the court's emphasis on reputation that makes it difficult for the victim to accuse an attacker without a countercharge of slander *(qadhf).* However, in the context of the court at 'Ayntab in 1540–41, several cases were brought to court with community support in prosecuting the crime.[51] That type of community effort in support of the cases was not found in the Aleppo registers, underscoring the burden of evidence placed on rape victims.

In conclusion, the court records for Aleppo contain a mixture of cases that reveal dynamics of gender in the legal system. First, the court records suggest that cases of spousal abuse had some success in the courts. It appears through these cases that a woman's well-being in a marriage, both emotional and physical, was a standard set in Islamic jurisprudence through the principle of *darar,* and the court upheld it. On the other hand, rape prosecutions were rarely successful. Furthermore, in some cases women were raped by men from out of town or absent from the court proceedings. It is suspicious that the women waited until they were well along in their pregnancies to report the rapes. Was it because only then their pregnancies were noticeable to the general public? It is arguable that with the cultural taboos concerning out-of-wedlock children, a woman would be very cautious and need to place the blame elsewhere. The court's failure in these cases to punish the rapists is also worth noting. It is possible that these cases served more as testimonials to events in order to avert future accusations of *zina* against the women. An unproven case of rape could have been countered with an accusation of *zina.* However, *zina* charges were not made, possibly owing to the court's strict adherence to rules of evidence requiring four male witnesses. It could also be an attempt by the court to diffuse these situations in the community by not pursuing *zina* convictions. Nonetheless, it is curious that women in Aleppo did not utilize the ability to take an oath that would have substantially strengthened their cases against their rapists.

Conclusion

It is only fitting to end this book with the only documented case of stoning in the history of Syria—the stoning of Mar Elias in the city of Homs in the third century. This case of stoning was not for *zina* but for the crime of spreading the revolutionary doctrine of Christianity. The stoning was performed not by Muslims but by Romans who were attempting to halt the spread of an ideology viewed as subversive to the empire. The persecution, and even stoning, of Christians is found in several instances in the history of early Christianity. However, Mar Elias, considered a martyr, was unique in that he suffered the excruciating punishment of stoning until dead by the hands of his own father, the Roman governor of Homs.[1]

The case of Mar Elias only emphasizes that stoning itself is not a punishment unique to Islam. However, it is a punishment documented in the hadith, a source that guides Muslim religious and legal practice. There it is documented that the early Islamic community endorsed stoning, and there is evidence, as best we have through oral transmissions of the hadiths, that the Prophet Muhammad practiced stoning in his lifetime, as did his immediate successors. Later, the Ottomans took pains to write *kanunnames* that continued to criminalize sex outside of circumscribed boundaries, yet they did not include stoning as a punishment for *zina* in those imperial codes. Despite the laborious construction of these criminal codes throughout the empire, there are no references to them in the various kinds of sexual indiscretion cases presented in Aleppo's shari'a courts. Furthermore, the practice of banishment in cases of *zina* versus the Ottoman mandated fine system is evidence that judges may have been using another legal basis for their legal rulings. Prostitutes and pimps were not documented as paying sums of cash to the Ottomans in court cases. The Ottoman officials were also remarkably absent from the process of apprehending and bringing offenders to court. Instead, the power of the local community is apparent in the records, as they policed their own communities and brought offenders to justice. The shari'a court was an important institution that offered official endorsement of the policing being performed by the quarters of the city. The court records do not indicate that the Ottomans coerced residents into "policing" their neighborhoods by punishing them outright when they did not apprehend offenders in their neighborhoods. Nonetheless, there is some evidence that the phenomenon of neighborhood policing may have existed long before the presence of the Ottoman state as a grassroots legal tradition that dated back to the Mamluk period. People were familiar with the law and trusted the courts to ensure justice in their communities. Quarters were also organized through local leadership via the *'arif al-hara.* Even today in Syria, these local forms of government persist in which *abaday* tend to be a crucial link between the community and government, using their contacts in high places to provide critical services to their communities. However, what is also apparent from quarter solidarity in court is that mass testimony could work to ensure the removal of an undesired neighbor. This fact, combined with vague definitions of moral wrongdoing, left plenty of room for abuse toward those Aleppines who did not walk "the straight path" and chose to deviate from accepted norms of their community.

Overall, this book documented the flexibility within Islamic law that is often portrayed as stagnant and draconian. *Zina,* as it was managed in Aleppo, offers an extreme example of the mutability of the law. It challenges our perceptions of gender in Islamic law, showing that prostitutes were given a proverbial slap on the wrist when brought to court. These women were removed from city quarters rather than subjected to death by stoning, as found in the historic juridical writings on Islamic law. The case of *zina* law and its application in Ottoman Aleppo demonstrates the way that Islamic law accommodated the needs of its community. It also calls into question our notions of honor in the Islamic world. As previously noted, the court records reveal families and couples engaged in prostitution together in 42 percent of the cases located in the Aleppo court records. Economic necessity sometimes overrode abstract notions of family honor, which complicates the dominant portrayal of family honor as immutable in the Islamic world.

How were the courts able to circumvent the edicts for *zina* punishment found in Islamic law? There was a tradition of jurists looking to *'urf* traditions of law that were deemed acceptable and given weight in local matters, so long as they did not contradict injunctions found in the Qur'an and Sunna. For Aleppo, it also may have been the process of *istihsan,* or realizing the public good, and the traditions of the local community. It may be that stoning was a foreign custom to the cosmopolitan community of Aleppo. Therefore, judges may have preferred to use the punishment familiar to the community rather than one that was alien. In either case, it appears that the term *Islamic law* inaccurately describes the system in the singular, when in actuality it appears to be a series of legal codes that differ according to time, place, and context. This message is an important lesson, as today multiple extremist ideologies claim to have a corner on Islamic law yet have diverging visions as to how to apply it.

So what can this study tell us about the path that lies ahead as debates over gender and morality in Islamic law become amplified and laden with increasing stakes in the Islamic world? This exercise has illuminated some of the forgotten discourse in Islamic law on sexual morality. However, it has not been a comprehensive study, and I hope it will be followed by others that will investigate the way that Muslim empires and their laws dealt with morality and practiced the law on a daily basis. Such studies will serve to alleviate the historical amnesia that pervades the Islamic world today as well as correct the assumptions of non-Muslims about the rigid nature of Islamic law that have long dominated discussions.

Part of this reassessment of Islamic law is already under way. Contemporary Muslim scholars have called for reinterpretation of Islamic law and its discourse on gender and morality. One scholar I would like to highlight is Tariq Ramadan, a moderate Muslim intellectual who has produced a number of writings in recent years, but is mostly known for the controversy surrounding his hiring at the University of Notre Dame in 2004. Ramadan was never able to take up his position at Notre Dame because he was denied a visa to the United States. However, the media coverage that followed his rejection included a public accusation in *Vanity Fair* that he endorsed stoning in Islamic law, and, even more, that he had publicly sanctioned the practice in his writing.[2] The following year, Ramadan publicly posted his article titled "An International Call for Moratorium on Corporal Punishment, Stoning, and the Death Penalty in the Islamic World" on an Internet site he created. It is in this article that Ramadan generally calls for ending corporal punishment altogether in the Islamic world and more specifically takes on the issue of stoning. He argues that most *'ulama* concede that the conditions under which stoning was prescribed are impossible to reestablish today. However, spiritual leaders today are under pressure by the masses who call for the implementation of corporal punishment *(hudud)*, yet, Ramadan argues, "they themselves will often be the first victims" of such punishments. An application of the *hudud* is desired by the masses because it provides evidence of the application of the shari'a, and "the harshness and intransigence of the application, gives an Islamic dimension to the popular psyche." The fact that the application of Islamic justice is greeted with condemnation by the West plays into a mutually reinforcing binary reasoning, according to Ramadan. Such condemnation provides "sufficient proof of the authentic Islamic character of the literal application of *hudud.*"[3] Western repulsion, which in many ways is fueled by the draconian measures employed by Islamists, only reassures the authenticity of the practice to the Islamists who apply it. By implementing the punishments, the *'ulama* have caved into popular demands for the *hudud* because they fear losing their power.

Ramadan justifies, in the end, his call for a moratorium on stoning based on a lack of consensus *(ijma')* among scholars, or even a clear majority. He finishes with a provocative argument based on Islamic justice as it forms a superior aspiration within the shari'a, arguing that stoning has been a tool of abuse and has targeted the weak throughout the Islamic world. In this way, Tariq Ramadan is one of many who are calling for a reevaluation of the shari'a's perspective on stoning as well as other matters such as reform, women's rights, and human rights.

Tariq Ramadan is one example of Muslim scholars who are continuing the long tradition of *ijtihad* and deliberation on the law that has been discussed in this book, despite attempts to silence the debate. For Muslim intellectuals today, the stakes are even higher, as they have authoritarian states and more deeply entrenched Orientalist notions of an essential Islamic tradition to challenge. There are also challenges being made within the Islamic tradition, as scholarly authority and authoritarianism are often interrelated. As the license to issue rulings on legal matters is no longer for the learned, and as shari'a is understood more as a normative applicable law rather than a loose discourse of guidelines meant to be used in conjunction with social practice, the understanding of the shari'a in both the East and the West has become rigid, the very opposite of the legal culture presented in this book. This struggle over shariʿa today has made investigating the historical space between the theory and practice of shariʿa vitally important. It is time to eliminate the historical amnesia that is so pervasive and begin to fill in the memory gap that has created so much political struggle over the true nature of the shariʿa.

Epilogue

While researching this book between 1999 to 2005, I had always lived in neighborhoods in the "new city" of Damascus. As I worked on revisions in 2005 I decided to live in the old city of Damascus for the first time. The last year of research and writing was spent in the old neighborhoods, much like the *harat* of days past with the exception that many parts of Bab Touma were destroyed during the sectarian violence of 1860 and are of relatively new construction. Life in Damascus is much like life in any large city: cars honking their horns, signs of global capitalism that can be observed through clothing and music, cell phones ringing in the narrow alleys of the old city. I found myself in an old *bayt ʿarabi,* much like the ones I describe in the book, living with several young Syrian women, professionals and students alike. I was excited about making new friends with this diverse group of seven women from Lebanon and Syria.

Among the renters was a Lebanese woman whom I will call Suzanne. She was a runaway who had left her troubled family, a mixed Christian and Muslim marriage that resulted in divorce, to be near her boyfriend, who lived in our neighborhood. She was young, eighteen at the time. Her boyfriend had helped her find the apartment and bought her food, clothes, and personal items since she was unemployed. I soon learned that this situation was not all that uncommon, since another woman from Aleppo lived in the house, and her boyfriend likewise paid for her living expenses so that she could live near him. Suzanne would spend her days smoking *nargila* and her nights out on the town with her boyfriend in cafés and dance clubs. She would often come home around four or five in the morning, sometimes drunk, and even afterward her boyfriend and other male friends from their group would call to her from the alleyway below. Despite the disruptions, her boyfriend and other male friends were usually careful not to enter the house at night. Within a week the landlord told her that she needed to move at the end of the month. By Syrian standards it was incredibly generous, since most would have kicked her out on the spot. But the landlord felt that she, being a runaway, would literally be out in the streets if he kicked her out immediately. His conscience demanded that he give her the opportunity to find other housing.

The other women in the house suffered through a month of disruptions in the night. On Suzanne's birthday, for example, she locked herself out of the house late at night while drunk; another night, she became sick and fell down at three o'clock; her boyfriend came to the house and took her to the hospital, only to find out her mysterious illness was the common cold.

Suzanne moved into a new house in the same neighborhood at the end of the month. She lasted only a day in the new place. The new house had a landlord who did not live in Damascus—something that would lead most to think that anything could happen in that house without his knowing. That may have been what she hoped for. When boys showed up on her very first day in her new apartment, however, whistling at her in the alleyway and calling to her, as they had at her old place, the neighbors surrounding her new residence gathered together, came to the house, and told Suzanne that she needed to leave. So, after one day, Suzanne was kicked out of her apartment, not by the landlord but by her neighbors!

Although this anecdote is based on contemporary experience, not Ottoman documents, I thought in some way it conveyed a perseverance of a cultural attitude toward community responsibility demonstrated in this study. Although the shari'a courts are in no way what they were, and the environs have changed, we can still see a civic action, a "quarter solidarity," that resembles the kind seen in the court records discussed in this book. Rather than call the police, who were only a five-minute walk away at the bustling entrance into Bab Touma, or even the landlord who actually owned the property, the neighbors acted on their own behalf to expel an undesirable resident from their midst. This example may further hint that the phenomenon of quarter solidarity may have been organic rather than the product of Ottoman coercion.

APPENDIXES

NOTES

BIBLIOGRAPHY

INDEX

Appendix 1

Sample Sijills *from the Aleppo Court Records*

DOCUMENT 1

Aleppo-shariʿa court record: *SMH* 1:185:1913 2 Safar 962 A.H./December 1554

Example of early court records from the first register in which ʿAbd al-Salam ibn Shams al-din the doorkeeper *(al-bawab)* was accused of drinking in the company of women. Courtesy of the Syrian National Archives (Dar al-Wathaʾiq al-Tarikhiyya), Damascus, Syria.

DOCUMENT 2

Shariʿa court record: *SMH* 45:154:372 19 Dhuʾl Hijja 1130 A.H./November 1718

Zina case resulting in pregnancy and expulsion from the quarter of al-Qasila. Courtesy of the Syrian National Archives (Dar al-Wathaʾiq al-Tarikhiyya), Damascus, Syria.

DOCUMENT 3

Aleppo-shariʿa court record: *SMH* 36:182:517 18 Dhuʾl Hijja 1098 A.H./October 1687

Two women are brought to court for "gathering strangers" in their home and being "off the straight path." They are expelled from the neighborhood of Shukr Agha. Courtesy of the Syrian National Archives (Dar al-Wathaʾiq al-Tarikhiyya), Damascus, Syria.

DOCUMENT 4

Aleppo-shari'a court record: *SMH* 55:53:175 4 Rajab 1147 A.H./November 1734.

Hajj Hijazi bin 'Abd al-Qadir, accused of being an evildoer, spreading harm, and harassing women in front of a coffeehouse in Bab al-Nasr. Courtesy of the Syrian National Archives (Dar al-Watha'iq al-Tarikhiyya), Damascus, Syria.

DOCUMENT 5

Aleppo-shari'a court record: *SMH* 34:97:533 17 Shawwal 1089 A.H./August 1687

Example of spousal abuse *(darar).* Case with colloquialisms and first-person narrative. Courtesy of the Syrian National Archives (Dar al-Watha'iq al-Tarikhiyya), Damascus, Syria.

DOCUMENT 6

Aleppo-shari'a court record: *SMH* 113:178:460 29 Rabi' al-Thani 1190 A.H./June 1776

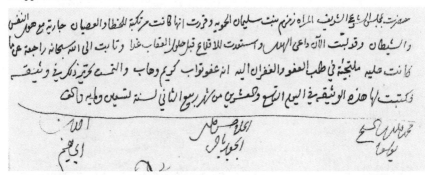

Testimonial of Zamzam bint Sulayman from Hama, documenting her repentance for the sins she committed in the past. Courtesy of the Syrian National Archives (Dar al-Watha'iq al-Tarikhiyya), Damascus, Syria.

Appendix 2

All Zina-Type Cases Found Within
the Selected Aleppo Sijills

TABLE A2.1

ALL *ZINA*-TYPE CASES FOUND WITHIN THE SELECTED ALEPPO *SIJILLS*

Case Type	Sijill	Page	Document	Defendant 1	Defendant 2	Defendant 3	Defendant 4	Defendant 5	Defendant 6
Criminal	1	22	214	Muhammad ibn Rasul					
Criminal	1	28	149	Sabah bint Sayyid Mustafa al-Qassab					
Criminal	1	185	1913	'Abd al-Salam ibn Shams al-Din al-Bawwab					
Criminal	2	159	273	Musa ibn 'Ali al-Musari'a					
Testimonial	3	386	1889	Myriam bint Khudhr					
Criminal	8	222	1163	Fatima bint Ahmad the foreigner	Mahmud ibn 'Issa	Yusuf ibn Hajj 'Amr	Hassan ibn Hajj Khalil		
Criminal	10	518	2557	Amhan bint Muhammad	Zahra bint Jamal al-Din				
Criminal	11	208	1109	Hajj Ahmad ibn Hajj 'Aqan al-'Akkam	Hijazi ibn Hajj Muhammad ibn Küçük				
Criminal	14	174	878	Nur al-Din al-Sawwari					
Criminal	27	102	437	Fatima bint Muhammad	Mustafa	Nabiha	Karim ibn Ibrahim		
Testimonial	27	311	1499	Sultan bint 'Abd al-'Az					
Criminal	28	18	63	Zahra bint (blank)					
Criminal	28	108	464	Burkhan bint Abi Bakr	Khadija bint 'Ali	Zahara bint Ahmad			
Criminal	28	181	721	Myriam bint Yusuf	Yara (mother)				
Criminal	28	265	1009	Myriam bint Suleyman	Boghos walad Yusuf				
Criminal	28	498	1708	Kulthum bint 'Abdallah					
Criminal	28	577	2093	Farha bint Sa'di					
Criminal	28	596	2167	'Affan ibn Shab al-Din					
Testimonial	28	611	2233	Khadija bint Rajab al-Sirminiyya					
Criminal	34	108	580	Paolo al-Afranji					
Criminal	34	110	595	Mustafa ibn 'Abdallah					
Criminal	34	146	739	Mamluk Yusuf					

↓ *(Columns continue on page 174)*

Defendant 7	Crime type 1	Crime type 2	Crime type 3	Religion	Neighborhood	Gender	Christian Date	Date Hijra	Punishment	Related?
	zina	drinking		Muslim	al-Shaykh 'Arabi	m	1555	16 Muharram 963	removed	n/a
	gathering	cursing		Muslim	al-Qasila	ff	1801	6 Dhu'l Qa'da 1215	removed	n/a
	drinking with women			Muslim	not listed	m	1554	2 Safar 962	not listed	n/a
	prostitution	picking up women		Muslim	Akyol	m	1707	11 Rabi' al-Thani 1119	removed Aleppo	n/a
	prostitution	despicable acts		Muslim	Karlik	f	1655	27 Jumada al-Akhir 1065	none	n/a
	gathering with women	despicable acts		Muslim	Bab Allah village (Jabal Sam'an)	mmf	1596	15 Jumada al-Akhir 1004	not listed	n/a
	Gathering	off the straight path		Muslim	Dudu	ff	1655	21 Ramadan 1065	removed	no
	fornication	corruption		Muslim	Qal'a	mm	1618	1 Jumada al-Awwal 1027	not listed	n/a
	gathering	harmful		Muslim	Sawayqat	m	1625	15 Sha'ban 1034	none	no
	gathering	off the straight path		Muslim	Bab al-Nasr	mmff	1650	26 Shawwal 1060	removed	yes
	prostitution			Muslim	Sahat Biza	f	1661	11 Rajab 1071	none	no
	gathering	evildoer	off the straight path	Muslim	Jami' 'Ubays	f	1660	21 Muharram 1071	removed	n/a
	gathering	off the straight path		Muslim	Sajilkhan	fff	1660	7 Rabi' al-Awwal 1071	removed	no
	gathering	off the straight path		Christian	Jubb Asad Allah	ff	1660	14 Rabi' al-Thani 1071	removed	yes
	zina	pregnancy		Christian	al-Hazzaza	f	1661	29 Jumada al-Awwal 1071	none	n/a
	gathering	off the straight path		Muslim	Sajilkhan	f	1662	14 Safar 1073	removed	n/a
	rape	evildoer (her)		Jewish	Jewish Quarter	f	1662	22 Rabi' al-Thani 1073	none	n/a
	picking up women	pinching women's thighs		Muslim	Village of Hayyan	m	1663	15 Jumada al-Akhir 1073	nafi (banishment)	n/a
	prostitution	off the straight path		Muslim	not listed	f	1663	18 Jumada al-Akhir 1073	none	n/a
	gathering	drinking		Christian	al-Jallum al-Kubra	m	1679	23 Shawwal 1089	removed	n/a
	gathering			Muslim	al Nuhiyya	m	1678	9 Dhu'l Qa'da 1089	not listed	n/a
	zina (rape)			Muslim	Saljikhan	m	1679	14 Muharram 1090	ta'zir	no

TABLE A2.1

ALL *ZINA*-TYPE CASES FOUND WITHIN THE SELECTED ALEPPO *SIJILLS*

Case Type	Sijill	Page	Document	Defendant 1	Defendant 2	Defendant 3	Defendant 4	Defendant 5	Defendant 6
Criminal	34	150	756	Shahin ibn 'Issa					
Criminal	36	24	67	'Aqil ibn al-Hajj 'Uthman	Hana bint 'Uthman (sister)	Alif bint Muhammad (mother)			
Criminal	36	84	230	Bulus walad Ishaq					
Criminal	36	130	359	Nerses walad 'Abdallah					
Criminal	36	182	517	Farah bint Hajj Mustafa	Kohar bint 'Attallah				
Criminal	43	175	702	Ghalia bint Qasim (absent)					
Criminal	45	5	2	Halim ibn Ma'tuq	'Abd al-Rahman ibn Hassan al-Qattan	Safiya bint Asad	Khizma bint Rizaq	Hajj Hussayn (Khizma's son, absent)	
Criminal	45	8	19	Muhammad ibn Hajj Hasan	Hasan ibn Ahmad	Hajj 'Ali ibn Hajj Rahim	Hajj Muhammad ibn Hajj Salih		
Criminal	45	65	158	Ibrahim Chalabi ibn 'Abdi Efendi					
Criminal	45	73	177	none					
Criminal	45	154	372	Fatima bint Hussein					
Criminal	45	182	446	Aslan ibn Khudr al-Mutajir					
Criminal	45	203	501	unnamed levend					
Criminal	45	224	555	Mustafa ibn Fathi	Fatima bint Musa (wife)				
Criminal	45	273	682	Milhem ibn Isma'il					
Criminal	45	276	689	Mustafa ibn Hajj Hijazi	Khadija bint (blank) his mother				
Criminal	55	48	162	Mustafa ibn Muhammad al-'Attar					
Criminal	55	52	173	Hajj Hijazi ibn 'Abd al-Qadir al-Mazzayik					
Criminal	55	53	175	Sayyid Abi al-Yemen ibn Hajj Ahmad					
Criminal	55	106	337	Hajj Muhammad ibn Hajj 'Ali al-Shami	'A'isha bint Hajj Na'ima (wife)	Khadija (daughter)	Fatima bint Hajj Muhammad (not related)	Fatima bint Hussein	'A'isha bint Musa
Criminal	55	107	340	Mustafa ibn 'Abdallah	Fatima bint Hadhr	'Abra			

⬇ *(Columns continue on page 176)*

Defendant 7	Crime type 1	Crime type 2	Crime type 3	Religion	Neighborhood	Gender	Christian Date	Date Hijra	Punishment	Related?
	gathering			Muslim	Akyol	m	1679	27 Muharram 1090	removed	n/a
	gathering	harmful		Muslim	Zuqaq Shimali	mff	1686	10 Jumada al-Awwal 1098	removed	yes
	zina (rape)			Christian	Arba'in	f	1687	28 Rajab 1098	none	n/a
	zina (rape)			Christian	Zuqaq al-Qir, outside Bab al-Nasr	m	1687	5 Shawwal 1098	none	no
	gathering	off the straight path		Muslim	Shukr Agha	ff	1687	18 Dhu'l Hijja 1098	removed	no
	gathering	evildoer	harmful	Muslim	village of Naghawla (Jabal Sam'an)	f	1710	6 Thu'l Qa'da 1122	none	n/a
	gathering	harmful		Muslim	al-Qasila	mmmff	1621	30 Jumada al-Awwal 1130	removed	yes
	homosexuality	pimping	qadhf	Muslim	al-Safsafah	mmmm	1718	16 Jumada al-Akhir 1130	ta'zir	no
	zina (rape)			Muslim	not listed	m	1621	26 Sha'ban 1130	none	yes
	gathering			not listed	Several quarters of Aleppo	n/a	1718	19 Ramadan 1130	none	n/a
	zina			Muslim	al-Qasila	f	1718	29 Dhu'l Hijja 1130	removed	no
	gathering	off the straight path		Muslim	al-Bandara	m	1718	20 Muharram 1131	removed	n/a
	zina (rape)			Muslim	village of Nayrab (Aleppo)	m	1719	18 Safar 1131	none	n/a
	gathering	evildoer		Muslim	Ma'adi (Bab al-Maqam)	mf	1719	29 Safar 1131	removed	yes
	zina (rape)	kidnapping		Muslim	al-Maliha (Nahiya al-Jabul)	m	1719	6 Jumada al-Awwal 1131	hadd	n/a
	gathering	evildoers		Muslim	Jubb Asad Allah	mf	1719	18 Rabi' al-Akhir 1131	removed	yes
	gathering	pimping		Muslim	al-'Aynayn (Bab al-Jenayn)	m	1734	2 Rajab 1147	removed	no
	picking up women	evildoer		Muslim	Outside Bab al-Nasr	m	1734	4 Rajab 1147	removed from guild	n/a
	picking up women	sex with young boys (ghilman)		Muslim	Bab Allah village (Jabal Sam'an)	m	1734	6 Jumada al-Akhir 1147	removed	n/a
Fatima bint Shaykh Ramadan	gathering	fornication		Muslim	Zuqaq al-Arba'in	mfffff	1735	17 Dhu'l Qa'da 1147	removed	yes
	gathering	fornication		Muslim	al-'Atawi al-Saghir	mf	1735	26 Dhu'l Qa'da 1147	removed	yes

TABLE A2.1

ALL *ZINA*-TYPE CASES FOUND WITHIN THE SELECTED ALEPPO *SIJILLS*

Case Type	Sijill	Page	Document	Defendant 1	Defendant 2	Defendant 3	Defendant 4	Defendant 5	Defendant 6
Criminal	55	115	363	Muhammad ibn Hajj 'Ali					
Criminal	55	124	395	Bayad ibn Ibrahim	Amina bint Sanduq (wife)	'A'isha bint Musa (unrelated)			
Criminal	55	137	434	Taha ibn Bilal					
Criminal	55	152	481	Muhammad ibn Ahmad	Hajj 'Ali ibn Hajj Ibrahim	Khadija bint Hussein (procuress)			
Criminal	55	163	517	Fatima bint Ibrahim					
Criminal	55	166	526	Basil walad Yusuf					
Criminal	55	271	822	Ahmad ibn Jasar	Hajj Hussein ibn 'Abdallah	Khalil ibn (blank) al-Birawi			
Criminal	55	272	824	Hagop walad Nerses the Armenian	Rumiya bint Halabsha (absent, mother-in-law)				
Criminal	55	322	974	Mustafa ibn 'Uthman al-Ghuayshabi	unnamed wife (absent)				
Criminal	55	328	991	'Abdallah ibn Ahmad	'Aud ibn 'Abdallah	Hajj Hussein ibn Isma'il		Mustafa (brother of Hajj Hussein)	
Criminal	64	85	233	Taha ibn Muhammad	Hajj Mustafa ibn Hajj Jum'a	Tayyiba bint Hilal (mother)	Hajj Muhammad ibn Hajj Asad	Sa'id ibn Hajj Hijazi	
Criminal	64	94	257	Fatima bint Darwish al-Kurdiyya	Ismail ibn Ya'qub al-Kurdi				
Criminal	64	153	432	Karima bint Hajj 'Ali al-Sisu	Hajj Haydar ibn 'Abd al-Latif (husband, absent)				
Criminal	64	172	495	Hajj Muhammad ibn Rajab	Mustafa (brother)	Fatima bint Muhammad			
Criminal	85	16	45	Hadhr and Ahmad sons of (blank)					
Criminal	85	32	85	Shaykh Mansur	Shaykh 'Abd al-Qadir (his son)	Sheikh Muhammad			
Criminal	85	78	211	Fatima bint Hajj 'Ali					
Criminal	85	92	249	Sayyid 'Abd al-Wahab ibn Sayyid Muhammad					

↓ *(Columns continue on page 178)*

Defendant 7	Crime type 1	Crime type 2	Crime type 3	Religion	Neighborhood	Gender	Christian Date	Date Hijra	Punishment	Related?
	fornication	homosexuality		Muslim	al-Masabin	m	1735	25 Dhu'l Qa'da 1147	removed	no
	gathering	prostitution	harmful	Muslim	Arba'in	mff	1735	23 Dhu'l Hijja 1147	removed/ ta'zir bi'l darb and imprisoned	yes
	drinking	fornication	homosexuality (ghilman)	Muslim	Sahat Biza	m	1735	8 Muharram 1148	ta'zir bi'l darb	no
gathering	fornication			Muslim	Tall 'Aran	mmf	1735	4 Safar 1148	ta'zir bi'l darb	no
	gathering	evildoer	harmful	Muslim	Jubb Asad Allah	f	1735	6 Rabi' al-Awwal 1148	removed	n/a
	rape			Christian	al-Qawwas, outside Bab al-Nasr	f	1735	16 Rabi' al-Awwal 1148	none	n/a
	gathering	fornication	harmful	Muslim	al-Hajjaj	mmm	1736	26 Sha'ban 1148	removed	no
fornication	drinking	harmful		Christian	Akyol	mf	1736	24 Sha'ban 1148	removed	yes
	gathering	fornication	harmful	Muslim	Dudu	mf	1736	3 Dhu'l Hijja 1148	removed	yes
gathering	cursing	evildoers		Muslim	inside Bab al-Nayrab	mmmm	1736	14 Dhu'l Hijja 1148	removed	yes
	gathering	prostitution	drinking	Muslim	Qal'a	mm	1741	4 Rabi' al-Awwal 1154	removed	yes
	zina (rape)			Muslim	Village of Matara (outside Aleppo)	f	1741	12 Rabi' al-Awwal 1154	none	no
gathering	evildoer			Muslim	Qal'a	mf	1741	23 Jumada al-Awwal 1154	removed	yes
	gathering	pimping		Muslim	al-Mugha'ir	mmf	1741	6 Rajab 1154	removed	yes
	picking up women	cursing	evildoers	Muslim	al-Balat	mm	1754	15 Rajab 1167	removed	yes
	gathering	cheating weights		Muslim	Cotton Market (Central Market)	mmm	1657	7 Sha'ban 1167	none	yes
	gathering	evildoer		Muslim	al-Qasila	f	1754	29 Shawwal 1167	removed	n/a
gathering	evildoer			Muslim	al-Jallum al-Kubra	m	1754	1 Dhu'l Hijja 1167	removed	n/a

TABLE A2.1

ALL *ZINA*-TYPE CASES FOUND WITHIN THE SELECTED ALEPPO *SIJILLS*

Case Type	Sijill	Page	Document	Defendant 1	Defendant 2	Defendant 3	Defendant 4	Defendant 5	Defendant 6
Criminal	85	146	200	Sayyid Ahmad ibn Hajj Muhammad al-Dawalibi					
Criminal	85	193	553	Sayyid Hashem ibn Sayyid Ahmad	Situt bint Muhammad	Layla bint Hajj 'Uthman			
Criminal	85	293	813	Hajj Ahmad ibn Ala' al-Din al-Hamrawi	his unnamed wife				
Criminal	85	298	829	Khadija bint Hajj Nasr					
Testimonial	94	40	80	Khadija bint Muhammad al-Kilisiyya					
Criminal	94	66	125	'Abd al-Qadir ibn Hajj Asad al-Samman					
Testimonial	94	81	166	Khadija bint Shaykh Salih					
Testimonial	94	82	171	Myriam bint 'Abdallah					
Testimonial	94	86	179	Khadija bint Sayyid Mustafa					
Criminal	94	123	269	Khanum bint Hajj 'Ali ibn Hajj Muhammad	Sayyid Bakri ibn Hajj Muhammad				
Testimonial	113	18	50	Rahmat bint Musa al-Shamiyya					
Testimonial	113	92	242	Myriam bint 'Abdallah (convert to Islam)					
Testimonial	113	127	302	Myriam bint Hajj Muhammad					
Criminal	113	128	304	Sayyid Ahmad ibn Hajj Muhammad	Khadija bint Bakri (wife)				
Testimonial	113	140	341	Zaynab bint Hajj Ahmad al-'Ayntabiyya					
Testimonial	113	178	460	Zamzam bint Suleyman al-Hamwiyya					
Criminal	113	181	443	Taha ibn Ahmad					
Criminal	113	233	584	Sayyid Qasim ibn Sayyid 'Ali					
Testimonial	113	234	585	Safiya bint Ramadan al-Birejikliyya					
Testimonial	113	276	691	Fatima bint Hajj 'Abd al-Karim					

↓ *(Columns continue on page 180)*

Defendant 7	Crime type 1	Crime type 2	Crime type 3	Religion	Neighborhood	Gender	Christian Date	Date Hijra	Punishment	Related?
picking up women	evildoer		harmful	Muslim	Hawarina	m	1764	13 Rabi' al-Awwal 1178	removed	n/a
	gathering	evildoers	cursing	Muslim	Dudu	mff	1764	14 Jumada al-Akhir 1178	removed	no
	gathering	drinking	cursing	Muslim	Mugha'ir	mf	1765	17 Shawwal 1178	removed	yes
	gathering	evildoer		Muslim	Muhammad Bey	f	1765	1 Dhu'l-Qa'da 1178	removed	n/a
	prostitution			Muslim	al-A'jam	f	1762	3 Rajab 1175	none	n/a
	picking up women	evildoer	vicious tongued	Muslim	Suq Bab al-Janayn	m	1762	6 Sha'ban 1175	removed	no
	prostitution			Muslim	Shaykh 'Arabi	f	1762	4 Ramadan 1175	none	n/a
	prostitution			Muslim	not listed	f	1762	3 Ramadan 1175	none	n/a
	prostitution			Muslim	al-A'jam	f	1660	13 Ramadan 1170	none	n/a
	gathering	cursing	evildoers	Muslim	Altunbogha	mf	1762	4 Dhu'l Hijja 1175	removed	yes
	prostitution			Muslim	Sahat Biza	f	1775	16 Rabi' al-Awwal 1189	none	n/a
prostitution				Muslim	Sahat Biza	f	1775	30 Sha'ban 1189	none	n/a
	prostitution			Muslim	Sahat Biza	f	1776	6 Muharram 1190	none	n/a
	gathering	harmful		Muslim	al-Bandara	mf	1776	8 Muharram 1190	removed	yes
	prostitution			Muslim	al-Qasila	f	1776	19 Muharram 1190	none	n/a
	prostitution			Muslim	Hama (Syria)	f	1776	29 Rabi' al-Thani 1190	none	n/a
	gathering	prostitution	harmful	Muslim	al-'Aynayn	m	1776	19 Rabi' al-Thani 1190	removed	n/a
		mixing non-Muslim and Muslim women		Muslim	al-Farafira (Hamam al-Zamr)	m	1776	17 Rajab 1190	none	n/a
	prostitution			Muslim	Birecik (Turkey)	f	1776	21 Rajab 1190	none	n/a
	prostitution			Muslim	al-Basha (at Bab al-Hadid)	f	1776	22 Jumada al-Akhir 1190	none	n/a

Table A2.1

All *Zina*-Type Cases Found Within the Selected Aleppo *Sijills*

Case Type	Sijill	Page	Document	Defendant 1	Defendant 2	Defendant 3	Defendant 4	Defendant 5	Defendant 6
Criminal	113	305	768	Fatima bint 'Abd al-Karim	Khadija (sister)	Sayyid Mustafa ibn Sayyid Hussein			
Testimonial	130	122	321	Sharf bint Hajj Mustafa ibn 'Abdallah					
Criminal	130	166	415	'Abd al-Baqi Lughud Badran					
Criminal	149	28	70	Sabah bint Sayyid Mustafa al-Qassab					
Criminal	149	155	420	'A'isha bint 'Ali	daughter (unnamed)				
Testimonial	153	18	45	Amina bint Ahmad al-Qattan					
Testimonial	153	25	70	Madul bint Yusuf					
Testimonial	154	1	2	Alif bint Ibrahim					
Testimonial	154	2	5	Ruqaya bint Isma'il					
Testimonial	154	2	6	'A'isha bint Hajj Ibrahim al-Niyyal					
Testimonial	208	8	14	'Azza bint Mikha'ak					
Testimonial	208	33	75	Zamzam bint Ibrahim al-Kabbal					
Testimonial	208	53	124	Kiz bint Yusuf al-Siriyaniyya					
Testimonial	208	85	198	Na'ma bint Qasim					
Testimonial	208	115	274	'Afiya bint Mustafa					
Testimonial	208	126	300	Haliba bint Hajj Hamid					
Testimonial	208	249	592	Fatima bint Yusuf al-Shamiyya					
Testimonial	208	294	723	Houriyya bint al-Sayyid Ahmad al-Antakiyya					
Testimonial	208	304	747	'A'isha bint Khalil al-Adanaliyya					
Testimonial	232	30	77	Saliha bint Abi Bakri al-???					
Testimonial	232	32	79	Amina bint Hajj 'Ali al-Shamiyya					
Testimonial	232	53	126	Myriam bint 'Abdallah (convert to Islam)					

↓ *(Columns continue on page 182)*

Defendant 7	Crime type 1	Crime type 2	Crime type 3	Religion	Neighborhood	Gender	Christian Date	Date Hijra	Punishment	Related?
gathering	harmful			Muslim	al-Akrad	mff	1777	16 Muharram 1191	removed	yes
	prostitution			Muslim	al-Qal'a	f	1786	4 Dhu'l Qa'da 1200	none	n/a
	gathering			Muslim	Qastal al-Zaytun ('Antar Quarter)	m	1786	15 Safar 1201	none	n/a
	gathering	cursing	harmful	Muslim	al-Qasila	f	1801	7 Dhu'l Qa'da 1215	removed	n/a
	gathering	cursing	harmful	Muslim	Shaykh 'Arabi	ff	1802	7 Shawwal 1216	removed	yes
	prostitution			Muslim	Bab al-Nayrab	f	1803	22 Rabi' al-Awwal 1218	none	n/a
	prostitution			Christian	unnamed	f	1803	3 Jumada al-Awwal 1218	none	n/a
	prostitution			Muslim	unnamed	f	1804	5 Rabi' al-Awwal 1219	none	n/a
	prostitution			Muslim	unnamed	f	1804	13 Rabi' al-Thani 1219	none	n/a
	prostitution			Muslim	unnamed	f	1804	16 Rabi' al-Thani 1219	none	n/a
	prostitution			Christian	Akyol	f	1826	14 Jumada al-Akhir 1241	none	n/a
	prostitution			Muslim	al-Qasila	f	1826	4 Jumada al-Thani 1241	none	n/a
	prostitution			Christian	not listed	f	1826	17 Jumada al-Akhir 1241	none	n/a
	prostitution			Muslim	al-A'jam	f	1826	19 Jumada al-Thani 1241	none	n/a
	prostitution			Muslim	Bab al-Nayrab	f	1826	16 Rajab 1241	none	n/a
	prostitution			Muslim	Karlik	f	1826	2 Sha'ban 1241	none	n/a
	prostitution			Muslim	Damascus (Syria)	f	1826	8 Sha'ban 1241	none	n/a
	prostitution			Muslim	Antakiya (Turkey)	f	1826	24 Shawwal 1241	none	n/a
	prostitution			Muslim	Adana (Turkey)	f	1826	9 Shawwal 1241	none	n/a
	prostitution			Muslim	al-Mashariqa	f	1837	6 Dhu'l Qa'da 1252	none	n/a
	prostitution			Muslim	Ibn Ya'qub	f	1837	19 Shawwal 1252	none	n/a
	prostitution			Muslim	Qastal al-Harami	f	1837	12 Dhu'l Qa'da 1252	none	n/a

TABLE A2.1

ALL *ZINA*-TYPE CASES FOUND WITHIN THE SELECTED ALEPPO *SIJILLS*

Case Type	Sijill	Page	Document	Defendant 1	Defendant 2	Defendant 3	Defendant 4	Defendant 5	Defendant 6
Testimonial	232	330	806	Myriam bint Bakri al-Shamiyya					
Testimonial	232	339	833	Fatima bint Shaykh Mustafa al-Antakiyaliyya					
Testimonial	232	???	470	Amina bint Muhammad al-Baroudi					
Testimonial	239	165	388	Ruqaya bint al-Sayyid Muhammad Barakat al-Ladaqiyya					
Testimonial	239	267	960	Fatima bint Muhammad al-Sharbaji al-Shamiyya					
Testimonial	239	337	868	'A'isha bint Hussein al-Hariri al-Shamiyya					
Testimonial	239	345	894	Myriam bint ?					
Testimonial	239	346	895	'A'isha bint Hajj 'Abd al-Qadir al-Durziyya					
Testimonial	261	3	5	Fatima bint N'ama al-Sarraj al-Mar'ashliyya					
Testimonial	261	140	100	Amina bint 'Abdallah al-Diyarbakirli al-Shamiyya					
Testimonial	261	242	452	'A'isha bint Ibrahim al-Mawda' al-Hamawiyya					
Testimonial	261	459	615	Fatima bint Mustafa					
Testimonial	296	15	22	Zaynab bint Ahmad ibn 'Abd al-Bari					
Testimonial	296	209	274	Fatima bint Hassan al-'Atari					
Testimonial	296	233	307	'A'isha bint Mustafa al-Ladaqiyya					
Testimonial	296	310	416	Nahda bint Muhammad al-Kilisiyya					

Defendant 7	Crime type 1	Crime type 2	Crime type 3	Religion	Neighborhood	Gender	Christian Date	Date Hijra	Punishment	Related?
	prostitution			Muslim	Khan al-Sabil	f	1837	2 Jumada al-Awwal 1253	none	n/a
	prostitution			Muslim	Antakiya (Turkey)	f	1837	6 Jumada al-Awwal 1253	none	n/a
	prostitution			Muslim	al-Jallum al-Kubra	f	1837	28 Muharram 1253	none	n/a
	prostitution			Muslim	Latakia (Syria)	f	1841	19 Jumada al-Awwal 1257	none	n/a
	prostitution			Muslim	Damascus (Syria)	f	1841	12 Dhu'l Qa'da 1257	none	n/a
	prostitution			Muslim	Damascus (Syria)	f	1841	10 Shawwal 1257	none	n/a
	prostitution			Muslim	Illegible	f	1841	20 Shawwal 1257	none	n/a
	prostitution			Druze	al-Almaji	f	1841	9 Shawwal 1257	none	n/a
	prostitution			Muslim	Marash (Turkey)	f	1851	12 Jumada al-Akhir 1267	none	n/a
	prostitution			Muslim	Damascus (Syria)	f	1851	17 Sha'ban 1267	none	n/a
	prostitution			Muslim	Bandara	f	1851	4 Rabi' al-Awwal 1268	none	n/a
	prostitution			Muslim	not listed	f	1851	28 Dhu'l Qa'da 1267	none	n/a
	prostitution			Muslim	village of Fafirtin	f	1866	6 Jumada al-Awwal 1283	none	n/a
	prostitution			Muslim	Al-Shamisatiyya	f	1866	11 Jumada al-Awwal 1283	none	n/a
	prostitution			Muslim	Al-Shamisatiyya	f	1866	25 Rajab 1283	none	n/a
	prostitution			Muslim	Al Shamisatiyya	f	1867	11 Ramadan 1283	none	n/a

Notes

1. *Sijillat al-Mahakim Halab* (hereafter cited as *SMH*) 27:18:63 21 Muharram 1071 A.H./September 1660.

2. More recent cases of convictions of stoning have occurred in places such as Iran, Nigeria, the United Arab Emirates (UAE), and Saudi Arabia. In Iran, a moratorium on stoning was issued in 2002 by Ayatollah Shahroudi, the head of the Iranian judiciary. Currently, there is a stay of execution for a couple who bore an out-of-wedlock child eleven years ago (Mark Tran, "Iran Stays Execution by Stoning"). A case in the UAE is detailed in Bassma al-Jandaly's article "Death by Stoning Case Goes to Supreme Court," *Gulf News*, January 31, 2007. Two Nigerian women, Safiya Husseini and Amina Lawal, successfully appealed their stoning convictions in Nigeria, and both happened to be cases of out-of-wedlock pregnancy ("Shari'a Court Frees Nigerian Woman"; and Dan Isaacs's article "Nigerian Woman Fights Stoning"). The Associated Press reported a stoning in a Mazar-e Sharif stadium in Afghanistan under the Taliban ("Taliban Stone Woman for Adultery," May 1, 2000). Janelle Brown describes an often broadcast video of a Taliban public execution of a woman accused of adultery in a Kabul soccer stadium; the woman identified only as Zarmina was killed with a rifle shot to the head ("The Taliban's Bravest Opponents"). A posting of the Associated Press article related to this case, as well as the original video of the execution, can be found on the Web site of the Revolutionary Association of Women of Afghanistan (RAWA) ("Taliban Publicly Execute Women").

3. For a full reference of all court registers consulted in this research as well as my research methodology, see chapter 3. Although I have found no cases of stoning in Aleppo, Fariba Zarinebaf has found a case mentioned in her unpublished paper, "Regulating Prostitution in 18th Century Istanbul." Zarinebaf's case from the seventeenth century was of a Muslim woman who married a Jew; he was forcibly converted to Islam, and they were both stoned to death. This study is part of her forthcoming book, "The Mediterranean's Metropolis: Urban Transformation, Crime, and Social Control in Eighteenth-Century Istanbul." The same *zina* case between a Muslim woman and a Jewish man, resulting in stoning, is discussed in Marc Baer's article "Islamic Conversion Narratives of Women: Social Change and Gendered Religious Heirarchy in Early Modern Ottoman Istanbul," 436. Madeline Zilfi first discussed this case earlier in her study *The Politics of Piety*. Boğaç Ergene has found few references to stoning but shared one case with me concerning the rape of a virgin

slave named Belkis from the Kastamonu registers from 1789. The rapist was sentenced to execution by stoning (personal communication).

4. Joseph Schacht, "Zina," in *Encyclopedia of Islam,* 4:1227.

5. I use the term *"zina"*-related because the courts sometimes used the term *zina* and sometimes used euphemisms to describe the crime. See chapter 4 on the use of euphemisms.

6. Abraham Marcus, *The Middle East on the Eve of Modernity: Aleppo in the Eighteenth Century*; Margaret L. Meriwether, *The Kin Who Count: Family and Society in Ottoman Aleppo, 1770– 1840*; Bruce Masters, *The Origins of Western Dominance in the Middle East: Mercantilism and the Islamic Economy in Aleppo, 1600–1750* and *Christians and Jews in the Ottoman Arab World: The Roots of Sectarianism*; Abdul Karim Rafeq, "The Syrian 'Ulama, Ottoman Law, and Islamic Shari'a," "Craft Organization, Work Ethics, and the Strains of Change in Ottoman Syria," and "Local Forces in Syria in the Seventeenth and Eighteenth Centuries."

7. Abdul Karim Rafeq, "Public Morality in 18th Century Damascus."

8. Preference was given to legal sources in this study owing to the wealth of documentation. Accordingly, chronicles and travel accounts were used occasionally for context but not similarly surveyed.

9. Two articles by Amira Sonbol exemplify her method of combining *fiqh* and *sijills.* See "Law and Gender Violence in Ottoman and Modern Egypt" and "Rape and Law in Ottoman and Modern Egypt." Judith Tucker's method of combining the fatwas of three muftis alongside *sijills* from Damascus, Nablus, and Jerusalem can be seen in her book *In the House of the Law: Gender and Law in Ottoman Syria and Palestine.* Leslie Peirce analyzes Hanafi *fiqh,* imperial fatwas, and *sijills* from 'Ayntab in *Morality Tales: Law and Gender in the Ottoman Court of Aintab.*

10. Recent examples of microhistories in Middle Eastern history include Peirce, *Morality Tales*; and Cem Behar, *A Neighborhood in Ottoman Istanbul: Fruit Vendors and Civil Servants in the Kasap İlyas Mahalle.*

11. Two classic examples of microhistorical approaches in European history include Carlo Ginzburg, *The Cheese and the Worms: The Cosmos of a Sixteenth-Century Miller*; and Natalie Zemon Davis, *The Return of Martin Guerre.*

12. Dror Ze'evi wrote a thought-provoking article that discusses the pitfalls of using the shari'a court records, particularly the speculative process of understanding what lies behind "the *sijill* façade" ("The Use of Ottoman Shari'a Court Records as a Source for Middle Eastern Social History: A Reappraisal").

13. Women may have practiced *ijtihad* before Fatima Mernissi, but it is not well documented. See Mernissi, *The Veil and the Male Elite: A Feminist Interpretation of Women's Rights in Islam.* There are too many studies inspired by Mernissi's work to name here. Examples include a great deal of feminist exegeses of sacred texts and reinterpretations of women in Islam, such as Leila Ahmed, *Women and Gender in Islam: Historical Roots of a Modern Debate*; Asma Barlas, *"Believing Women" in Islam: Unreading Patriarchal Interpretations of the Qur'an*; Denise A. Spellberg, *Politics, Gender, and the Islamic Past: The Legacy of 'A'isha bint Abi Bakr*; Barbara Freyer Stowasser, *Women in the Qur'an, Traditions, and Interpretation*; and Amina Wadud, *Qur'an and Woman: Rereading the*

Sacred Text from a WomanXs Perspective. Judith Tucker has noted that she follows in the path of Mernissi (*In the House of the Law,* 9).

14. This theme has been explored by Sami Zubaida in *Law and Power in the Islamic World.*

15. Mernissi, *Veil and the Male Elite,* 19.

16. Karl Wlttfogel, *Oriental Despotism: A Comparative Study of Total Power.* The history and development of Oriental despotism is well documented by Ervand Abrahamian in "Oriental Despotism: The Case of Qajar Iran," 3–9.

17. This description has been taken from the work of Lawrence Rosen, which draws heavily on the Weberian notions of Islamic justice (*The Anthropology of Justice: Law as Culture in Islamic Society,* 59).

18. See Max Weber, *Max Weber on Law in Economy and Society,* 213; and Bryan S. Turner, *Weber and Islam: A Critical Study,* 107–21.

19. Some more recent studies have continued to adhere to the Orientalist position that the "gates of *ijtihad*" were closed. See Dror Ze'evi, *Producing Desire: Changing Sexual Discourse in the Ottoman Middle East, 1500–1900,* 49. I have also noticed the argument being advanced, without including the revisionist arguments against the closing, in texts such as Mohammad Hashim Kamali's "Law and Society: The Interplay of Revelation and Reason in the Shariah," 115–16.

20. See, for example, Brinkley Messick, *The Calligraphic State: Textual Domination and History in Muslim Society*; and David Powers, "Kadijustiz or Qadi-Justice? A Paternity Dispute from Fourteenth-Century Morocco." Both authors edited several articles, along with Muhammad Khaled Masud, in a volume titled *Islamic Legal Interpretation: Muftis and Their Fatwas.* Many of the contributors to this volume are engaged in this important field of study and are regular contributors to a journal dedicated to this field titled *Islamic Law and Society,* published by E. J. Brill. See also Wael Hallaq, *A History of Islamic Legal Theories: An Introduction to Sunni "Usul al-Fiqh."*

21. Haim Gerber, "Rigidity Versus Openness in Late Classical Islamic Law: The Case of the Seventeenth-Century Palestinian Mufti Khayr al-Din al-Ramli," 181n. 67.

22. Messick, *Calligraphic State*; Masud, Messick, and Powers, *Islamic Legal Interpretation*; David Powers, "Kadijustiz or Qadi-Justice?"; Tucker, *In the House of the Law.*

23. A few works came to the defense of Joseph Schacht and the argument about the closing of the gates of *ijtihad* soon after Hallaq's original article. See Norman Calder, "Al-Nawawi's Typology of Muftis and Its Significance for a General Theory of Islamic Law"; and Sherman Jackson, "*Taqlid,* Legal Scaffolding, and the Scope of Legal Injunctions in Post-formative Theory: *Mutlaq* and *'Amm* in the Jurisprudence of Shihab al-Din al-Qarafi." These works are referenced in Gerber, "Rigidity Versus Openness," 181n. 67. For the connection between fatwas and positive law, see Wael Hallaq, "From Fatwas to *Furu':* Growth and Change in Islamic Substantive Law."

24. The term *doctrine* is one that I have borrowed from David Powers that connotes law as found in the prescriptive literature of *fiqh* that stands in contrast to the everyday practice of law (personal conversation at Harvard University, May 2002).

25. Tucker, *In the House of the Law,* 10.

26. See table 3.1, which documents the court registers examined in this study as dating from 1507 to 1866.

27. Michel Foucault, "Truth and Juridical Forms," 2.

28. Yusuf Qushaqji, *Al-Amthal al-sha'biyya al-halabiyya wa amthal Mardin*, 1:155.

29. Jean Sauvaget, "Halab," 85.

30. Marcus, *Middle East*, 17.

31. Sauvaget, "Halab," 85.

32. Masters, *Origins of Western Dominance*, 13.

33. Marcus, *Middle East*, 19–21.

34. André Raymond, *The Great Arab Cities in the 16th and 17th Centuries: An Introduction*, 15.

35. Masters, *Origins of Western Dominance*, 42. See also André Raymond, *Urban Networks and Popular Movements in Cairo and Aleppo (End of the 18th–Beginning of the 19th Centuries)*, 255–56.

36. Masters, *Origins of Western Dominance*, 10.

37. Ibid.

38. Qushaqji, *Al-Amthal*, 155.

39. Masters, *Origins of Western Dominance*, 76. Meriwether also argues for increased integration into the world economy during the period 1750 to 1850 (*Kin Who Count*, 18).

40. Masters, *Origins of Western Dominance*, 3.

41. Masters discusses these alliances in *Christians and Jews*, specifically chap. 3, "Merchants and Missionaries in the Seventeenth Century: The West Intrudes," 68–97.

42. Yasser Tabbaa, *Constructions of Power and Piety in Medieval Aleppo*, 23.

43. Marcus, *Middle East*, 44, 318. This lack of segregation in Aleppo's quarters was true of later periods as well. See the detailed tables of the various quarters in Heinz Gaube and Eugen Wirth, *Aleppo: Historische and geographische Beiträge zur baulichen Gestaltung, zur sozialen Organisation und zur wirtschaftlichen Dynamik einer vorderasiatischen Fernhandelsmetropole*, 427–41. The intermixing of social classes within the city quarters is mentioned in Antoine Abdel Nour, *Introduction à l'histoire urbaine de la Syrie Ottomane (XVIè–XVIIIè siècle)*, 165; and Raymond, *Great Arab Cities*, 57.

44. Jean Sauvaget, *Alep: Essai sur le développement d'une grande ville syrienne, des origins au milieu du xixe siècle*, 224; André Raymond, *Alep à l'époque ottomane (XVIe–XIXe siècle)*, 95. Charles Wilkins has noted that the 1678 Tapu Tahrir of Aleppo shows the Bab al-Nasr region as the major commercial district of Aleppo (personal communication).

45. Sauvaget, *Alep*, 225.

46. One court record specifically cites the existence of a Jewish court in Aleppo. The case is of a Jewish woman who sold property to a Jewish man, yet the record makes a reference to the existence of the Jewish court of Aleppo (*SMH* 34:270:1212 8 Rajab 1090 A.H./August 1679, incorrectly numbered no. 1312 in the *sijill*).

47. Some early studies of non-Muslims in the courts can be found in the two-volume collection edited by Bernard Lewis and Benjamin Braude: see the articles by Amnon Cohen and Adnan Bakhit in *Christians and Jews in the Ottoman Empire: The Functioning of a Plural Society*.

More recent scholarship on non-Muslims in the empire can be found in Masters's *Christians and Jews* and in articles by M. Baer, "Islamic Conversion Narratives"; Fatma Müge Göçek, "The Legal Resource of Minorities in History: Eighteenth-Century Appeals to the Islamic Court of Galata"; and Najwa al-Qattan, "Across the Courtyard: Residential Space and Sectarian Boundaries in Ottoman Damascus."

48. Masters, *Origins of Western Dominance*, 19 (quote), 20.

49. Marcus, *Middle East*, 81.

50. Masters, *Origins of Western Dominance*, 23. Abdel Nour has argued that this shift did not affect Aleppo as much as other places because the city had strong links of trade with its hinterland (*Introduction à l'histoire urbaine*, 271).

51. Masters, *Origins of Western Dominance*, 30–33.

52. Herbert L. Bodman Jr., *Political Factions in Aleppo, 1760–1826*, viii.

53. Raymond, *Urban Networks and Popular Movements*, 262, 244–45 (quote on 245).

54. Marcus, *Middle East*, 73.

55. For more information on this period, see Moshe Ma'oz, *Ottoman Reform in Syria and Palestine, 1840–1861: The Impact of the Tanzimat on Politics and Society*, 15–20.

56. Meriwether, *Kin Who Count*, 20.

57. Ma'oz, *Ottoman Reform*, 22–23.

58. Roderic Davison, "Tanzimat," 204.

59. See Bruce Masters, "The 1850 Events in Aleppo: An Aftershock of Syria's Incorporation into the World Capitalist System,"

60. See Ma'oz, *Ottoman Reform*; and Iris Agmon, *Family and Court: Legal Culture and Modernity in Late Ottoman Palestine*.

61. The Nizami court is discussed further in chapter 3.

1. *ZINA* IN ISLAMIC LEGAL DISCOURSE

1. The Tanzimat and its impact on the courts is discussed in more detail in chapter 3. For information about the Tanzimat reforms and their purpose in "reordering" the Ottoman Empire, see Roderic Davison, *Reform in the Ottoman Empire, 1856–1876*; Ira Lapidus, *A History of Islamic Societies*, 598–601; and Ma'oz, *Ottoman Reform*. Its impact on Ottoman law can be found in Dora Glidewell Nadolski, "Ottoman and Secular Civil Law." For more recent scholarship critiquing the Tanzimat, see Ussama Makdisi, "Ottoman Orientalism," 770. A more recent critique of Davison's study can be found in Milen V. Petrov, "Everyday Forms of Compliance: Subaltern Commentaries on Ottoman Reform, 1864–1868."

2. This thesis is clearly articulated in the introduction and several articles found within Amira Sonbol, ed., *Women, the Family, and Divorce Laws in Islamic History*. Sonbol focuses elsewhere on the institution of domestic incarceration (*"Ta'a* and Modern Legal Reform: A Rereading"). Ann Elizabeth Mayer questions the impact of reform in modern North Africa toward women's rights in "Reform of Personal Status Laws in North Africa: A Problem of Islamic or Mediterranean Laws?"

3. Khaled Abou el Fadl, *Speaking God's Name: Islamic Law, Authority, and Women*, 173.

4. This argument also appears in Aziz al-Azmeh, *Islams and Modernities*, 12.

5. Haim Gerber, *Islamic Law and Culture, 1600–1840*, 80.

6. The scholarship concerning this debate has already been cited in the Introduction of this book.

7. J. Burton, "Naskh," 1011.

8. Joseph Schacht, *An Introduction to Islamic Law*, 77.

9. Colin Imber, *Ebu's-su'ud: The Islamic Legal Tradition*, 37.

10. Ze'evi, *Producing Desire*, 49.

11. B. F. Musallam, *Sex and Society in Islam: Birth Control Before the Nineteenth Century*. Musallam touches on a number of these issues in his groundbreaking analysis of birth control and sexuality. See his discussion of masturbation on p. 33, concubinage on p. 31, and birth control on pp. 15–16.

12. Ze'evi, *Producing Desire*, 55.

13. James A. Bellamy, "Sex and Society in Islamic Popular Literature," 30, 37; Rudolph Peters, *Crime and Punishment in Islamic Law: Theory and Practice from the Sixteenth to the Twenty-first Century*, 61.

14. I will be using Sunni hadith in this study since the court records used in the latter part of the study are in the Hanafi court of law.

15. Several modern gender historians have examined 'A'isha in the past couple decades. The most comprehensive study to date is Spellberg's examination of the early and later Muslim sources that include both Sunni and Shiite variations (*Politics, Gender, and the Islamic Past*). Spellberg uses several of the early Muslim histories that provided narratives of the "affair of the lie." See examples from Ibn Sa'd's *Tabaqat al-Kubra*, Ibn Hisham's *Kitab sirat rasul Allah*, and al-Baladhuri's *Ansab* in her study. Other gender histories include Mernissi, *Veil and the Male Elite*; and "'A'isha bint Abi Bakr," in *Middle Eastern Muslim Women Speak*, edited by Elizabeth Warnock Fernea and Basima Qattan Bezirgan, 27–36. These works were preceded by the work of Nabia Abbott in her biography, *Aishah, the Beloved of Muhammed*.

16. Spellberg, *Politics, Gender, and the Islamic Past*, 66.

17. Ibid., 72.

18. J. W. Wright, "Masculine Allusion and the Structure of Satire in Early 'Abbasid Poetry," 11.

19. A. A. Duri, *The Rise of Historical Writing among the Arabs*, 22–23. Duri's book is an important contribution to a debate about Arab and Islamic history. Often hadiths, in that they are a form of oral history, are dismissed by scholars of the Middle East who argue that they are not a genre of history writing. Like Duri, Tarif Khalidi has argued that hadiths are a form of science that developed out of a tradition of oral transmission performed by professional memorizers, and developed into a science of hadith scholarship (*Arabic Historical Thought in the Classical Period*).

20. Khalidi, *Arabic Historical Thought*, 17.

21. For a better discussion of the hadith of 'A'isha bint Abi Bakr, see "A Tradition of Misogyny (2)," chap. 4 of Mernissi, *Veil and the Male Elite*.

22. Mernissi frames her study in response to a schoolteacher who hurled a patriarchal hadith her way while she was shopping in a grocery story in Morocco (*Veil and the Male Elite*, 1–2).

23. Muhammad ibn Ahmad al-Sarakhsi, *Kitab al-Mabsut*, 9:36.

24. Abu 'Abdallah Muhammad ibn Isma'il al-Bukhari, *Sahih al Bukhari*, 8:529. Also found in Ahmad ibn Ali ibn Hajar al-Asqalani, *Fath al-bari sharh sahih al-Bukhari*, 12:153.

25. Bukhari, *Sahih al-Bukhari*, 8:537. The same hadith is recounted in Muhammad Ibn Ishaq, *The Life of Muhammad: A Translation of Ishaq's "Sirat Rasul Allah,"* 684–85; and 'Abdur Rahman I. Doi, *Shari'ah: The Islamic Law*, 239–40.

26. Burton, "Naskh," 1011.

27. Maurice Gaudefroy-Demombynes and T. Fahd, "Radjm," 379.

28. The punishment of public humiliation called *tajbiya* is reserved for those individuals guilty of unlawful intercourse where both offenders were mounted back-to-back on a donkey, paraded in humiliation, and driven out of town (Sir James W. Redhouse, *A Turkish and English Lexicon*, 497).

29. Al-Bukhari, *Sahih al-Bukhari*, 8:530.

30. The full text of this longer version of the hadith of Ma'iz is translated by Peters in *Crime and Punishment*, 55.

31. Hallaq, *History of Islamic Legal Theories*, 70.

32. Burhan al-Din Abu'l Hasan 'Ali ibn Abi Bakr ibn 'Abd al-Jalil al-Farghani al-Marginani, *Hedaya*, trans. Charles Hamilton (Lahore: Premier Book House, 1975), 177; single-volume second edition.

33. Ibid.; al-Sarakhsi, *Kitab al-Mabsut*, 9:37.

34. Al-'Asqalani, *Fath al-bari sharh sahih al-Bukhari*, 12:144.

35. Al-Marginani, *Hedaya*, 176.

36. Al-Bukhari, *Sahih al-Bukhari*, 8:531.

37. Peters, *Crime and Punishment*, 20.

38. Bellamy, "Sex and Society," 37.

39. Al-Bukhari, *Sahih al-Bukhari*, 8:545; Bellamy, "Sex and Society," 36.

40. Bellamy, "Sex and Society," 37.

41. Wright, "Masculine Allusion," 7.

42. Musallam notes that the Shafi'i jurist al-Nawawi also agreed with Ibn Malik on masturbation (*Sex and Society*, 33, 34).

43. See Wahba al-Zuhayli, *Al-fiqh al-islami wa 'adillatuhu*, 7:5350; and Khaled Fahmy, *All the Pasha's Men: Mehmed Ali, His Army, and the Making of Modern Egypt*, 150n. 167.

44. Barbara von Schlegell, "Sufism in the Ottoman Arab World: Sheikh 'Abd al-Ghani al-Nabulsi (d. 1143/1731)," 75.

45. Peters, *Crime and Punishment*, 61.

46. See also Bouhdiba, *Sexuality in Islam*, 187.

47. The two accounts are found in Bouhdiba, *Sexuality in Islam*, 188.

48. Mernissi, *Veil and the Male Elite*, 182–83.

49. Schacht, *Introduction to Islamic Law*, 29.

50. Schacht, "Hanafiyya."

51. Schacht, *Introduction to Islamic Law,* 43.

52. Ibid., 46.

53. Peters, *Crime and Punishment,* 71.

54. Schacht argues that the Hanafi code was chosen by the Ottomans because it "had always been a favourite of the Turkish peoples" (*Introduction to Islamic Law,* 89).

55. See Imber, *Ebu's-su'ud,* chap. 3, which discusses the role of the sultan in Hanafi jurisprudence.

56. Ibid., 30; Peirce, *Morality Tales,* 114.

57. Imber, *Ebu's-su'ud,* 30–31; Peirce, *Morality Tales,* 123.

58. Al-Marginani, *Hedaya,* 182 (emphasis added).

59. Ahmed Hafiz Nur, *Jarimat al-zina fi al-qanun al-misri wa al-muqarin,* 18.

60. Imber, *Ebu's-su'ud,* 236, concerning the legal category of *ghasb*; Hans Wehr, *A Dictionary of Modern Written Arabic,* 675; Schacht, "Zina."

61. Al-Sarakhsi, *Kitab al-Mabsut,* 5:78, 184. Also cited in Colin Imber, "*Zina* in Ottoman Law," 176.

62. Al-Sarakhsi, *Kitab al-Mabsut,* 5:81; al-Marginani, *Hedaya,* 44.

63. Al-Marginani, *Hedaya,* 44. Note that *darahim* is the plural of *dirham,* a unit of currency. The use of ten *darahim* as dowry is also noted in many Christian marriage contracts found in the Aleppo court, most noticeably in the eighteenth century, in which women consistently asked for dowries of 10 *ghrush* (the standard monetary unit in Ottoman Aleppo). Because of the consistency of the cases, it appears the courts used this hadith of the Prophet Muhammad as a basis for dowry. See some sample court cases in *SMH* 55 85:269 2 Shawwal 1146 A.H./March 1734; *SMH* 64:10:25 11 Dhu'l-Qa'da 1154 A.H./January 1742; *SMH* 64:122:336 15 Rabi' al-Thani 1154 A.H./June 1741; *SMH* 94:127:305 22 Muharram 1176 A.H./August 1762; *SMH* 130:74:194 12 Sha'ban 1200 A.H./June 1786; and *SMH* 157:61:140 5 Sha'ban 1220 A.H./October 1805.

64. E. Tyan, "Diya." See also Peters on *diya* and *arsh* (*Crime and Punishment,* 49–53).

65. Imber, *Ebu's-su'ud,* 238.

66. Ibrahim al-Halabi, *Al-Multaqa al-abhur,* 87. Also noted in Leslie Perice, *Morality Tales,* 89.

67. Peters, *Crime and Punishment,* 7.

68. Lawrence Rosen, *The Justice of Islam: Comparative Perspectives on Islamic Law and Society,* 75.

69. Gerber, *Islamic Law and Culture,* 39; Peters, *Crime and Punishment,* 65–67.

70. Peters, *Crime and Punishment,* 66.

71. Schacht, *Introduction to Islamic Law,* 179: Fadl Ilahi, *Al-Tadabir al-waqiya min al-zina fi al-fiqh al-Islami,* 48.

72. It is worth noting that during my study in the Aleppo archives, I did not find any cases of *li'an* divorce. But this fact could also be owing to the unique characteristics of the Aleppo archives in that *zina* is a word rarely used. Another possibility is that this type of divorce procedure existed more in theory than in practice.

73. Al-Bukhari, *Sahih al-Bukhari,* 9:67.

74. Sonbol, "Rape and Law," 223.

75. Peirce, *Morality Tales*, 90, 132.

76. Al-Marginani, *Hedaya*, 178. For the Hanbali reference, see the fatwa of Ibn Taymiyya in Ahmad ibn 'Abd al-Halim ibn Taymiyya, *Fatawa al-nisa'*, 294.

77. Muhammad Sharaf al-Din Khattab, *Jarimat al-zina wa 'uqubituha fi al-fiqh al-islami dirasah muqaranah*, 218. See also Gaudefroy-Demombynes and Fahd, "Radjm."

78. Peters, *Crime and Punishment*, 61. For a full definition of *muhsan*, see Shaykh Asad Muhammad Sa'id al-Saghirji, *Al-fiqh al-hanafi wa 'adillatuhu*, 2:294.

79. Peters, *Crime and Punishment*, 61, 63.

80. Muhammad Faruq al-Nabhan, *Mabahith fi al-tashri' al-jina'i al-Islami: Al-qatl, al-zina, al-sariqah*, 306.

81. This problem is addressed in Asifa Quraishi, "Her Honor: An Islamic Critique of the Rape Laws of Pakistan from a Woman-Sensitive Perspective," 119–20. Peirce discusses the problematic treatment of women's testimony in *Morality Tales*, 147.

82. Al-Nabhan, *Mabahith fi al-tashri'*, 306, 309.

83. Ibid., 308; al-Halabi, *Al-Multaqa al-abhur*, 87; Peters, *Crime and Punishment*, 37.

84. Peters, *Crime and Punishment*, 37; Sadiq ibn Muhammad al-Saqazi, *Surat al-fatawa al-Saqazi*, 62.

85. Al-Halabi, *Al-Multaqa al-abhur*, 78; Khattab, *Jarimat al-zina*, 251. The size of the stones is also mentioned in Peters, *Crime and Punishment*, 37.

86. Al-Halabi, *Al-Multaqa al-abhur*, 88; Khattab, *Jarimat al-zina*, 249.

87. Al-Marginani, *Hedaya*, 180.

88. All accounts of the stoning of al-Ghamidiyya are taken from al-'Asqalani, *Fath al-bari sharh sahih al-Bukhari*, 12:454–58.

89. Al-Marginani, *Hedaya*, 181. See also al-Sarakhsi, *Kitab al-Mabsut*, 9:101. Al-'Asqalani, *Fath al-bari sharh sahih al-Bukhari*, discusses it in 12:174–77.

90. Al-Marginani, *Hedaya*, 179–80; Peters, *Crime and Punishment*, 37.

91. Al-Marginani, *Hedaya*, 180.

92. Freidoune Sahebjam, *The Stoning of Soraya M.* The biblical passage noted reads: "The dogs shall eat Jezebel in the territory of Jezreel, and no one shall bury her" (2 Kings 9:10).

93. Al-Marginani, *Hedaya*, 178.

94. Ibid., 182; al-Sarakhsi, *Kitab al-Mabsut*, 9:73; al-'Asqalani, *Fath al-bari sharh sahih al-Bukhari*, 12:455.

95. Cited in al-Marginani, *Hedaya*, 176.

96. Al-Halabi, *Al-Multaqa al-abhur*, 87.

97. *Ta'zir* amongst the Ottomans was bastinado: "The culprit was laid on the ground and his feet were immobilised between a stout pole or board (*falaka*) and a rope passed through two holes at its ends. Two men lifted the pole so that only the offender's shoulders touched the ground. Two others then inflicted strokes on the bare soles (and other parts of the body) with long pliant sticks about one finger thick" (Uriel Heyd, *Studies in Old Ottoman Criminal Law*, 273).

98. Muhammad ibn 'Abd al-Rahman al-'Uthmani, *Rahmat al-ummah fi ikhtilaf al-a'immah: Fatawa a'immat al-madhahib al-arba'ah, Abu Hanifah, Malik, al-Shafi'i, Ahman ibn Hanbal*, 284; al-Sarakhsi, *Kitab al-Mabsut*, 9:43; al-Saqazi, *Surat al-fatawa al-Saqazi*, 63.

99. Doi notes that some jurists found the lashing prior to stoning for married offenders redundant and contradictory to other hadiths where the Prophet prescribed only stoning (*Shari'ah*, 238; see also al-Marginani, *Hedaya*, 181; and al-Sarakhsi, *Kitab al-Mabsut*, 9:43–44).

100. Al-Marginani, *Hedaya*, 179; al-Halabi, *Al-Multaqa al-abhur*, 88.

101. Al-Marginani, *Hedaya*, 179.

102. Al-Nabhan, *Mabahith fi al-tashri'*, 307, 306.

103. Al-Marginani, *Hedaya*, 179; al-Halabi, *Al-Multaqa al-abhur*, 87.

104. Al-Marginani, *Hedaya*, 179.

105. Al-Nabhan, *Mabahith fi al-tashri'*, 305; al-Sarakhsi, *Kitab al-Mabsut*, 9:100.

106. Fahmy, *All the Pasha's Men*, 128.

2. ZINA IN OTTOMAN LAW

1. Parts of this chapter were previously published in a book chapter titled "Gender Violence in *Kanunnames* and *Fetvas* of the Sixteenth Century."

2. For consistency in style, I will use the Arabic spelling of *fatwa* versus the Turkish term *fetva* for juridical opinions in the Ottoman tradition.

3. Some studies have used Ottoman fatwas from Arab muftis to varying degrees. A few examples include Masud, Messick, and Powers, *Islamic Legal Interpretation*; Tucker, *In the House of the Law*; and von Schlegell, "Sufism in the Ottoman Arab World."

4. Good examples of provincial fatwas can be found in Tucker, *In the House of the Law*; and von Schlegell, "Sufism in the Ottoman Arab World."

5. Imber, *Ebu's-su'ud*, 6.

6. Heyd, *Old Ottoman Criminal Law*, 196; Peirce, *Morality Tales*, 313–18.

7. Imber, "*Zina* in Ottoman Law," 182; al-Marginani, *Hedaya*, 176; Heyd, *Old Ottoman Criminal Law*, 280; Schacht, *Introduction to Islamic Law*, 69.

8. Imber, "*Zina* in Ottoman Law," 183.

9. *Shubha* is also discussed by Powers in "Kadijustiz or Qadi-Justice?" 339, 358.

10. Al-Marginani, *Hedaya*, 182; Imber, "*Zina* in Ottoman Law," 177.

11. Imber, "*Zina* in Ottoman Law," 179.

12. Al-Saqazi, *Surat al-fatawa al-Saqazi*, 63; Tucker, *In the House of the Law*, 161. The prevalence of prostitution is fully documented in chapter 5.

13. Imber, "*Zina* in Ottoman Law," 177, 178 (quote). Imber cites examples from Hanafi jurists al-Kuduri and al-Sarakhsi.

14. Imber, *Ebu's-su'ud*, 6.

15. Dick Douwes, *The Ottomans in Syria: A History of Justice and Oppression*, 212.

16. Heyd, *Old Ottoman Criminal Law*, 177.

17. Boğaç A. Ergene, *Local Court, Provincial Society, and Justice in the Ottoman Empire: Legal Practice and Dispute Resolution in Çankırı and Kastamonu, 1652–1744*, 104.

18. This ideal vision of Ottoman justice has been challenged in recent studies. See Douwes, *Ottomans in Syria*; Ergene, *Local Court*, 104; and Van Den Boogert, *The Capitulations and the Ottoman Legal System: Qadis, Consuls, and Beratlıs in the 18th Century*.

19. Huri İslamoğu-İnan, *State and Peasant in the Ottoman Empire: Agrarian Power and Regional Economic Development in Ottoman Anatolia During the Sixteenth Century*, 7.

20. Douwes, *Ottomans in Syria*, 153.

21. Imber, *Ebu's-su'ud*, 38 (quote), 95.

22. Ibid., 89–90. See chapter 3 of the same work for a discussion of the role of the sultan in Hanafi jurisprudence.

23. Uriel Heyd, *"Kanun and Shari'a in Old Ottoman Criminal Justice,"* 3.

24. Halil Inalcik, "Suleiman the Lawgiver and Ottoman Law," 116; Inalcik, *The Ottoman Empire: The Classical Age, 1300–1600*, 70.

25. Inalcik, "Suleiman the Lawgiver," 116.

26. The *kanunnames* of Aleppo are found in the Başbakanlık Archives in Istanbul as folio no. 493, *Kanunname Liwa' Haleb*. I would like to thank Charles Wilkins of Harvard University for giving me a copy of it. The earlier version of the *Kanunname Liwa' Haleb* issued by Sultan Süleyman is published along with the *kannuname* of Selim I for Bilad al-Sham in Ahmed Akgündüz, *Osmanlı Kanunnâmeleri ve Hukukî Tahlilleri*, vols. 5 and 3. Neither of the *kanunnames* deals with criminal matters. Heyd affirms that provincial *kanunnames* did not contain criminal codes, as the Ottoman criminal code was already in place. There were three exceptions: Niğbolu (Nikopol), Cephalonia, and Montenegro (*Old Ottoman Criminal Law*, 38, 41).

27. I would like to thank Yvonne Seng, who introduced me to the *kanunname* of Selim I when she taught Ottoman Turkish at Georgetown from 1996 to 1998. That being said, any errors in translation or interpretation are my own. For Heyd's translation of the *kanunname* of Süleyman, see his *Old Ottoman Criminal Law*. There are several untranslated copies of Ottoman *kanunnames* that have been published in both the original Ottoman script and transliteration by Ahmed Akgündüz. These resources are excellent for anyone who seeks to systematically chart the development of the *kanunname*. See *Osmanlı Kanunnâmeleri ve Hukukî Tahlilleri*.

28. Inalcik, "Suleiman the Lawgiver," 118, 126.

29. Imber, *Ebu's-su'ud*, 245.

30. Heyd, *Old Ottoman Criminal Law*, 95.

31. Ibid., 96 (quotes). Heyd argues that the husband is viewed as being liable because he condoned her actions (96).

32. Al-Marginani, *Hedaya*, 181; Imber, *"Zina* in Ottoman Law," 188. The text reads, "Eğer bir kişi püzavinklik itşe kazi ta'zir idüb teşhir ağaça bir cürm alına" (Selami Pulaha and Yaşar Yücel, "I. Selim Kanunnamesi (1512–1520) ve XVI. Yüzyılın İkinci Yarısının kimi kanunları." *Belgeler* 53.

33. Heyd, *Old Ottoman Criminal Law*, 102, 110.

34. Ibid., 201, 136.

35. Heyd relates that only two *siyasetnames* have been located, one from the period of Mehmet II and the other Selim I (ibid., 16, 59, 98, 114, 265).

36. Inalcik, *Ottoman Empire*, 50–51.

37. The text reads, "kız ya avret çikup cebr ile" (Pulaha and Yücel, *Derbeyan-i Kanunname-i 'Osmanı*, 51).

38. Ibid. Also found in Süleyman's *kanunname* (Heyd, *Old Ottoman Criminal Law*, 97).

39. Heyd, *Old Ottoman Criminal Law*, 98, 59.

40. Tucker, *In the House of the Law*, 164.

41. This point has been made in several works by Beshara Doumani, including "Palestinian Islamic Court Records: A Source for Socioeconomic History," 157n6; and *Rediscovering Palestine: Merchants and Peasants in Jabal Nablus, 1700–1900*, 11. Meriwether makes the same argument in *Kin Who Count*, 13.

42. Heyd, *Old Ottoman Criminal Law*, 100.

43. Pulaha and Yücel, "I. Selim Kanunnamesi (1512–1520) ve XVI. Yüzylını İkinci Yarısım Kimi Kanunları," 51; Heyd, *Old Ottoman Criminal Law*, 100.

44. I would like to thank Katherine Coughlin-De for her comments on this section when parts of it were presented as a paper in Yvonne Seng's graduate seminar in Ottoman history at Georgetown University in 1997. She interpreted the cutting of a woman's hair as a metaphor for shaming a woman.

45. Heyd, *Old Ottoman Criminal Law*, 110.

46. Ibid., 98.

47. Al-Marginani, *Hedaya*, 185.

48. Heyd, *Old Ottoman Criminal Law*, 103.

49. See Ralph Hattox, *Coffee and Coffeehouses: The Origins of a Social Beverage in the Medieval Near East*, 109.

50. Pulaha and Yücel, *Derbeyan-i Kanunname-i 'Osmanı*, 52.

51. Heyd, *Old Ottoman Criminal Law*, 136.

52. Pulaha and Yücel, *Derbeyan-i Kanunname-i 'Osmanı*, 51.

53. Redhouse, *Turkish and English Lexicon*, 1156.

54. Frederic M. Goadby, *Commentary on Egyptian Criminal Law*, 84.

55. Haim Gerber, *State, Society, and Law in Islam: Ottoman Law in Comparative Perspective*, 53.

56. Heyd, *Old Ottoman Criminal Law*, 99.

57. Pulaha and Yücel, *Derbeyan-i Kanunname-i 'Osmanı*, 51; Heyd, *Old Ottoman Criminal Law*, 99, Peirce, *Morality Tales*, 273–74.

58. Heyd, *Old Ottoman Criminal Law*, 98.

59. Ibid., 109–10.

60. Pulaha and Yücel, *Derbeyan-i Kanunname-i 'Osmanı*, 51.

61. Al-Marginani, *Hedaya*, 176 (emphasis added). See also Imber, "*Zina* in Ottoman Law," 187; and Doi, *Shari'ah*, 237.

62. von Schlegell, "Sufism in the Ottoman Arab World," 74.

63. Pulaha and Yücel, *Derbeyan-i Kanunname-i 'Osmanı*, 53.

64. Sonbol, "Rape and Law," 214.

65. Tucker, *In the House of the Law,* 152.

66. For a case in which a woman was stoned based on her husband's suspicion of bad intentions with a neighbor, see Sahebjam, *Stoning of Soraya M.,* 60; and Quraishi, "Her Honor," 118.

67. Discussed in Fedwa Malti-Douglas, *Woman's Body, Woman's Word: Gender and Discourse in Arabo-Islamic Writing,* 57–59; and Stowasser, *Women in the Qur'an,* 50–56.

68. Malti-Douglas, *Woman's Body,* 6; Stowasser, *Women in the Qur'an,* 51.

69. Malti-Douglas's analysis of patriarchal themes in Arabic literature illuminates the subject covered in this paragraph. She outlines the entire frame story of the *1001 Nights* in *WomanXs Body,* 14.

70. Ibid., 87–88.

71. Ibid., 54, 55 (quote).

72. Peirce has noted, "Again, no term for 'honor' appears in the 'Ayntab records, yet it was clearly at stake in many cases at court" (*Morality Tales,* 179).

73. Imber, *Ebu's-su'ud,* 7.

74. It may be a point of contention whether Ottoman fatwas and *kanunnames* have much relevance outside of Anatolia. Future study on the use of fatwas in different social contexts may demonstrate such variety of uses. Moreover, how much Ebu's Su'ud's fatwas were used in the provinces has yet to be investigated. For instance, Ibn 'Abidin of Damascus cites Ebu's Su'ud quite often, even in the nineteenth century. His fatwas were also cited occasionally in the court records of Aleppo. The full impact of the *kanunnames* in the Ottoman provinces has yet to be studied.

75. Uriel Heyd, "Aspects of the Ottoman *Fatwa,*" 46.

76. Ibid. The fatwas of muftis mentioned in Tucker's study *In the House of the Law,* such as Khayr ad-Din ibn Ahmad al-Ramli, al-'Imadi, and al-Tamimi, have more elaborate answers than Ebu's Su'ud's, whose answers are sometimes extremely brief.

77. See Messick, *Calligraphic State.*

78. Douwes, *Ottomans in Syria,* 81.

79. *SMH* 45:604:243 20 Rabi' al-Awwal 1131 A.H./February 1719.

80. See Tucker, *In the House of the Law.*

81. Hallaq, *History of Islamic Legal Theories,* 160. Imber disagrees with Hallaq on this point in particular (*Ebu's-su'ud,* 272n5).

82. Ebu's Su'ud's fatwas have been used extensively in two studies by Imber, "*Zina* in Ottoman Law" and *Ebu's-su'ud,* and to a lesser extent by Peirce in *Morality Tales.*

83. Imber, "*Zina* in Ottoman Law," 201.

84. Mehmet Ertuğrul Duzdağ, *Şeyhülislam Ebussuud Efendi Fetvaları Işığında 16 Asır Türk Hayatı,* 157.

85. Al-Sarakhsi, *Kitab al-Mabsut,* 17:23. Alternatively, this punishment is stated in al-Marginani, *Hedaya,* 178.

86. Gerber, *State, Society, and Law in Islam*; Marcus, *Middle East*; Rafeq, "Public Morality"; Yvonne Seng, "Standing at the Gates of Justice: Women in the Law Courts of Early-Sixteenth-Century Üsküdar, Istanbul"; Sonbol, "Law and Gender Violence."

87. Quraishi, "Her Honor," 133; Sonbol, *Women of Jordan: Islam, Labor, and the Law,* 203.

88. Duzdağ, *Şeyhülislam Ebussuud Efendi,* 158; Imber, "*Zina* in Ottoman Law," 214.

89. Gerber, *State, Society, and Law,* 53.

90. Peters, *Crime and Punishment,* 25.

91. Duzdağ, *Şeyhülislam Ebussuud Efendi,* 158.

92. Tucker, *In the House of the Law,* 65.

93. Imber, "*Zina* in Ottoman Law," 187.

94. See Gerber, *State, Society, and Law;* Sonbol, "Law and Gender Violence"; and Sonbol, "Rape and Law." See part 2, "Ine's Story," which discusses a rape case from 'Ayntab, in Peirce, *Morality Tales,* 129–42.

95. Duzdağ, *Şeyhülislam Ebussuud Efendi,* 158.

96. Imber, "*Zina* in Ottoman Law," 80.

97. Peters, *Crime and Punishment,* 26; Schacht, *Introduction to Islamic Law,* 184.

98. Duzdağ, *Şeyhülislam Ebussuud Efendi,* 158.

99. Imber, *Ebu's-su'ud,* 251, 252.

100. Natalie Zemon Davis, *Fiction in the Archives: Pardon Tales and Their Tellers in Sixteenth-Century France,* 12, 95. The full transcript of this court case is translated by Ze'evi in *An Ottoman Century: The District of Jerusalem in the 1600s,* 177–78.

101. Tucker, *In the House of the Law,* 152.

102. Douwes, *Ottomans in Syria,* 152.

103. Heyd, *Old Ottoman Criminal Law,* 274.

104. Ibid., 263.

105. Heyd, *Old Ottoman Criminal Law,* 32; Heyd, "*Kanun* and Shari'a," 15–16.

3. PEOPLE AND COURT: POLICING PUBLIC MORALITY IN THE STREETS OF ALEPPO

1. See Rafeq, "Public Morality."

2. Cengiz Kırlı, "The Struggle over Space: Coffeehouses of Ottoman Istanbul, 1780–1845," 72–73.

3. Peirce, *Morality Tales,* 169. See also Kırlı, "Struggle over Space," 76.

4. These sources may have been used by local historians and genealogists who frequent the archives today and do not publish their work academically. For examples of earlier work done in the field of Ottoman history with Syrian court records, see Jon E. Mandeville, "The Ottoman Court Records of Syria and Jordan"; Abdul Karim Rafeq, "The Law-Court Registers and Their Importance for a Socio-economic and Urban Study of Ottoman Syria"; and James A. Reilly, "Shari'a Court Registers and Land Tenure Around Nineteenth-Century Damascus," 167.

5. Unique in this respect is the work of Ergene, who has addressed both the administration of law and comparisons with other courts in *Local Court.*

6. More critical readings of the court record as a source can be found in Iris Agmon, "Muslim Women in Court According to the *Sijill* of Late Ottoman Jaffa and Haifa: Some Methodological

Notes"; Doumani, *Rediscovering Palestine*; Ergene, *Local Court*; Peirce, *Morality Tales*; and Ze'evi, "Use of Ottoman Shari'a Court Records."

7. Ze'evi systematically critiques the quantification, narrative, and microhistory written with the help of court records. He lays out two agendas for future research, the study of court narratives and the study of the actual structure of the court ("Use of Ottoman Shari'a Court Records," 43).

8. Ibid., 38. Similar methodological problems concerning the court records are posed by Ronald C. Jennings in "Kadi, Court, and Legal Procedure in 17th Century Ottoman Kayseri," 133.

9. A good example is Peirce's discussion of Ottoman 'Ayntab in which she looks to *kanunnames* for guidance on punishments because no record of their taking place exists in the court record (*Morality Tales,* 188).

10. Examples of cases in which *ta'zir bi'l-darb* was administered as punishment can be seen in *SMH* 34:80:469 2 Shawwal 1098 A.H./August 1687 (drinking); *SMH* 55:124:395 23 Dhu'l Hujja 1147 A.H./May 1735 (prostitution); *SMH* 55:137:434 8 Muharram 1148 A.H./May 1735 (homosexuality and drinking); *SMH* 55:152:481 4 Safar 1148 A.H./June 1735 (prostitution); *SMH* 55:251:770 6 Rajab 1148 A.H./November 1735 (cursing and evildoing); and *SMH* 64:566:197 23 Ramadan 1154 A.H./December 1741 (harmful).

11. Ergene, *Local Court*, 130.

12. These arguments are found in ibid., 126-27; and Peirce, *Morality Tales,* 101. Examples from the Aleppo records include *SMH* 28:18:63 21 Muharram 1071 A.H./September 1660; and *SMH* 85:16:45 15 Rajab 1167 A.H./May 1754

13. Doumani, *Rediscovering Palestine,* 11; Ze'evi, "Use of Ottoman Shari'a Court Records," 37.

14. Davis, *Return of Martin Guerre.*

15. Ergene, *Local Court,* 134.

16. See the court record located in appendix 1. Note the awkward use of the letters *kaf* and *ya* to indicate second-person feminine in the document, an example of the idiosyncrasies of the scribe (*SMH* 94:123:269 4 Dhu'l-Qa'da 1175 A.H./May 1762).

17. In some cases, a full sense of the colloquial language is noted through the use of first-person colloquial speech patterns. See the rape case discussed in chapter 6 (*SMH* 94:123:269 4 Dhu'l-Qa'da 1175 A.H./May 1762).

18. Some of the early volumes in particular are missing. Therefore, I have significant gaps in the formative years of Ottoman rule over Aleppo from 1515 to 1540 (see table 3.1). See Ze'evi's critique of quantitative analysis ("Use of Ottoman Shari'a Court Records," 39-45).

19. Doumani, *Rediscovering Palestine,* 11; Meriwether, *Kin Who Count,* 13; Jennings, "Kadi, Court, and Legal Procedure," 147; Ergene, *Local Court,* 177.

20. Ergene has devoted an entire chapter of his book *Local Court* to this very subject (chap. 5, "Costs of Court Usage," 76-98).

21. An example of plaintiffs seeking another ruling is *SMH* 94:123:269 4 Dhu'l-Qa'da 1175 A.H./May 1762. The full document is translated and discussed in chapter 5. Ergene discusses the role of the governor in administration of justice in Ottoman Çankırı and Kastamonu (*Local Court,* 107, 176).

22. The police prison *(habs al-dhabt)* is mentioned in documents *SMH* 113:164:454 25 Rabi'
al-Awwal 1190 A.H./May 1776 and *SMH* 113:200:491 10 Jumada al-Ula 1190 A.H./June 1776. For an
example of the sultan's prison *(al-sijin al-sultani)* see *SMH* 34:167:828 18 Safar 1090 A.H./March 1679
and *SMH* 34:135:601 25 Dhu'l Hijja 1089 A.H./February 1679 (this document was numbered incorrectly as document no. 701 in the original *sijill*).

23. Alexander Russell, *The Natural History of Aleppo*, 1:333.

24. Bodman, *Political Factions*, 13. On the subject of *tufɪnkjis*, see Marcus, *Middle East*, 115.
Only four cases of the police actually entering the court were found during the research conducted
for this study. For instance, in one court case a *subaşı* (police chief) appeared in court to relate the
details of a case in which a man destroyed the property of another, then fled the scene. The second case in which a *subaşı* appeared was in 1555, where the officer apprehended three men "drunk
on alcohol." See *SMH* 10:938:4567 14 Jumada al-Akhir 1019 A.H./September 1610; *SMH* 1:294:284
8 Shawwal 962 A.H./August 1555; *SMH* 27:102:437 26 Shawwal 1068 A.H./July 1659; *SMH* 28: 265:
1009 Jumada al-Awwal 1071 A.H./January 1661. Peirce notes that the *subaşı* frequently appeared at
court in Ottoman 'Ayntab. She found that in the year under study, two-thirds of the *zina-* and other
related offenses were brought to court by Ottoman officials, one-third by private individuals (*Morality Tales*, 288, 358). This dynamic stands in stark contrast to the cases brought to court in Aleppo,
almost exclusively by individuals and communities.

25. Heyd, *Old Ottoman Criminal Law*, 235, 238.

26. Ibid.; Ronald C. Jennings, "The Judicial Registers *(Ser'i Mahkeme Sicilleri)* of Kayseri
(1590–1630) as a Source of Ottoman History"; Jennings, "Kadi, Court, and Legal Procedure"; and
Gamal al-Nahal, *Judicial Administration in Ottoman Egypt in the Seventeenth Century*. Ergene's
Local Court and Agmon's *Family and Court* are nice follow-ups to these earlier studies.

27. Marcus, *Middle East*, 80–82; Abdul Karim Rafeq, *The Province of Damascus, 1723–1783*,
44. An exception would be the use of local judges, often from the same family (Kaylani) in smaller
towns such as Hama, as recorded in Douwes, *Ottomans in Syria*, 82. For Damascus, Stephen
Edmond Tamari has noted that judges were regularly rotated ("Teaching and Learning in 18th-
Century Damascus: Localism and Ottomanism in an Early Modern Arab Society," 96).

28. Marcus, *Middle East*, 80.

29. Linda Schatowski Schilcher, *Families in Politics: Damascene Factions and Estates of the 18th
and 19th Centuries*, 116.

30. Marcus, *Middle East*, 103. An example can be seen in the annulment of the Bedouin woman
Fatima bint 'Abdallah to her absent husband. See *SMH* 55:171:544 25 Rabi' al-Awwal 1148 A.H./
August 1735 and from the Shafi'i court itself, *SMH* 155:68:270 12 Safar 1220 A.H./May 1805.

31. Court registers missing this title page may have been damaged, as the volumes have been
bound and rebound throughout the years.

32. Iris Agmon has been able to track down the names of several levels of scribes in her study of
late Ottoman Haifa (*Family and Court*, chap. 3). The Aleppo registers do no specifically name court
scribes. On the office of scribe, see Schilcher, *Families in Politics*, 117. Tamari has noted that court
scribes are rarely mentioned in al-Muradi's biographical dictionary ("Teaching and Learning," 117).

33. Tamari, "Teaching and Learning," 96.

34. Meriwether, *Kin Who Count*, 13.

35. Judith Tucker, "Muftis and Matrimony: Islamic Law and Gender in Ottoman Syria and Palestine," 296.

36. The structure of the court records of Ottoman Syria are discussed in more detail in Rafeq, "Law-Court Registers."

37. Brigitte Marino and Tomoki Okawara, eds., *Dalil sijillat al-mahakim al-shar'iyya al-'uthmaniyya*, 44.

38. Fariba Zarinebaf has found police records in Istanbul, as mentioned during the delivery of her unpublished paper ("Regulating Prostitution").

39. The officials at the Syrian archives claimed that the *nizami* court records, which were the criminal court records for the city of Aleppo, were destroyed (burned) during the French mandate period. I continued to search in vain for these records in the shari'a court of Aleppo, the Ministry of Waqfs (Dar al-Awqaf), and the Saray (Shourta Jina'iah), which is where contemporary criminal cases are delivered. I never found any criminal court records for the Tanzimat era. I received this information, along with a tour of both localities, from Suleyman Nasr, a lawyer who served as minister of endowments *(awqaf)* from 1959 to 1979 and the district chief *(ra'is baladiyya)* for Aleppo in 1961.

40. This information was also obtained from Suleyman Nasr.

41. Marino and Okawara, *Dalil sijillat*, 44.

42. Marcus, *Middle East*, 315–16. André Raymond notes that the earliest Tapu register from 1537–38 records seventy quarters in Aleppo ("The Population of Aleppo in the Sixteenth and Seventeenth Centuries According to Ottoman Census Documents," 453).

43. Abdel Nour, *Introduction à l'histoire urbaine*, 174.

44. Raymond, "Population of Aleppo." The Christian composition of the quarter of Saliba al-Judayda is also discussed in Meriwether, *Kin Who Count*, 28.

45. Lapidus, *History of Islamic Societies*, 85. Marcus says, "There was no neighborhood exclusively Jewish or Christian in its composition" (*Middle East*, 44).

46. Muhsin 'Ali Shuman, *Al-yahud Fi misr al-'uthmaniyah hatta awa'il al-qarn al-tasi' 'ashar*, 1:29; al-Qattan, "Across the Courtyard"; Kırlı, "Struggle over Space," 92.

47. *SMH* 34:80:369 2 Shawwal 1089 A.H./November 1678. This document was numbered incorrectly as no. 469 but actually appears as no. 369 in the *sijill*.

48. Lapidus, *History of Islamic Societies*, 87. Marcus, basing his argument on real estate prices, finds the most affluent neighborhoods to be in the center of the city (*Middle East*, 318–22).

49. Although using *walad* instead of *ibn* is improper use of the Arabic language, I have written the names exactly as they appear in the documents. The court records differentiated between Christian and Muslim names on several levels. Christian names were not written using *ibn* as in Muslim names. Instead, *walad* was used in the original document to signify a Christian name. Furthermore, Christian names were often misspelled purposely by the scribe; for example, the shared Muslim and Christian name of Yusuf (in Arabic), spelled in proper Arabic, was purposely misspelled as (in

Arabic with Sad) when a Christian was documented. This type of differentiation has been studied by Najwa al-Qattan in her article "Textual Differentiation in the Damascus *Sijill:* Religious discrimination or Politics of Gender?"

50. *SMH* 64:276:795 23 Safar 1155 A.H./April 1742.

51. *SMH* 34:106:473 (misnumbered in the *sijill*) 23 Shawwal 1087 A.H./December 1676 and *SMH* 34:108:480 (misnumbered in the *sijill*) 23 Shawwal 1087 A.H./December 1676. These cases are discussed later in chapter 6.

52. Ira Lapidus, *Muslim Cities in the Later Middle Ages,* 80.

53. Marcus, *Middle East,* 51.

54. Lapidus, *Muslim Cities,* 82; Marcus, *Middle East,* 51.

55. Schilcher, *Families in Politics,* 124.

56. Raymond, *Urban Networks and Popular Movements,* 250.

57. Albert Hourani, "Ottoman Reform and the Politics of Notables." Additional studies have tested Hourani's paradigm in several Arab provinces (in Mosul, Dina Rizq Khoury, *State and Provincial Society in the Ottoman Empire: Mosul, 1540–1834*; in Damascus, Rafeq, *Province of Damascus*; and Philip Khoury, *Urban Notables and Arab Nationalism: The Politics of Damascus, 1860–1920*).

58. Meriwether, *Kin Who Count,* 31. Tamari examines the role of Damascene *'ulama* in local Ottoman government in his dissertation ("Teaching and Learning").

59. Meriwether, *Kin Who Count,* 19.

60. Marcus, *Middle East,* 74.

61. Ibid., 66.

62. Lapidus, *Muslim Cities,* 82, 83.

63. Amira El-Azhary Sonbol, *The New Mamluks: Egyptian Society and Modern Feudalism,* xxviii.

64. This documentation is also observed in Jennings, "Kadi, Court, and Legal Procedure," 142.

65. The full record cases in which the defendant(s) bore social titles can be observed in the names of defendants convicted of *zina*-related crimes in appendix 2. See sample cases of sayyids in *SMH* 85:92:249 1 Dhu'l Hijja 1167 A.H./September 1754; *SMH* 113:233:584 17 Rajab 1190 A.H./September 1776; and *SMH* 55:53:175 6 Jumada al-Akhir 1147 A.H./November 1734; and hajjis in *SMH* 64:172:495 6 Rajab 1154 A.H./September 1741; *SMH* 55:152:481 4 Safar 1148 A.H./June 1735; and *SMH* 45:8:19 16 Jumada al-Akhir 1130 A.H./May 1718.

66. This finding is in stark contrast to a recent study by Boğaç Ergene that found a majority of litigants, in all cases that appeared in three *sijills* in Kastamonu, were from the military and religious establishment ("Social Identity and Patterns of Interaction in the Shari'a Court of Kastamonu, 1740–44").

67. Lapidus, *Muslim Cities,* 92; Abdel Nour, *Introduction à l'histoire urbaine,* 162–63; Raymond, *Great Arab Cities,* 15.

68. Abdel Nour, *Introduction à l'histoire urbaine,* 156.

69. Lapidus, *Muslim Cities,* 93.

70. Abdel Nour, *Introduction à l'histoire urbaine,* 162–63; Raymond, *Great Arab Cities,* 3.

71. Amy Singer, *Palestinian Peasants and Ottoman Officials: Rural Administration Around Sixteenth-Century Jerusalem,* 36. Cem Behar describes a similar position of the *mukhtar,* who was a local community leader who was also officially connected with Ottoman authorities in the Kasap İlyas quarter in Istanbul (*Neighborhood in Ottoman Istanbul,* 160–71).

72. Lapidus, *Muslim Cities,* 94.

73. Heyd, "*Kanun* and Shari'a," 15–16.

74. Marcus, *Middle East,* 116.

75. Peirce, *Morality Tales,* 90.

76. Heyd, *Old Ottoman Criminal Law,* 130–31, 242.

77. Marcus, *Middle East,* 117. Ze'evi makes a similar argument in *Producing Desire,* 60.

78. Heyd, *Old Ottoman Criminal Law,* 106, 115.

79. Imber, *Ebu's-su'ud,* 89. Ze'evi has also argued that communities were responsible for monitoring morality, expelling criminals, and handing them over to the police (*Producing Desire,* 60).

80. Imber, *Ebu's-su'ud,* 127.

81. Peirce, *Morality Tales,* 274. Pulaha and Yücel, "I. Selim Kanunnamesi (1512–1520) ve XVI. Yüzyılını İkinci Yarısım Kimi Kanunları." *Belgeler,* 53. This passage is also discussed in chapter 2.

82. See individual punishments for wine consumption and distribution in codes 61 and 62. For a lack of collective punishment for *zina* crimes, see codes 29 and 30 in Heyd, *Old Ottoman Criminal Law,* 111, 102, respectively.

83. Ibid., 130. Also mentioned in Peirce, *Morality Tales,* 263.

84. Heyd, *Old Ottoman Criminal Law,* 229.

85. Peirce, *Morality Tales,* 169.

86. Heyd, *Old Ottoman Criminal Law,* 130.

87. Rafeq, "Public Morality," 180, 181.

88. Scholarship on the local tradition of the *qabaday* is very meager at the moment. Philip Khoury has described the institution and written a biography of a local Damascene *qabaday* (pronounced *abaday* in Syrian colloquial Arabic) he interviewed ("Abu Ali al-Kilawi: A Damascus *Qabaday*").

89. Russell, *Natural History of Aleppo,* 2:55–56.

90. Cases located that express a fear of possible fines placed on the community include *SMH* 36:53:145 28 Jumada al-Akhir 1098 A.H./May 1687; *SMH* 45:350:869 28 Ramadan 1131 A.H./August 1719; *SMH* 55:276:833 21 Sha'ban 1148 A.H./January 1736; *SMH* 85:103:283 7 Dhu'l Hijja 1176 A.H./June 1763; *SMH* 64:198:566 23 Ramadan 1154/December 1741; and *SMH* 113:89:208 18 Rajab 1189 A.H./September 1775.

91. Lapidus, *Muslim Cities,* 93.

92. Ergene, *Local Court,* 151 (quote), 72, 151–52.

93. Ibid., 137, 154–55.

94. Ergene comes to a similar conclusion in ibid.; see chap. 6 in particular.

95. Ibid., 152–53.

96. Rafeq, "Public Morality," 190.

97. Kırlı, "Struggle over Space," 77.

98. One document, *SMH* 94:66:125 6 Sha'ban 1175 A.H./March 1762, mentions the *ta'ifat al-nisa' al-masturat* (virtuous women) in a case in which a man was bothering women passersby. Gabriel Baer also mentions the use of *ta'ifat al-nisa'* in Egypt (*Egyptian Guilds in Modern Times,* 17).

99. Rafeq, "Craft Organization," 495.

100. Marcus, *Middle East,* 159. Raymond puts the number of guilds in Aleppo at 130 at the end of the seventeenth century (*Great Arab Cities,* 19).

101. Information on the use of the title *shaykh* is discussed in Schilcher, *Families in Politics,* 109. The document citation is *SMH* 4:144:717 28 Rabi' al-Thani 1052 A.H./July 1642.

102. Amnon Cohen also notes that there were no prostitute guilds in Jerusalem either, attributing it to the holy nature of the city (*The Guilds of Ottoman Jerusalem,* 185).

103. G. Baer, *Egyptian Guilds,* 35.

104. Ibid., 35–37. See also Judith Tucker, *Women in Nineteenth-Century Egypt,* 150–51, on prostitution in Egypt during the nineteenth century.

105. Fahmy, "Prostitution in Egypt," 78.

106. G. Baer, *Egyptian Guilds,* 38–39.

107. Marcus, *Middle East,* 177.

108. G. Baer, *Egyptian Guilds,* 11.

109. Marcus, *Middle East,* 173; Heyd, *Old Ottoman Criminal Law,* 231, 233; Marcus, *Middle East,* 173. See also Bodman, *Political Factions,* 25. Jennings makes the same observation for seventeenth-century Ottoman Kayseri ("Kadi, Court, and Legal Procedure," 155).

110. Cohen, *Guilds of Ottoman Jerusalem,* 190.

111. *SMH* 27:383:1856 14 Jumada al-Thani 1072 A.H./February 1662; Cohen, *Guilds of Ottoman Jerusalem,* 190.

112. Marcus, *Middle East,* 173–74; *SMH* 113:226:558 3 Jumada al-Ula 1190 A.H./June 1776; *SMH* 130:83:222 3 Sha'ban 1200 A.H./June 1786.

113. Rafeq, "Craft Organization," 496.

114. *SMH* 34:180:887 3 Rabi' al-Awwal 1090 A.H./April 1679. This record was numbered incorrectly as no. 887 in the original *sijill.*

115. Ibid., "Craft Organization," 508. For discussion of the *futuwwa* and the mystic ceremonies of initiation, see André Raymond, *Artisans et commerçants au Caire au XVIIIe siècle,* 2:506, 529–30.

116. Raymond, *Artisans et commerçants,* 2:506, 523–24; *SMH* 85:185:527 6 Jumada al-Akhir 1168 A.H./March 1755; Masters, *Origins of Western Dominance,* 84–85.

117. *SMH* 55:344:1138 18 Dhu'l Hijja 1148 A.H./April 1736; *SMH* 27:432:2180 23 Dhu'l Hijja 1072 A.H./August 1662.

4. PROSTITUTES, SOLDIERS, AND THE PEOPLE:
MONITORING MORALITY THROUGH CUSTOMARY LAW

1. Some of the material from this chapter has been published in article form in "Sinful Professions: Illegal Occupations of Women in Ottoman Aleppo, Syria."

2. Court procedure and the various ranks of scribe, such as chief scribe *(başkatib)* as well as *katib, zabt katibi,* and *mukayyid,* are illuminated in Agmon, *Family and Court,* chap. 3 more generally and p. 71 specifically for scribe rankings.

3. Foucault, "Truth and Juridical Forms," 2; Kathleen M. Brown, *Good Wives, Nasty Wenches, and Anxious Patriarchs: Gender, Race, and Power in Colonial Virginia,* 97, 102-3.

4. Abdul Karim Rafeq, "New Light on the 1860 Riots in Ottoman Damascus," 415.

5. Examples of this language can be seen in the primary source documents located in appendix 1. Rafeq lists a number of euphemisms used in the shari'a courts of Damascus in "Public Morality," 180-83. Fahmy notes that prostitutes in Egypt were often referred to as *ashrar,* or "evil people" ("Prostitution in Egypt," 90).

6. *SMH* 55:272:733 24 Sha'ban 1148 A.H./January 1736.

7. Rafeq, "Public Morality," 182. "Gathering strange men and women in their home" is a common quote from the court records that will be repeated often in this chapter. The term *ajanab* is tricky and needs to be read in context. Reading it with modern sensibilities would create an interpretation that all of these crimes were committed by foreigners. However, it is easy to detect foreign-born individuals at court, as their names are often furnished with a *nisba,* which indicates the town of origin.

8. Peters, *Crime and Punishment,* 13 (quote), 15, 16.

9. Ergene, *Local Court,* 159-60. This exact phrasing was not found in the breaches of public morality found in the Aleppo record. Instead, variations on this phrase, such as "spread harm [*yas'a fi adrar*]" and "spreading evil through their crimes and fines [*yas'a fi tajrimuhum wa taghrimuhum*]," indicating fear of possible fining, were used. See examples of these phrases in *SMH* 64:241:674 13 Dhu'l Hijja 1157 A.H./January 1745; *SMH* 130:83:222 3 Sha'ban 1200 A.H./May 1786; *SMH* 85:103:283 7 Dhu'l Hijja 1176 A.H./June 1763; *SMH* 64:198:566 23 Ramadan 1154 A.H./December 1741; and *SMH* 113:89:208 18 Rajab 1189 A.H./October 1775.

10. Heyd, *Old Ottoman Criminal Law,* 196; Ergene, *Local Court,* 159.

11. Peters, *Crime and Punishment,* 16.

12. The three cases in question are *SMH* 55:115:363 25 Dhu'l-Qa'da 1147 A.H./April 1735; *SMH* 45:8:19 16 Jumada al-Akhir 1130 A.H./May 1718; and *SMH* 55:53:175 6 Jumada al-Akhir 1147 A.H./November 1734. Rafeq, "Public Morality," 187.

13. Fahmy notes a similar phenomenon in nineteenth-century Cairo ("Prostitution in Egypt," 83).

14. The two accounts are found in Bouhdiba, *Sexuality in Islam,* 188.

15. Mernissi, *Veil and the Male Elite,* 182-83.

16. Examples of this description can be found in al-Budayri al-Hallaq, *Hawadith dimashq al-yawmiyya, 1154-1176 A.H./1741-1763,* 127; *SMH* 85:293:813 16 Shawwal 1168 A.H./July 1755; and *SMH* 94:123:269 4 Dhu'l-Qa'da 1175 A.H./May 1762, fully translated in this chapter.

17. Rudi Matthee, "Prostitutes, Courtesans, and Dancing Girls: Women Entertainers in Safavid Iran," 129.

18. Bouhdiba, *Sexuality in Islam,* 192.

19. Matthee, "Prostitutes, Courtesans, and Dancing Girls," 133.

20. Bouhdiba, *Sexuality in Islam,* 189.

21. Shirley Guthrie, *Arab Women in the Middle Ages: Private Lives and Public Roles,* 99.

22. G. Baer, *Egyptian Guilds,* 35.

23. Zarinebaf, "Regulating Prostitution," part of her forthcoming book, "Mediterranean's Metropolis."

24. Tucker, *Women in Nineteenth-Century Egypt,* 151–52.

25. Support for this argument can be found in neighborhood policing for similar crimes, such as illegal distillation of liquor and distribution. It was not illegal to produce and sell alcohol as a Christian or Jew, yet there is evidence that it was illegal to do so without being subjected to regulation and taxation, most likely through the guild structure. See *SMH* 4:130:678 Jumada al-Ula 1052 A.H./July 1642; *SMH* 113:1:3 23 Dhu'l Hijja 1189 A.H./February 1776; and *SMH* 113:146:355 20 Safar 1190 A.H./April 1776.

26. Fahmy describes this phenomenon in his article "Prostitution in Egypt."

27. Bouhdiba, *Sexuality in Islam,* 191.

28. The work of al-Budayri was the subject of a dissertation written by Dana Sajdi, "Peripheral Visions: The Worlds and Worldviews of Commoner Chroniclers in the Eighteenth-Century Ottoman Levant." Sajdi examines the original manuscript located in the Chester Beatty library in Dublin, Ireland, that is the basis of a published rendition compiled by a nineteenth-century scholar, Muhammad Sa'id al-Qasimi, and used by many scholars of Damascus. Importantly, she notes that the *nisba* al-Budayri is inaccurate, as the original manuscript refers to him as al-Budayr. The dissertation explores several chronicles written by commoners, including ones by Muhammad al-Makki, Muhammad Ibn Kannan, Hasan Agha al-'Abd, Haydar Rida al-Rukayni, Ibrahim al-Danafi, and Mikha'il Burayk.

29. Sajdi, "Peripheral Visions," 75.

30. Ibid., 164. Also related in James Grehan, "The Mysterious Power of Words: Language, Law, and Culture in Ottoman Damascus (17th–18th Centuries)," 1001.

31. Dana Sajdi, "A Room of His Own: The 'History' of the Barber of Damascus (Fl. 1762)," 28.

32. Sajdi, "Peripheral Visions," 163–64; Sajdi, "Room of His Own," 26, 29.

33. Rafeq, "Public Morality," 183.

34. Guthrie, *Arab Women,* 200.

35. Matthee, "Prostitutes, Courtesans, and Dancing Girls," 126; Raymond, *Great Arab Cities,* 46. Bruce Masters documents the number of caravansaries in the city as fifty-three, slightly lower than Raymond's assessment ("Aleppo: The Ottoman Empire's Caravan City," 26).

36. Rafeq, "Public Morality," 190.

37. Sajdi, "Room of His Own," 28.

38. This implication of the troops is illustrated in cases from chapter 4 as well as cases where *levend* openly associated with prostitutes. See *SMH* 55:107:340 26 Dhu'l-Qa'da 1147 A.H./April 1735; *SMH* 55:284:871 29 Ramadan 1148 A.H./February 1736; *SMH* 21:174:420 3 Ramadan 1049 A.H./December 1639; and *SMH* 21:173:419 2 Ramadan 1049 A.H./December 1639.

39. The Janissaries' struggle for power against the *ashraf* in eighteenth-century Aleppo is documented in Herbert Bodman's seminal study on the subject, *Political Factions,* esp. chap. 5. Bodman also draws connections between political corruption and moral disorder.

40. A vivid description of the *devṣirme* system and its educational program is related in Barnette Miller, *The Palace School of Muhammad the Conqueror.*

41. V. L. Ménage, "Devshirme."

42. Colin Imber, *The Ottoman Empire, 1300–1650,* 134–40.

43. Schilcher, *Families in Politics,* 111.

44. Rafeq, *Province of Damascus,* 37; Douwes, *Ottomans in Syria,* 112; Rafeq, *Province of Damascus,* 37.

45. Constantine François Volney, *Travels Through Egypt and Syria in the Years 1783, 1784, and 1785,* 144, 143.

46. Ibid., 409. *Lawend* is the Arabic pronunciation of the Turkish term *levend.*

47. This story can be found in Abdul-Karim Rafeq, "Local Forces in Syria," 292.

48. *SMH* 45:134:319 7 Dhu'l-Qaʿda 1030 A.H./September 1621.

49. Singer, *Palestinian Peasants and Ottoman Officials,* 126; Ergene, *Local Court.*

50. Cases of rape involving *levend* are discussed along with other rape cases in chapter 6.

51. *SMH* 55:107:340 26 Dhu'l-Qaʿda 1147 A.H./April 1736.

52. Bodman, *Political Factions,* 104.

53. *SMH* 55:284:861 29 Ramadan 1148 A.H./February 1736.

54. Jennings, "Judicial Registers," 159, 146 (quote).

55. See differing interpretations in Sajdi, "Peripheral Visions," 163; and Rafeq, "Public Morality," 183.

56. Rafeq, "Local Forces," 305–6.

57. Matthee, "Prostitutes, Courtesans, and Dancing Girls," 131 (quote), 129.

58. I only found one suicide in the Aleppo *sijills* used in this study (*SMH* 4:74:360 28 Ramadan 1090 A.H./November 1679).

59. Al-Budayri, *Hawdith dimashq,* 127 (my translation). This case is also cited in Rafeq, "Public Morality," 183.

60. Rafeq, "Public Morality," 189, 183; Tucker, *Women in Nineteenth-Century Egypt,* 151–52; Fahmy, "Prostitution in Egypt," 83.

61. See *SMH* 149:28:70 7 Dhu'l-Qaʿda 1215 A.H./1801; *SMH* 261:3:5 12 Jumada al-Akhir 1267 A.H./April 1851; *SMH* 232:470 28 Muharram 1253 A.H./May 1837; *SMH* 261:242:452 4 Rabiʿ al-Awwal 1268 A.H./December 1851; and *SMH* 296:209:274 11 Jumada al-Awwal 1283 A.H./September 1866.

62. *SMH* 28:498:1708 14 Safar 1073 A.H./September 1662; *SMH* 94:82:171 3 Ramadan 1175 A.H./ March 1762; *SMH* 113:92:242 30 Shaʿban 1189 A.H./October 1775; *SMH* 232:53:126 12 Dhu'l-Qaʿda 1252 A.H./February 1837.

63. The registering of foreign prostitutes is particularly evident in nineteenth-century cases where the court registers include information on place of origin. See appendix 2.

64. Rafeq, "Public Morality," 182.

65. This information is based on the study of Marcus of real estate values in Aleppo during the eighteenth century (*Middle East*, 318).

66. Bodman, *Political Factions*, 63.

67. Raymond, *Urban Networks and Popular Movements*, 252, 255.

68. Ibid., 256; Bodman, *Political Factions*, 63.

69. Matthee, "Prostitutes, Courtesans, and Dancing Girls," 126; Tucker, *Women in Nineteenth-Century Egypt*, 151–52; Fahmy, "Prostitution in Egypt," 83.

70. To be specific, the last criminal prostitution case I located was in 1802 (see appendix 2). I am still perplexed by the lack of criminal prostitution cases in the nineteenth century as opposed to the peak in the eighteenth century. My only guess is that there may have been a shift in jurisdiction whereby these cases were adjudicated elsewhere, because prostitution, as evidenced by these testimonials, was still present in the city.

71. *SMH* 94:82:171 3 Ramadan 1175 A.H/March 1762.

72. Peirce, *Morality Tales*, 356; Peters, *Crime and Punishment*, 27; Peirce, *Morality Tales*, 355.

73. *SMH* 94:81:167 4 Ramadan 1175 A.H./March 1664; *SMH* 130:122:321 4 Dhu'l-Qaʻda 1200 A.H./August 1786; *SMH* 261:3:5 12 Jumada al-Akhir 1267 A.H./April 1851.

74. Behar, *Neighborhood in Ottoman Istanbul*, 164–65.

75. The lack of privacy afforded residents and the importance of reputation have been topics of several studies, including two works by Abraham Marcus, "Privacy in Eighteenth-Century Aleppo: The Limits of Cultural Ideals" and *Middle East*. Peirce addresses the connection between community and reputation in her discussion of *töhmet*, the negative mark given an individual that damaged his or her reputation and made his or her word unacceptable in the court of law. The collective memory of the community was used to determine who had a tarnished reputation through *töhmet* and how many offenses (*Morality Tales*, 113).

76. *SMH* 28:181:721 14 Rabiʻ al-Thani 1071 A.H./December 1660.

77. *SMH* 113:128:304 2 Muharram 1196 A.H./December 1781.

78. In this study I use the term *family* to means people who are immediate family members, meaning related within degrees by which they are not marriageable. Meriwether has called it an elementary or conjugal family consisting of a husband, wife or wives, and children as opposed to a larger lineal family. In some cases in-laws are included in the elementary family household. Moreover, the context of these court cases indicates that these families may have lived in the same households. See Meriwether's discussion defining family in eighteenth- and nineteenth-century Aleppo (*Kin Who Count*, 16–18).

79. *SMH* 36:24:67 1 Jumada al-Ula 1098 A.H./March 1687.

80. *SMH* 45:224:555 29 Safar 1031 A.H./January 1622; *SMH* 36:232:657 6 Safar 1099 A.H./December 1687.

81. *SMH* 64:172:490 6 Rajab 1154 A.H./September 1741.

82. *SMH* 55:314:947 14 Dhu'l Qaʻda 1148 A.H./March 1736.

83. Rafeq, "Public Morality," 187; Marcus, *Middle East*, 197.

84. Alain Corbin, *Women for Hire: Prostitution and Sexuality in France after 1850,* 69.

85. Raymond, *Great Arab Cities,* 69, 81–87. This type of housing is also discussed in Abdel Nour, *Introduction à l'histoire urbaine,* 110, 130–35.

86. *SMH* 36:182:517 18 Dhu'l Hijja 1098 A.H./October 1687; *SMH* 113:305:768 16 Muharram 1191 A.H./February 1777.

87. Ergene, *Local Court,* 152.

88. Charles Wilkins and I shared a number of cases during the course of our research from 1999 to 2001 in the Syrian archives. I thank Charles for sharing these two documents with me. They are *SMH* 34:106:473 (misnumbered in the *sijill*), 23 Shawwal 1087 A.H./December 1676 and *SMH* 34:108:480 (misnumbered in the *sijill*) 23 Shawwal 1087 A.H./December 1676.

89. *SMH* 94:123:269 4 Dhu'l-Qaʿda 1175 A.H./May 1762. The power of the *hakim al-ʿurf* to make legal judgments has been documented in part by Marcus, *Middle East,* 105; and Gerber, *Islamic Law and Culture,* 57–58.

90. The nickname "Abi Ras," meaning "father of the head," may be indicative of a physical peculiarity that inspired the nickname, possibly a larger-sized head.

91. Ergene, *Local Court,* 107.

92. *SMH* 45:8:19 16 Jumada al-Akhir 1130 A.H./May 1718; *SMH* 45:53:123 10 Shaʿban 1130 A.H./July 1718; *SMH* 94:139:309 4 Muharram 1176 A.H./July 1762.

93. *SMH* 55:137:434 8 Muharram 1148 A.H./May 1735; *SMH* 85:146:400 23 Rabiʿ al-Awwal 1187 A.H./June 1773.

94. *SMH* 113:181:443 19 Rabiʿ al-Thani 1190 A.H./June 1776; Marcus, *Middle East,* 117.

95. Marcus, *Middle East,* 328.

96. M. Baer, "Islamic Conversion Narratives," 435–36; von Schlegell, "Sufism in the Ottoman Arab World," 82. For a more thorough discussion of the movement, see Madeline Zilfi, "The Kadizadelis: Discordant Revivalism in Seventeenth-Century Istanbul."

97. M. Baer, "Islamic Conversion Narratives," 436. See also Zilfi, "Kadizadelis"; and von Schlegell, "Sufism in the Ottoman Arab World" on the Kadızâdeli movement (for context).

98. Imber, "*Zina* in Ottoman Law," 182–83; Haim Gerber, "Position of Women in an Ottoman City, Bursa, 1600–1700," 239; Heyd, *Old Ottoman Criminal Law,* 273. A similar description is found in Alexander Russell's account in *Natural History of Aleppo,* 1:334.

99. Gerber, "Position of Women," 239; Russell, *Natural History of Aleppo,* 1:334.

100. Seng, "Standing at the Gates of Justice," 199; Zeʾevi, *Ottoman Century,* 179.

101. Ronald C. Jennings, "Women in Early 17th Century Ottoman Judicial Records: The Shariʿa Court of Anatolian," 96.

102. Marcus argues that when women were "expelled" or "ordered to leave" by the court, they often moved to another quarter with the approval of their new neighbors. See the case of Fatima bint ʿAbdallah, who was most likely a manumitted slave (*Middle East,* 118). See also *SMH* 2:159:673 20 Rabiʿ al-Thani 1119 A.H./July 1707; *SMH* 45:170:415 17 Dhu'l Hijja 1130 A.H./November 1718; and *SMH* 28:216:731 17 Rabiʿ al-Thani 1071 A.H./December 1660.

103. Al-Marginani, *Hedaya*, 181; *SMH* 2:159:273 11 Rabi' al-Thani 1119 A.H./July 1707; *SMH* 45:170:415 17 Dhu'l Hijja 1130 A.H./November 1718; *SMH* 28:216:731 17 Rabi' al-Thani 1071 A.H./December 1660.

104. Russell, *Natural History of Aleppo*, 1:335.

105. Peirce, *Morality Tales*, 332.

106. Here I have adopted the explanation of Gerber as related in his article "Rigidity Versus Openness," 166.

107. Schacht, *Introduction to Islamic Law*, 60–61. Some of these variations among schools of law are discussed in ibid., 60–63.

108. Ibid., 204.

109. Gerber dedicates an article to discussing the way in which Mufti Khayr ad-Din ibn Ahmad al-Ramli referenced *istihsan* in his fatwas ("Rigidity Versus Openness").

110. Rosen, *Justice of Islam*, 95–96, 97.

111. Masters, *Origins of Western Dominance*, 50.

112. Felicitas Opwis, *"Maslaha* in Contemporary Islamic Legal Theory," 188.

113. For more information on the Ash'ari and Mu'tazila debate, see W. Montgomery Watt, "Al-Ash'ari"; and D. Gimaret, "Mu'tazila."

114. Opwis, *"Maslaha* in Contemporary Theory," 190 (quote), 191.

115. Ibid., 194.

116. Rosen, *Anthropology of Justice*, 48.

117. Lawrence Rosen, "Equity and Discretion in a Modern Islamic Legal System," 234.

118. Ahmad Zaki Yamani, *Islamic Law and Contemporary Issues*, 11; Rosen, "Equity and Discretion," 235.

119. Rafeq, "Public Morality," 306.

5. IN HARM'S WAY: DOMESTIC VIOLENCE AND RAPE
IN THE SHARI'A COURTS OF ALEPPO

1. Two recent nonacademic yet mainstream and popular publications that continue to perpetuate notions that Islamic law endorses violence against women can be found in Irshad Manji, *The Trouble with Islam: A Muslim's Call for Reform in Her Faith*; and Ayaan Hirsi 'Ali, *Infidel*.

2. Hina Jilani, "Whose Laws? Human Rights and Violence Against Women in Pakistan," 73.

3. John Esposito, *Women in Muslim Family Law*; 26; Tucker, *In the House of the Law*, 63.

4. Isma'il ibn 'Umar Ibn Kathir, *Mukhtasir tafsir ibn Kathir*, 1:386; Abu Ja'far Muhammad ibn Jarir al-Tabari, *Tafsir al-Tabari*, 4:71.

5. Sonbol, "Law and Gender Violence," 281.

6. Tucker, *In the House of the Law*, 63; Sonbol, "Law and Gender Violence"; and Dalenda Largueche, "Confined, Battered, and Repudiated Women in Tunis since the Eighteenth Century," both latter articles found in *Women, the Family, and Divorce Laws*, edited by Sonbol. Sonbol also has an

article exclusively dedicated to the issue of *taʿa* and the development of *bayt al-taʿa* as an institution ("*Taʿa* and Modern Legal Reform").

7. Tucker, *In the House of the Law,* 65.

8. See Esposito, *Women in Muslim Family Law,* 32.

9. See Colin Imber, "Why You Should Poison Your Husband: A Note on Liability in Hanafi Law in the Ottoman Period."

10. Davis, *Fiction in the Archives,* 78–79.

11. Tucker, *In the House of the Law,* 66.

12. Duzdağ, *Şeyhülislam Ebussuud Efendi,* 54; Imber, *Ebu's-suʿud,* 216.

13. Muhammad Ibn ʿAbidin, *Radd al-muhtar ʿala al-durr al-mukhtar,* 3:190.

14. *SMH* 36:78:214 16 Rajab 1098 A.H./May 1687.

15. *SMH* 313:312:323 22 Shawwal 1301 A.H./August 1884.

16. *SMH* 50:171:465 19 Jumada al-Ula 1136 A.H./February 1724.

17. Imber, "*Zina* in Ottoman Law," 186–87.

18. Quraishi, "Her Honor," 129.

19. *SMH* 45:145:372 27 Dhu'l Hijja 1030 A.H./November 1621.

20. Peters, *Crime and Punishment,* 62.

21. This terminology is close to the Turkish rendering *cebran zina* that Peirce found in the ʿAyntab court (*Morality Tales,* 206).

22. Also related in Peirce, *Morality Tales,* 352.

23. Sonbol, "Law and Gender Violence," 287.

24. Al-Zuhayli, *Al-fiqh al-islami wa ʿadillatuhu,* 7:5351.

25. Ahmad ibn Muhammad ibn Qudama, *Al-Mughni,* 12:347–48; al-Zuhayli, *Al-fiqh al-islami wa ʿadillatuhu,* 6:4448; Muhammad ibn Hamza al-ʿAlaʾi, *Naqd al-fatawa al-imam al-ʿalama,* 324, Manuscript Collection, Asad Library, Damascus, Syria.

26. Muhammad ibn Muhammad al-Bazzazi, *Al-Fatawa al-Bazzaziya,* 352; Khayr ad-Din ibn Ahmad al-Ramli, *Al-Fatawa al-khayriya li nafʿ al-birriya,* 80.

27. Al-Ramli, *Al-Fatawa,* 80.

28. Al-Bukhari, *Sahih al-Bukhari,* 9:67. Also related in Ibn Qudama, *Al-Mughni,* 12:347.

29. Peirce, *Morality Tales,* 132–33 (including quote from al-Marginani). See also Heyd, *Old Ottoman Criminal Law,* 99.

30. Peters, *Crime and Punishment,* 62; Peirce, *Morality Tales,* 133.

31. *SMH* 36:84:230 28 Rajab 1098 A.H./May 1687.

32. Restrictions placed on oath taking are explained by Peters in *Crime and Punishment,* 13.

33. Grehan, "Mysterious Power of Words," 991 (quote), 1003.

34. *SMH* 45:273:682 6 Jumada al-Ula 1131 A.H./March 1719; Sonbol, "Law and Gender Violence," 287.

35. *SMH* 45:65:158 26 Shaʿban 1030 A.H./July 1621.

36. This case is related in Ergene, *Local Court,* 153.

37. Boğaç Ergene presents a rape case from the court of Çankırı in which the victim, a woman named Emine, reported her rape after six months had passed (ibid.).

38. Amira El-Azhary Sonbol, "Adoption in Islamic Society: A Historical Survey," 60.

39. Al-Asqalani, *Fath al-bari sharh sahih al-Bukhari,* 12:153. An article has been published on the subject: Uri Rubin, "'Al-Walad Li-l-Firash' on the Islamic Campaign Against *'Zina,'*" 5.

40. Tucker, *In the House of the Law,* 173.

41. See Muhammad Ibn 'Abidin, *Al-'Uqud al-Durriyya fi Tanqih al-Fatawa al-Hamdiyya,* 1:75.

42. All references in the paragraph are taken from Tucker, *In the House of the Law,* 173–74.

43. Peirce, *Morality Tales,* 192.

44. This Egyptian case is mentioned in Sonbol, "Law and Gender Violence," 286.

45. Russell, *Natural History of Aleppo,* 1:55–56.

46. Peirce, *Morality Tales,* 362.

47. Sonbol, "Law and Gender Violence," 288.

48. *SMH* 36:130:359 5 Shawwal 1098 A.H./August 1687.

49. *SMH* 45:203:501 18 Safar 1131 A.H./January 1719.

50. Peirce, *Morality Tales,* 365.

51. Ibid., 206.

CONCLUSION

1. *Mar* is the Greek word for "saint."

2. This incident is referenced in Tariq Ramadan's op-ed piece "Too Scary for the Classroom?" *New York Times,* September 1, 2004.

3. Tariq Ramadan, "An International Call for Moratorium on Corporal Punishment, Stoning, and the Death Penalty in the Islamic World," March 30, 2005, http://www.tariqramadan.com.

Bibliography

Unpublished Primary Sources

Al-Bazzazi, Muhammad ibn Muhammad. *Al-Fatawa al-Bazzaziya.* Manuscript Collection, Asad Library, Damascus, Syria, 867 A.H./1471–1472.

Kanunname Liwa' Haleb, Kanunname for Aleppo Vilayet. Tapu Tahrir #493, Başbakanlık Archives, Istanbul, Turkey, 978 A.H./1570–1571.

al-Ramli, Khayr ad-Din ibn Ahmad. *Al-Fatawa al-khayriya li naf' al-birriya.* Manuscript Collection, Asad Library, Damascus, Syria, 1081 A.H./1670–1671.

al-Saqazi, Sadiq ibn Muhammad. *Surat al-fatawa al-Saqazi.* Manuscript Collection Asad Library, Damascus, Syria, 1099 A.H./1688.

Sijillat al-Mahakim Halab (SMH) [Islamic court records]. Syrian National Archives *(Markaz al-Watha'iq al-Tarikhiya).* Damascus, Syria.

Published Primary Sources

Akgündüz, Ahmed. *Osmanlı Kanunnâmeleri ve Hukukî Tahlilleri.* 9 vols. Istanbul: Faysal Eğitim ve Yardimlaşma Vakfı, 1990.

al-'Asqalani, Ahmad ibn Ali ibn Hajar. *Fath al-bari sharh sahih al-Bukhari.* 13 vols. Beirut: Dar al-kutb, 1989.

al-Budayri al-Hallaq. *Hawadith dimashq al-yawmiyya, 1154–1176 A.H./1741–1763.* Edited by Ahmad 'Izzat 'Abd al-Karim. Cairo: n.p., 1959.

al-Bukhari, Abu Abdallah Muhammad ibn Isma'il. *Sahih al-Bukhari.* Translated by Muhammad Muhsin Khan. Arabic and English edition. 9 vols. Beirut: Dar al-Arabia, 1985.

Çelebi, Katib. *The Balance of the Truth.* Translated by G. L. Lewis. New York: Macmillian, 1957.

Duzdağ, Mehmet Ertuğrul. *Şeyhülislam Ebussuud Efendi Fetvaları Işığında 16 Asır Türk Hayatı.* Istanbul: Enderun Kitabevi, 1972.

Grandmoulin, J. *Droit Pénal Egyptian Indigène.* 2 vols. Cairo: Imprimerie Nationale, 1908.

al-Halabi, Ibrahim. *Al-Multaqa al-abhur.* Beirut: Maktabat al-Umumiyya, n.d.

Ibn 'Abidin, Muhammad. *Radd al-muhtar 'ala al-durr al-mukhtar.* 7 vols. Cairo, n.d.

———. *Al-'Uqud al-Durriyya fi Tanqih al-Fatawa al-Hamdiyya.* 2 vols. Beirut: Dar al-Taba't al-Amiriyya, 1853.

Ibn Ishaq, Muhammad. *The Life of Muhammad: A Translation of Ishaq's Sirat Rasul Allah.* Translated by A. Guillaume. 1955. Reprint, New York: Oxford Univ. Press, 2003.

Ibn Kathir, Isma'il ibn 'Umar. *Mukhtasir tafsir ibn Kathir.* 3 vols. Beirut: Dar al-Qur'an al-Karim, 1981.

Ibn al-Nujaym, Zayn al-Din. *Al-Bahr al-ra'iq sharh kanz al-daqa'iq.* 8 vols. Beirut: Dar al-Ma'rifah, 1993.

Ibn Qudama, Ahmad ibn Muhammad. *Al-Mughni.* 16 vols. Cairo: Hajr, 1990.

Ibn Taymiyya, Ahmad ibn 'Abd al-Halim. *Fatawa al-nisa'.* Cairo: Maktabah al-Qur'an, 1983.

Lane, Edward William. *An Account of the Manners and Customs of the Modern Egyptians Written in Egypt During the Years 1833–1835.* 1836. Reprint, London: East-West Publications, 1895.

al-Marginani, Burhan al-Din Abu'l Hasan 'Ali ibn Abi Bakr ibn 'Abd al-Jalil al-Farghani. *Al-Hadaya sharh badayat al-mubtadi.* 4 vols. Beirut: Shirkat dar al-urqam bin abi al-urqam, n.d.

———. *The Hedaya; or, The Guide: A Commentary on the Mussulman Laws.* Translated by Charles Hamilton. 4 vols. London: New Book, 1957.

———. *Hedaya or Guide. A Commentary on the Mussulman Laws.* Translated by Charles Hamilton. Lahore: Premier Book House, 1975. Single volume second edition.

Pulaha, Selami, and Yaşar Yücel. "I. Selim Kanunnamesi (1512–1520) ve XVI. Yüzyılın İkinci Yarısının kimi kanunları." *Belgeler* (Türk Tarih Kurumu Basımevi) 12, no. 16 (1987).

Qu'ran. Translated by 'Abd Allah Yusuf 'Ali. Beirut: Dar al-'Arabiah, n.d.

Qushaqji, Yusuf. *Al-Amthal al-sha'biya al-halabiya wa amthal Mardin.* 2 vols. 2d ed. Aleppo: Mutb'at al-ihsan, 1984.

Russell, Alexander. *The Natural History of Aleppo.* 2 vols. London: G. G. and J. Robinson, 1794.

al-Sarakhsi, Muhammad ibn Ahmad. *Kitab al-Mabsut.* 30 vols. Beirut: Dar al-Ma'rifah, 1986.

al-Tabari, Abu Ja'far Muhammad ibn Jarir. *Tafsir al-Tabari.* 13 vols. Beirut: Dar al-Kutub al-'Ilmiyya, 1999.

Volney, Constantine François. *Travels Through Egypt and Syria in the Years 1783, 1784, and 1785*. 2 vols. New York: Printed by T. Tiebour, for E. Duyckinck and Company, Booksellers, 1798.

SECONDARY SOURCES

Abbott, Nabia. *Aishah, the Beloved of Muhammed*. Chicago: Univ. of Chicago Press, 1942.

Abdel Nour, Antoine. *Introduction à l'histoire urbaine de la Syrie Ottomane (XVIè–XVIIIè siècle)*. Beirut: Publications de l'Université Libanaise, 1982.

Abou el Fadl, Khaled. *Speaking God's Name: Islamic Law, Authority, and Women*. Oxford: One World, 2001.

Abrahamian, Ervand. "Oriental Despotism: The Case of Qajar Iran." *International Journal of Middle East Studies* 5, no. 1 (1974): 3–31.

Abu-Odeh, Lama. "Comparatively Speaking: The 'Honor' of the 'East' and the 'Passion' of the 'West.'" *Utah Law Review* 2 (1997): 287–307.

———. "Crimes of Honor and the Construction of Gender in Arab Societies." In *Feminism and Islam: Legal and Literary Perspectives*, edited by Mai Yamani, 141–94. New York: New York Univ. Press, 1996.

Agmon, Iris. *Family and Court: Legal Culture and Modernity in Late Ottoman Palestine*. Syracuse: Syracuse Univ. Press, 2006.

———. "Muslim Women in Court According to the *Sijill* of Late Ottoman Jaffa and Haifa: Some Methodological Notes." In *Women, the Family, and Divorce Laws in Islamic History*, edited by Amira El-Azhary Sonbol. Syracuse: Syracuse Univ. Press, 1996.

Ahmed, Leila. *Women and Gender in Islam: Historical Roots of a Modern Debate*. New Haven: Yale Univ. Press, 1993.

al-Asadi, Khayr al-Din. *Ahiya' halab wa aswaqha*. Damascus: Wizarat al-Thaqafah wa-al-Irshad al-Qawm , 1990.

al-Aswad, Nizar. *Karagöz bilad al-Sham*. Damascus: al-Matba'a al-Jumhuriyya, 1994.

al-Azmeh, Aziz. *Islams and Modernities*. London: Verso, 1993.

Baer, Gabriel. *Egyptian Guilds in Modern Times*. Jerusalem: Israel Oriental Society, 1964.

Baer, Marc. "Islamic Conversion Narratives of Women: Social Change and Gendered Religious Hierarchy in Early Modern Ottoman Istanbul." *Gender and History* 16, no. 2 (Aug. 2004): 425–58.

Barlas, Asma. *"Believing Women" in Islam: Unreading Patriarchal Interpretations of the Qur'an*. Austin: Univ. of Texas Press, 2002.

Behar, Cem. *A Neighborhood in Ottoman Istanbul: Fruit Vendors and Civil Servants in the Kasap İlyas Mahalle.* Albany: State Univ. of New York Press, 2003.

Bellamy, James. "Sex and Society in Islamic Popular Literature." In *Society and the Sexes in Medieval Islam,* edited by Afaf Lutfi al-Sayyid Marsot. Malibu: Undena Publications, 1979.

Bodman, Herbert L., Jr. *Political Factions in Aleppo, 1760–1826.* Chapel Hill: Univ. of North Carolina Press, 1963.

Bouhdiba, Abdelwahab. *Sexuality in Islam.* Translated from the French by Alan Sheridan. London: Routledge, 1985.

Brown, Janelle. "The Taliban's Bravest Opponents." Salon.com, October 2, 2001. http://archive.salon.com/mwt/feature/2001/10/02/fatima/index.html.

Brown, Kathleen M. *Good Wives, Nasty Wenches, and Anxious Patriarchs: Gender, Race, and Power in Colonial Virginia.* Chapel Hill: Univ. of North Carolina Press, 1996.

Burton, J. "Naskh." In *Encyclopaedia of Islam,* 7:1009–12. 2d ed. Leiden: E. J. Brill, 1993.

Calder, Norman. "Al-Nawawi's Typology of Muftis and Its Significance for a General Theory of Islamic Law." *Islamic Law and Society* 3, no. 2 (1996): 137–64.

Cattenoz, H. G. *Tables de concordance des ères chrétienne et hégirienne.* 2d ed. Rabat: Les Éditions Techniques Nord-Africaines, 1954.

Chamberlain, Michael. *Knowledge and Social Practice in Medieval Damascus, 1190–1350.* New York: Cambridge Univ. Press, 1994.

Cohen, Amnon. *The Guilds of Ottoman Jerusalem.* Leiden: E. J. Brill, 2001.

Cohen, Amnon, and Bernard Lewis. *Population and Revenue in the Towns of Palestine in the Sixteenth Century.* Princeton: Princeton Univ. Press, 1978.

Corbin, Alain. *Women for Hire: Prostitution and Sexuality in France after 1850.* Translated by Alan Sheridan. Cambridge: Harvard Univ. Press, 1990.

Davis, Natalie Zemon. *Fiction in the Archives: Pardon Tales and Their Tellers in Sixteenth-Century France.* Stanford: Stanford Univ. Press, 1987.

———. *The Return of Martin Guerre.* Cambridge: Harvard Univ. Press, 1984.

Davison, Roderic. *Reform in the Ottoman Empire, 1856–1876.* Princeton: Princeton Univ. Press, 1963.

———. "Tanzimat." In *Encyclopaedia of Islam,* 10:201–9. Leiden: E. J. Brill, 2000.

Doi, 'Abdur Rahman I. *Shari'ah: The Islamic Law.* London: Ta Ha Publishers, 1984.

Doumani, Beshara. "Endowing Family: Waqf, Property, Devolution, and Gender in Greater Syria, 1800–1860." *Comparative Studies in Society and History* 40, no. 1 (1998): 3–41.

———. "Palestinian Islamic Court Records: A Source for Socioeconomic History." *MESA Bulletin* 19 (1985): 155–72.

———. *Rediscovering Palestine: Merchants and Peasants in Jabal Nablus, 1700–1900.* Berkeley and Los Angeles: Univ. of California Press, 1995.

Douwes, Dick. *The Ottomans in Syria: A History of Justice and Oppression.* New York: I. B. Taurus, 2000.

Duri, A. A. *The Rise of Historical Writing among the Arabs.* Edited and translated by Lawrence I. Conrad. Princeton: Princeton Univ. Press, 1983.

Ergene, Boğaç A. *Local Court, Provincial Society, and Justice in the Ottoman Empire: Legal Practice and Dispute Resolution in Çankırı and Kastamonu, 1652–1744.* Leiden: E. J. Brill, 2003.

———. "Social Identity and Patterns of Interaction in the Shari'a Court of Kastamonu, 1740–44." *Islamic Law and Society* 15, no. 1 (2008): 20–54.

Esposito, John. *Women in Muslim Family Law.* New York: Syracuse Univ. Press, 1982.

Fahmy, Khaled. *All the Pasha's Men: Mehmed Ali, His Army, and the Making of Modern Egypt.* New York: Cambridge Univ. Press, 1998.

———. "Prostitution in Egypt in the Nineteenth Century." In *Outside-In: On the Margins of the Modern Middle East,* edited by Eugene Rogan, 77–103. New York: I. B. Taurus, 2002.

Fernea, Elizabeth Warnock, and Basima Qattan Bezirgan, eds. *Middle Eastern Muslim Women Speak.* Austin: Univ. of Texas Press, 1990.

Foucault, Michel. *Discipline and Punish: The Birth of the Prison.* Translated by Alan Sheridan. 2d ed. New York: Random House, 1977.

———. "Truth and Juridical Forms." In vol. 3 of *Power: Essential Works of Foucault, 1954–1984,* edited by James D. Faubion and translated by Robert Hurley et al. New York: New Press, 2000.

Gaube, Heinz, and Eugen Wirth. *Aleppo: Historische and geographische Beiträge zur baulichen Gestaltung, zur sozialen Organisation und zur wirtschaftlichen Dynamik einer vorderasiatischen Fernhandelsmetropole.* Wiesbaden: Dr. Ludwig Reichert, 1984.

Gaudefroy-Demombynes, Maurice, and T. Fahd. "Radjm." In *Encyclopaedia of Islam,* 8:379–81. Leiden: E. J. Brill, 1995.

Gerber, Haim. *Islamic Law and Culture, 1600–1840.* Leiden: E. J. Brill, 1999.

———. "Position of Women in an Ottoman City, Bursa, 1600–1700." *International Journal of Middle Eastern Studies* 12 (1980).

———. "Rigidity Versus Openness in Late Classical Islamic Law: The Case of the Seventeenth-Century Palestinian Mufti Khayr al-Din al-Ramli." *Islamic Law and Society* 5, no. 2 (1998): 165–95.

———. *State, Society, and Law in Islam: Ottoman Law in Comparative Perspective.* New York: State Univ. of New York Press, 1994.

Gibb, H. A. R., and H. Bowen. *Islamic Society and the West: A Study of the Impact of Western Civilization on Moslem Culture in the Near East.* 2 vols. 1950. Reprint, London, 1957.

Gimaret, D. "Mu'tazila." In *Encyclopaedia of Islam,* 7:783–93. Leiden: E. J. Brill, 1986.

Ginzburg, Carlo. *The Cheese and the Worms: The Cosmos of a Sixteenth-Century Miller.* Translated by John Tedeschi and Anne Tedeschi. Baltimore: Johns Hopkins Univ. Press, 1992.

Glidewell Nadolski, Dora. "Ottoman and Secular Civil Law." *International Journal of Middle East Studies* 8 (1977): 517–43.

Goadby, Frederic M. *Commentary on Egyptian Criminal Law.* Pt. 1. Cairo: Government Press, 1914.

Göçek, Fatma Müge. "The Legal Resource of Minorities in History: Eighteenth-Century Appeals to the Islamic Court of Galata." In vol. 12 of *Minorities in the Ottoman Empire,* edited by Molly Green. Princeton: Markus Weiner, 2005.

Grehan, James. "The Mysterious Power of Words: Language, Law, and Culture in Ottoman Damascus (17th–18th Centuries)." *Journal of Social History* 37, no. 4 (2004): 991–1015.

———. "Smoking and 'Early Modern' Sociability: The Great Tobacco Debate in the Ottoman Middle East (Seventeenth to Eighteenth Centuries)." *American Historical Review* 3, no. 5 (Dec. 2006): 1352–77.

Guthrie, Shirley. *Arab Women in the Middle Ages: Private lives and Public Roles.* London: Saqi, 2001.

Haeri, Shahla. "The Politics of Dishonor: Rape and Power in Pakistan." In *Faith and Freedom: Women's Human Rights in the Muslim World,* edited by Mahnaz Afkhami, 161–75. Syracuse: Syracuse Univ. Press, 1995.

Hallaq, Wael. "From Fatwas to *Furu':* Growth and Change in Islamic Substantive Law." *Islamic Law and Society* 1 (1994): 29–65.

———. *A History of Islamic Legal Theories: An Introduction to Sunni Usul al-Fiqh.* New York: Cambridge Univ. Press, 1997.

———. "Was the Gate of *Ijtihad* Closed?" *International Journal of Middle East Studies* 16 (1984): 3–41.

Hattox, Ralph. *Coffee and Coffeehouses: The Origins of a Social Beverage in the Medieval Near East.* Seattle: Univ. of Washington Press, 1985.

Heyd, Uriel. "Aspects of the Ottoman *Fatwa.*" *Bulletin of the School of Oriental and Asian Studies* 32 (1969): 35–56.

———. "*Kanun* and Shari'a in Old Ottoman Criminal Justice." In *Proceedings of the Israel Academy of Sciences and Humanities,* 3:1–18. Jerusalem: Litho-Offset Ziv, 1969.

———. *Studies in Old Ottoman Criminal Law.* Edited by V. L. Ménage. Oxford: Clarendon Press, 1973.

Hirsi 'Ali, Ayaan. *Infidel.* New York: Free Press, 2007.

"'Honour Killings' Law Blocked." http://bbc.co.uk. Sept. 8, 2003.

Hourani, Albert. "Ottoman Reform and the Politics of Notables." In *Beginnings of Modernization in the Middle East,* edited by William Polk and Richard Chambers. Chicago: Univ. of Chicago Press, 1966.

Human Rights Watch. "Honoring the Killers: Justice Denied for 'Honor' Crimes in Jordan." http://www.hrw.org/reports/2004/jordan0404/index.htm. Apr. 2004.

Ilahi, Fadl. *Al-Tadabir al-waqiya min al-zina fi al-fiqh al-Islami.* Riyad: Al-Maktabah al-Islami, 1983.

Imber, Colin. *Ebu's-su'ud : The Islamic Legal Tradition.* Edinburgh: Edinburgh Univ. Press, 1997.

———. *The Ottoman Empire, 1300–1650.* London and New York: Palgrave, 2002.

———. "Why You Should Poison Your Husband: A Note on Liability in Hanafi Law in the Ottoman Period." *Islamic Law and Society* 1, no. 2 (1994): 206–16.

———. "*Zina* in Ottoman Law." In *Studies in Ottoman History and Law,* 175–206. Istanbul: ISIS, 1996.

Inalcik, Halil. *The Ottoman Empire: The Classical Age, 1300–1600.* 1973. Reprint, London: Phoenix, 2000.

———. "Suleiman the Lawgiver and Ottoman Law." In *The Ottoman Empire: Conquest, Organization, and Economy,* 105–38. London: Variorum Reprints, 1978.

Isaacs, Dan. "Nigerian Woman Fights Stoning." *BBC News,* July 8, 2002. http://news.bbc.co.uk/1/hi/world/africa/2116540.stm.

İslamoğu-İnan, Huri. *State and Peasant in the Ottoman Empire: Agrarian Power and Regional Economic Development in Ottoman Anatolia During the Sixteenth Century.* Leiden: E. J. Brill, 1994.

Jackson, Sherman. "*Taqlid,* Legal Scaffolding, and the Scope of Legal Injunctions in Post-formative Theory: *Mutlaq* and *'Amm* in the Jurisprudence of Shihab al-Din al-Qarafi." *Islamic Law and Society* 3, no. 2 (1996): 165–92.

al-Jandaly, Bassma. "Death by Stoning Case Goes to Supreme Court." *Gulf News,* January 31, 2007.

Jennings, Ronald C. "The Judicial Registers (*Ser'i Mahkeme Sicilleri*) of Kayseri (1590–1630) as a Source of Ottoman History." Ph.D. diss., Univ. of California at Los Angeles, 1972.

———. "Kadi, Court, and Legal Procedure in 17th Century Ottoman Kayseri." *Studia Islamica* 48 (1978): 133–72.

———. "Women in Early 17th Century Ottoman Judicial Records: The Shari'a Court of Anatolian Kayseri." *Journal of Economic and Social History of the Orient* 18, no. 1 (1975): 53–114.

Jilani, Hina. "Whose Laws? Human Rights and Violence Against Women in Pakistan." In *Freedom from Violence: Women's Strategies Around the World,* edited by Margaret Schuler, 63–74. New York: Widbooks, 1992.

Kamali, Mohammad Hashim. "Law and Society: The Interplay of Revelation and Reason in the Shariah." In *The Oxford History of Islam,* edited by John Esposito. Oxford: Oxford Univ. Press, 1999.

Kasmieh, Khairia. "Social Life in Damascus at the Beginning of the 20th Century as Perceived by Some Contemporaries." In *Histoire économique et sociale de l'Empire ottoman et de la Turquie (1326–1960),* edited by Daniel Panzac, 373–82. Collection Turcica 8. Paris: Peeters, 1995.

Khalidi, Tarif. *Arabic Historical Thought in the Classical Period.* New York: Cambridge Univ. Press, 1994.

Khattab, Muhammad Sharaf al-Din. *Jarimat al-zina wa 'uqubituha fi al-fiqh al-islami dirasah muqaranah.* Cairo, 1983.

Khoury, Dina Rizq. *State and Provincial Society in the Ottoman Empire: Mosul, 1540–1834.* New York: Cambridge Univ. Press, 1997.

Khoury, Philip. "Abu Ali al-Kilawi: A Damascus *Qabaday.*" In *Struggle and Survival in the Modern Middle East,* edited by Edmund Burke, 3:179–90. Berkeley and Los Angeles: Univ. of California, 1993.

———. *Urban Notables and Arab Nationalism: The Politics of Damascus, 1860–1920.* New York: Cambridge Univ. Press, 1983.

Kırlı, Cengiz. "The Struggle over Space: Coffeehouses of Ottoman Istanbul, 1780–1845." Ph.D. diss., State Univ. of New York at Binghamton, 2000.

Lapidus, Ira. *A History of Islamic Societies.* Cambridge: Cambridge Univ. Press, 1988.

———. *Muslim Cities in the Later Middle Ages.* Cambridge: Harvard Univ. Press, 1967.

Largueche, Dalenda. "Confined, Battered, and Repudiated Women in Tunis since the Eighteenth Century." In *Women, the Family, and Divorce Laws in Islamic History,* edited by Amira El-Azhary Sonbol. Syracuse: Syracuse Univ. Press, 1996.

Lewis, Bernard. *The Emergence of Modern Turkey.* 2d ed. New York: Oxford Univ. Press, 1968.

Lewis, Bernard, and Benjamin Braude, eds. *Christians and Jews in the Ottoman Empire: The Functioning of a Plural Society.* New York: Holmes and Meier Publishers, 1982.

Makdisi, Ussama. "Ottoman Orientalism." *American Historical Review* 107, no. 3 (June 2002): 768–96.

Malti-Douglas, Fedwa. *Woman's Body, Woman's Word: Gender and Discourse in Arabo-Islamic Writing*. Princeton: Princeton Univ. Press, 1991.

Mandeville, Jon E. "The Ottoman Court Records of Syria and Jordan." *Journal of the American Oriental Society* 86 (1966): 311–19.

Manji, Irshad. *The Trouble with Islam: A Muslim's Call for Reform in Her Faith*. New York: St. Martin's, 2005.

Ma'oz, Moshe. *Ottoman Reform in Syria and Palestine, 1840–1861: The Impact of the Tanzimat on Politics and Society*. New York: Oxford Univ. Press, 1968.

Marcus, Abraham. *The Middle East on the Eve of Modernity: Aleppo in the Eighteenth Century*. New York: Columbia Univ. Press, 1989.

————. "Privacy in Eighteenth-Century Aleppo: The Limits of Cultural Ideals." *International Journal of Middle East Studies* 18 (1986): 165–83.

Marino, Brigitte. "Cafés et cafetiers de Damas aux XVIIIe et XIXe siècles." *Revue du Monde Musulman et de la Méditerranée* 75–76 (1995): 275–94.

Marino, Brigitte, and Tomoki Okawara, eds. *Dalil sijillat al-mahakim al-shar'iyya al-'uthmaniyya*. Damascus: Institute Français d'Études Arabes de Damas, 1999.

Masters, Bruce. "Aleppo: The Ottoman Empire's Caravan City." In *The Ottoman City Between East and West: Aleppo, Izmir, and Istanbul*, by Edhem Eldem, Daniel Goffman, and Bruce Masters. Cambridge: Cambridge Univ. Press, 1999.

————. *Christians and Jews in the Ottoman Arab World: The Roots of Sectarianism*. Cambridge: Cambridge Univ. Press, 2001.

————. "The 1850 Events in Aleppo: An Aftershock of Syria's Incorporation into the World Capitalist System." *International Journal of Middle East Studies* 22 (1990): 3–20.

————. *The Origins of Western Dominance in the Middle East: Mercantilism and the Islamic Economy in Aleppo, 1600–1750*. New York: New York Univ. Press, 1988.

Masud, Muhammad Khalid, Brinkley Messick, and David Powers, eds. *Islamic Legal Interpretation: Muftis and Their Fatwas*. Cambridge: Harvard Univ. Press, 1996.

Matthee, Rudi. "Prostitutes, Courtesans, and Dancing Girls: Women Entertainers in Safavid Iran." In *Iran and Beyond: Essays in Middle Eastern History in Honor of Nikkie R. Keddie*, edited by Rudi Matthee and Beth Baron, 121–50. Costa Mesa, Calif.: Mazda Publishers, 2000.

————. *The Pursuit of Pleasure: Drugs and Stimulants in Iranian History, 1500–1900*. Princeton: Princeton Univ. Press, 2005.

Mayer, Ann Elizabeth. "Reform of Personal Status Laws in North Africa: A Problem of Islamic or Mediterranean Laws?" *Middle East Journal* 49, no. 3 (Summer 1993): 432–46.

Ménage, V. L. "Devshirme." In *Encyclopaedia of Islam,* 2:210. 2d ed. Leiden: E. J. Brill, 1991.

Meriwether, Margaret L. *The Kin Who Count: Family and Society in Ottoman Aleppo, 1770–1840.* Austin: Univ. of Texas Press, 1999.

Mernissi, Fatima. *The Veil and the Male Elite: A Feminist Interpretation of Women's Rights in Islam.* Translated by Mary Jo Lakeland. 1987. Reprint, New York: Addison-Wesley Publishing, 1991.

Messick, Brinkley. *The Calligraphic State: Textual Domination and History in Muslim Society.* Berkeley and Los Angeles: Univ. of California Press, 1992.

Miller, Barnette. *The Palace School of Muhammad the Conqueror.* 1941. Reprint, New York: Arno Press, 1973.

Musallam, B. F. *Sex and Society in Islam: Birth Control Before the Nineteenth Century.* New York: Cambridge Univ. Press, 1983.

al-Nabhan, Muhammad Faruq. *Mabahith fi al-tashri' al-jina'i al-Islami: Al-qatl, al-zina, al-sariqah.* Beirut: Dar al-qalam, 1977.

al-Nahal, Gamal. *Judicial Administration in Ottoman Egypt in the Seventeenth Century.* Minneapolis: Bibliotheca Islamica, 1985.

"News Reports from Afghanistan." *Reproductive Health Matters* 9 (Nov. 18, 2001): 15–18.

Nu'aisa, Yusuf Jamil. *Mujtama' madinat damashq.* 2 vols. Damascus: Dar Talas, 1994.

Nur, Ahmed Hafiz. *Jarimat al-zina fi al-qanun al-misri wa al-muqarin.* Cairo, 1958.

Opwis, Felicitas. "*Maslaha* in Contemporary Islamic Legal Theory." *Islamic Law and Society* 12, 2 (2005): 182–223.

Owen, Roger. "The Middle East in the Eighteenth Century—an 'Islamic' Society in Decline? A Critique of Gibb and Bowen's Islamic Society and the West." *Bulletin* (British Society for Middle Eastern Studies) 3, no. 2 (1976): 110–17.

Peirce, Leslie. *Morality Tales: Law and Gender in the Ottoman Court of Aintab.* Berkeley and Los Angeles: Univ. of California Press, 2003.

Peters, Rudolph. *Crime and Punishment in Islamic Law: Theory and Practice from the Sixteenth to the Twenty-first Century.* Cambridge: Cambridge Univ. Press, 2005.

Petrov, Milen V. "Everyday Forms of Compliance: Subaltern Commentaries on Ottoman Reform, 1864–1868." *Comparative Studies in Society and History* 46, no. (2004): 730–59.

Powers, David. "Kadijustiz or Qadi-Justice? A Paternity Dispute from Fourteenth-Century Morocco." *Islamic Law and Society* 1, no. 3 (1994): 332–66.

al-Qattan, Najwa. "Across the Courtyard: Residential Space and Sectarian Boundaries in Ottoman Damascus." In *Minorities in the Ottoman Empire,* edited by Molly Greene, 12:13–46. Princeton: Markus Weiner, 2005.

———. "Textual Differentiation in the Damascus *Sijill:* Religious Discrimination or Politics of Gender?" In *Women, the Family, and Divorce Laws in Islamic History,* edited by Amira El-Azhary Sonbol, 191–202. Syracuse: Syracuse Univ. Press, 1996.

Quraishi, Asifa. "Her Honoi: An Islamic Critique of the Rape Laws of Pakistan from a Woman-Sensitive Perspective." In *Windows of Faith: Muslim Women Scholar-Activists in North America,* edited by Gisla Webb, 102–35. Syracuse: Syracuse Univ. Press, 2000.

Rafeq, Abdul Karim. "Craft Organization, Work Ethics, and the Strains of Change in Ottoman Syria." *Journal of the American Oriental Society* 111, no. 3 (1991): 495–511.

———. "The Law-Court Registers and Their Importance for a Socio-economic and Urban Study of Ottoman Syria." In *L'éspace social de la ville arabe,* edited by Dominique Chevallier, 51–58. Paris: Maisonneuve et Larose, 1979.

———. "Local Forces in Syria in the Seventeenth and Eighteenth Centuries." In *War, Technology, and Society in the Middle East,* edited by V. J. Parry and M. E. Yapp, 277–307. London: Oxford Univ. Press, 1975.

———. "New Light on the 1860 Riots in Ottoman Damascus." *Die Welt des Islams* 28 (1988): 412–30.

———. *The Province of Damascus, 1723–1783.* Beirut: Khayats, 1966.

———. "Public Morality in 18th Century Damascus." *Revue du Monde Musulman et de la Méditerranée* 55–56 (1990): 180–96.

———. "The Syrian 'Ulama, Ottoman Law, and Islamic Shari'a." In *Turcica: Revue d'études Turques peuples, langues, cultures, états,* 26:9–32. Strasbourg: Editions Peeters, 1994.

Ramadan, Tariq. "An International Call for Moratorium on Corporal Punishment, Stoning, and the Death Penalty in the Islamic World." http://www.tariqramadan.com. Mar. 30, 2005.

Raymond, André. *Alep à l'époque ottomane (XVIe–XIXe siècle).* Damas: Institut Français de Damas, 1998.

———. *Artisans et commerçants au Caire au XVIIIe siècle.* 2 vols. Damas: IFEAD, 1999.

———. *The Great Arab Cities in the 16th and 17th Centuries: An Introduction.* New York: New York Univ. Press, 1984.

———. "The Population of Aleppo in the Sixteenth and Seventeenth Centuries According to Ottoman Census Documents." *International Journal of Middle East Studies* 16 (1984): 447–60.

———. *Urban Networks and Popular Movements in Cairo and Aleppo (End of the 18th–Beginning of the 19th Centuries).* Urbanism in Islam: The Proceedings of the International Conference on Urbanism in Islam (ICUIT, Session 12). Vol. 2. Tokyo: Middle Eastern Culture Center, 1989.

Redhouse, Sir James W. *A Turkish and English Lexicon.* 1890. Reprint, Beirut: Librarie du Liban, 1996.

Reilly, James A. "Shari'a Court Registers and Land Tenure Around Nineteenth-Century Damascus." *Middle East Studies Association Bulletin* 21 (1987): 157–67.

Rhoded, Ruth. "Social Patterns among the Urban Elite of Syria During the Late Ottoman Period, 1876–1918." In *Palestine in the Late Ottoman Period: Political, Social, and Economic Transformation,* edited by David Kushner. Jerusalem: Yad Izhak Ben-Zvi, 1986.

Rosen, Lawrence. *The Anthropology of Justice: Law as Culture in Islamic Society.* 1989. Reprint, New York: Cambridge Univ. Press, 1996.

———. "Equity and Discretion in a Modern Islamic Legal System." *Law and Society Review* 15, no. 2 (1980): 217–45.

———. *The Justice of Islam: Comparative Perspectives on Islamic Law and Society.* New York: Oxford Univ. Press, 2000.

Rosenthal, Franz. *The Herb: Hashish Versus Medieval Muslim Society.* Leiden: E. J. Brill, 1971.

Rubin, Uri. "'Al-Walad Li-l-Firash' on the Islamic Campaign Against 'Zina.'" *Studia Islamica* 78 (1993): 5–26.

al-Saghirji, Shaykh Asad Muhammad Sa'id. *Al-fiqh al-hanafi wa 'adillatuhu.* 3 vols. Damascus: Dar al-Kalam al-Tayyibi, 2000.

Sahebjam, Freidoune. *The Stoning of Soraya M.* Translated from French by Richard Sever. New York: Arcade Publishing, 1990.

Sajdi, Dana. "Peripheral Visions: The Worlds and Worldviews of Commoner Chroniclers in the Eighteenth-Century Ottoman Levant." Ph.D. diss., Columbia Univ., 2002.

———. "A Room of His Own: The 'History' of the Barber of Damascus (Fl. 1762)." *MIT Electronic Journal of Middle East Studies* 3 (Fall 2003): 19–35.

Sauvaget, Jean. *Alep: Essai sur le développement d'une grande ville syrienne, des origins au milieu du xixe siècle.* Paris: Librairie Orientaliste Paul Geuthner, 1941.

———. "Halab." In *Encyclopaedia of Islam,* 3:85–90. Leiden: E. J. Brill, 1986.

Schacht, Joseph. "Hanafiyya." In *Encyclopedia of Islam,* 3:162. London: E. J. Brill, 1971.

———. *An Introduction to Islamic Law.* Oxford: Clarendon Press, 1964.

———. "Zina." In *Encyclopedia of Islam,* 4:1227. Leiden: E. J. Brill, 1934.

Schilcher, Linda Schatowski. *Families in Politics: Damascene Factions and Estates of the 18th and 19th Centuries.* Stuttgart: Franz Steiner Verlag Wiesbaden, 1985.

Semerdjian, Elyse. "Gender Violence in *Kanunnames* and *Fetvas* of the Sixteenth Century." In *Beyond the Exotic: Women's Histories in Islamic Societies,* edited by Amira El-Azhary Sonbol, 180–97. Syracuse: Syracuse Univ. Press, 2005.

————. "Sinful Professions: Illegal Occupations of Women in Ottoman Aleppo, Syria." *Hawwa* 1, no. 1 (2003): 60–85.

Seng, Yvonne. "Standing at the Gates of Justice: Women in the Law Courts of Early-Sixteenth-Century Üsküdar, Istanbul." In *Contesting States: Law, Hegemony, and Resistance,* edited by Mindie Lazarus-Black and Susan F. Hirsch. New York: Routledge, 1994.

"Shari'a Court Frees Nigerian Woman." *BBC News,* March 25, 2002. http://news.bbc.co.uk/2/hi/africa/1891395.stm.

Shuman, Muhsin 'Ali. *Al-yahud fi misr al-'uthmaniyah hatta awa'il al-qarn al-tasi' 'ashar.* 2 vols. Cairo: Al-hay'ah al-misriyah al-'ammah lil-kitab, 2000.

Singer, Amy. *Palestinian Peasants and Ottoman Officials: Rural Administration Around Sixteenth-Century Jerusalem.* New York: Cambridge Univ. Press, 1994.

Skaine, Rosemarie. *The Women of Afghanistan under the Taliban.* London: McFarland, 2001.

Sonbol, Amira El-Azhary. "Adoption in Islamic Society: A Historical Survey." In *Children in the Muslim Middle East,* edited by Elizabeth Warnock Fernea. Austin: Univ. of Texas Press, 1995.

————. "Law and Gender Violence in Ottoman and Modern Egypt." In *Women, the Family, and Divorce Laws in Islamic History,* edited by Amira El-Azhary Sonbol, 277–89. Syracuse: Syracuse Univ. Press, 1996.

————. *The New Mamluks: Egyptian Society and Modern Feudalism.* Syracuse: Syracuse Univ. Press, 2000.

————. "Rape and Law in Ottoman and Modern Egypt." In *Women in the Ottoman Empire: Middle Eastern Women in the Early Modern Era,* edited by Madeline C. Zilfi, 214–32. Leiden: E. J. Brill, 1997.

————. "*Ta'a* and Modern Legal Reform: A Rereading." *Islam and Christian-Muslim Relations* 9, no. 3 (1998): 285–94.

————. *Women of Jordan: Islam, Labor, and the Law.* Syracuse: Syracuse Univ. Press, 2003.

————, ed. *Women, the Family, and Divorce Laws in Islamic History.* Syracuse: Syracuse Univ. Press, 1996.

Spellberg, Denise A. *Politics, Gender, and the Islamic Past: The Legacy of 'A'isha bint Abi Bakr.* New York: Columbia Univ. Press, 1994.

Stillman, Norman A. *The Jews of Arab Lands in Modern Times.* New York: Jewish Publication Society, 1991.

Stowasser, Barbara Freyer. *Women in the Qur'an: Traditions and Interpretation.* New York: Oxford Univ. Press, 1994.

Tabbaa, Yasser. *Constructions of Power and Piety in Medieval Aleppo.* University Park: Univ. of Pennsylvania Press, 1997.

"Taliban Publicly Execute Women." Associated Press, November 17, 1999. Available online at http://www.rawa.org/murder-w.htm.

"Taliban Stone Woman for Adultery." Associated Press, May 1, 2000. Available online at http://www.rawa.org/stoning.htm. Reproduced in "News Reports from Afghanistan," *Reproductive Health Matters* 9, No. 18 (Nov. 2001), 15–18.

Tamari, Stephen Edmond. "Teaching and Learning in 18th-Century Damascus: Localism and Ottomanism in an Early Modern Arab Society." Ph.D. diss., Georgetown Univ., 1998.

Tran, Mark. "Iran Stays Execution by Stoning." *Guardian,* June 20, 2007.

Tucker, Judith. *In the House of the Law: Gender and Law in Ottoman Syria and Palestine.* Berkeley and Los Angeles: Univ. of California Press, 1998.

———. "Muftis and Matrimony: Islamic Law and Gender in Ottoman Syria and Palestine." *Islamic Law and Society* 1, no. 3 (1994): 265–300.

———. *Women in Nineteenth-Century Egypt.* New York: Cambridge Univ. Press, 1984.

Turner, Bryan S. *Weber and Islam: A Critical Study.* London: Routledge and Kegan Paul, 1974.

Tyan, E. "Diya." In *Encyclopedia of Islam,* 2:340. Leiden: E. J. Brill, 1965.

al-'Uthmani, Muhammad ibn 'Abd al-Rahman. *Rahmat al-ummah fi ikhtilaf al-a' immah: Fatawa a'immat al-madhahib al-arba'ah, Abu Hanifah, Malik, al-Shafi'i, Ahmad ibn Hanbal.* Baghdad: Maktabat al-As'ad, 1990.

Van Den Boogert, Maurits H. *The Capitulations and the Ottoman Legal System: Qadis, Consuls, and Beratlıs in the 18th Century.* Leiden: E. J. Brill, 2005.

Voll, John. "Old 'Ulama Families and Ottoman Influence in Eighteenth-Century Damascus." *American Journal of Arabic Studies* 3 (1975): 48–59.

von Schlegell, Barbara. "Sufism in the Ottoman Arab World: Sheikh 'Abd al-Ghani al-Nabulsi (d. 1143/1731)." Ph.D. diss., Univ. of California at Berkeley, 1997.

Wadud, Amina. *Qur'an and Woman: Rereading the Sacred Text from a Woman's Perspective.* Oxford: Oxford Univ. Press, 1999.

Watt, W. Montgomery. "Al-Ash'ari." In *Encyclopaedia of Islam,* 1:694–95. Leiden: E. J. Brill, 1986.

Weber, Max. *Max Weber on Law in Economy and Society.* New York: Simon and Schuster, 1967.

Wehr, Hans. *A Dictionary of Modern Written Arabic.* Edited by J. Milton Cowan. Beirut: Librarie du Liban, 1980.

Wittfogel, Karl. *Oriental Despotism: A Comparative Study of Total Power.* New Haven: Yale Univ. Press, 1957.

Wright, J. W., Jr. "Masculine Allusion and the Structure of Satire in Early 'Abbasid Poetry." In *Homoeroticism in Classical Arabic Literature,* edited by J. W. Wright, Jr., and Everett Rowson. New York: Columbia Univ. Press, 1997.

Yamani, Ahmad Zaki. *Islamic Law and Contemporary Issues.* Jidda: Saudi Publishing, 1968.

Zarinebaf, Fariba. "The Mediterranean's Metropolis: Urban Transformation, Crime, and Social Control in Eighteenth-Century Istanbul." Forthcoming.

———. "Regulating Prostitution in 18th Century Istanbul." Middle East Studies Association Conference, Washington, D.C., 2005.

Ze'evi, Dror. *An Ottoman Century: The District of Jerusalem in the 1600s.* Albany: State Univ. of New York Press, 1996.

———. *Producing Desire: Changing Sexual Discourse in the Ottoman Middle East, 1500–1900.* Berkeley and Los Angeles: Univ. of California Press, 2006.

———. "The Use of Ottoman Shari'a Court Records as a Source for Middle Eastern Social History: A Reappraisal." *Islamic Law and Society* 5, no.1 (1998): 35–56.

Zenner, Walter P. *A Global Community: The Jews from Aleppo, Syria.* Detroit: Wayne State Univ. Press, 2000.

Zilfi, Madeline. "The Kadizadelis: Discordant Revivalism in Seventeenth-Century Istanbul." *Journal of Near Eastern Studies* 45, no. 4 (1986): 251–69.

———. *The Politics of Piety: The Ottoman Ulema in the Post-Classical Age.* Chicago: Bibliotheca Islamica, 1987.

al-Zirikli, Khayr al-Din. *Al-'Alam.* 3d ed. 8 vols. Beirut: Dar al-'ilm, 1990.

Zubaida, Sami. *Law and Power in the Islamic World.* London: I. B. Tauris, 2005.

al-Zuhayli, Wahba. *Al-fiqh al-islami wa 'adillatuhu.* 11 vols. Beirut: Dar al-Fikr, 1997.

INDEX

Italic page number denotes illustration or table.